BEN JONSON: AUTHORITY: CRITICISM

Ben Jonson
Authority
Criticism

Richard Dutton

First published in Great Britain 1996 by
MACMILLAN PRESS LTD
Houndmills, Basingstoke, Hampshire RG21 6XS
and London
Companies and representatives
throughout the world

A catalogue record for this book is available
from the British Library.

ISBN 0-333-62981-7

 First published in the United States of America 1996 by
ST. MARTIN'S PRESS, INC.,
Scholarly and Reference Division,
175 Fifth Avenue,
New York, N.Y. 10010

ISBN 0-312-15848-3

Library of Congress Cataloging-in-Publication Data
Dutton. Richard, 1948–
Ben Jonson, authority, criticism / Richard Dutton.
p.   cm.
Includes bibliographical references and index.
ISBN 0-312-15848-3
1. Jonson, Ben, 1573?-1637—Knowledge—Literature.   2. Criticism–
-England—History—17th century.   3. Authority in literature.
I. Title.
PR2642.L5D88   1996
822'.3—dc20   95-26794
                                                                    CIP

Transferred to digital printing 1998
02/780

Contents

To Maura

List of Plates

Preface

Ben Jonson has been with me all my academic career, from studying *The Alchemist* at school (and playing Sir Epicure Mammon), via a doctoral dissertation, through articles in journals, to a book and editions of his masques and his poetry. With each encounter I have found the man bigger than the frame within which I confronted him, more complex and challenging than I had been led to suppose. My most recent book, on the censorship of English Renaissance drama, largely grew from having no real explanation of how it was that Jonson – whose plays antagonised the authorities more often than those of any other dramatist of the period – very nearly became himself Master of the Revels, the official who censored and licensed works for the public stage.

In as much as I can say I found an answer to that question, it lay in a complete reconsideration of the history of the period, of its power relations, and of the place of the theatres – strung between courtly patronage, commercial imperatives and the opposition of the London authorities – within those power relations. Questions of patronage, of rival factions, of differences between the style and the substance of power, of the distance between Westminster and London, of the mixed nature of audiences, came to predominate over earlier notions of a seamless, unproblematic Elizabethan or Jacobean 'world picture'. And the drama, rather than parroting universally held opinions, increasingly seemed to interrogate the era it represented. That is, it gave voice not to certainties but to the tensions inherent in a period when unprecedented social and economic changes (most obviously reflected in the growth of London to be the largest city and busiest trading centre in the known world) were subtly but remorselessly transforming the traditional political structures of monarchy, aristocracy and their underpinnings.[1] Parallel to this, the nature and status of all writing was changing as literacy spread and the printed word became an increasingly familiar commodity. In this book I hope to show how Jonson's criticism, which once struck me as rather predictable and unimaginative, is a similarly complex response to those tensions and pressures.

Over the past decade these issues, as they relate to Renaissance literature, have been addressed most urgently by critics variously described as new historicist, cultural materialist and revisionist. Some of my own recent writing has been described (rather loosely, I should say) as 'new historicist', but I do not consciously ally myself with any of these camps. I share with some of them, however, a conviction that writing does not simply mirror the society that produces it, but rather is involved in that society's definition of itself, in its structures and its norms (which are the sites of power). That is (as the new historicists would argue) writing is essentially shaped by the configurations of power from which it emanates and by which it is 'authorised', and in the end its only function *may* be to reiterate that authority. But, in articulating the configurations of power, it may (as the cultural materialists have argued) firstly expose those configurations as changeable constructs, not immutable ones, and secondly help to shape – or give credibility to – alternative configurations.[2] Where I part company from both camps is in the conviction that either scenario is always *necessarily* the case: that writing inevitably reinscribes the authority that begets it *or* that the 'alternative configurations' which it articulates thereby acquire authority of their own. These seem to me matters determined by forces other than writing itself – politics, economics, technology, demographics, war: the processes of social and cultural change. Writing, in and of itself, is only an enabling agency, and must meet as many dead ends as it does open doors, depending on the circumstances of its reception. The contradictions within, and mixed fortunes of, Jonson's literary criticism seem to me to bear out the truth of this with peculiar force.

Stephen Greenblatt has described the reciprocal processes of literary and societal interaction as part of 'the circulation of social energy', and a peculiar fascination of observing it in the early modern period is that we see there the shapings of our own world. In particular, we see the shapings of modern authorship, and the beginnings of the development whereby certain writings have acquired a special status as 'literature', distinguishing them from other, less prestigious writings. The *Oxford English Dictionary* informs us that the term 'literature' only acquired this distinctive sense in the early nineteenth century, but the cultural pressures that led to its emergence – and the attitudes that lie behind such a usage – go back much further.[3] Indeed, they might be traced back to the emergence of the term 'critic' in what is now (at least in academic circles) its primary sense – 'one skilful in judging of the qualities and merits of literary or artistic works'. The *OED* gives the first use of critic in this sense as by Francis Bacon in *The Advancement of Learning* (1605). Bacon figures in Jonson's *Discoveries*, as we shall see, as something of a cultural hero, and *The Advancement* appeared when Jonson was approaching the height of his powers.

This book is an exploration of the ways in which Jonson's own literary criticism relates to the emergence of this sense of 'critic' as a term during his lifetime, to the developments in the culture that required such a coinage. The chronology which follows attempts to highlight the complexities and inflections of his career, which epitomised many of those developments. That career is often represented (not least by Jonson himself) as more rounded and self-determined than it actually was, and it will be a particular concern of this book, starting with the Chronology, to emphasise its more fortuitous and less-than-coherent elements, since – as we shall see – they generated much of his criticism.

Acknowledgements

I want to thank a number of people and institutions who helped to make this book a better one than it might otherwise have been, and to bring it to press despite numerous other pressures on my time. Firstly thanks to David Kay and Scott Wilson, who both read the book at an advanced stage, saved me from numerous errors and made many helpful suggestions. Secondly, my thanks to the Huntington Library in San Marino, California, which awarded me a Short-Term Fellowship to work on the book in the summer of 1992; and to the British Academy, which gave me a travel grant for that fellowship. And thirdly, to the staff of the libraries of Lancaster University and the University of Notre Dame, who were unfailingly helpful in producing material I needed.

The book neared its completion while I was a Visiting Professor at the University of Notre Dame, and the secretarial staff of the College of Arts and Letters there were extremely helpful with the typescript of the Appendix. I have given a number of papers associated with the book, at the University of Keele, at Notre Dame and at the 'Refashioning Ben Jonson' Conference at the University of Warwick (January 1995), and I am grateful for the feedback and constructive criticism I received on each of those occasions. Finally, thanks to Charmian Hearne at Macmillan, whose support for this project at critical times should not go unremarked.

As ever, Maura, Katie and Claire saw less of me, for the writing of this book, than they would otherwise have done. That is a debt for which words are inadequate.

Chronology of Jonson's Life and Work

1561   Birth of Francis Bacon.

1564   Births of William Shakespeare, Christopher Marlowe.

1572   Benjamin Johnson born, 11 June, posthumous son of a clergyman.[1]
His mother remarries; his step-father a master bricklayer of Westminster, probably Robert Brett, who lived in Hartshorn Lane, near Charing Cross.
Attends private school in St Martin's Church, later Westminster School, where taught by the historian William Camden (see *Ep* XIV).
Birth of John Donne.

1586   Death of Sir Philip Sidney.

1588?   Taken from school and put to 'another craft', presumably bricklaying.
The defeat of the Spanish Armada.

c.1590–
92   Brief military service in the Low Countries, where 'he had, in the face of both the camps, killed an enemy and taken *opima spolia* from him'; 'but returning soon he betook himself to his wonted studies' (*Drummond*, 199–200, 198–9).

1594   'Benjamine Johnson and Anne Lewis maryed' (parish register of St Magnus Martyr, 14 November); Jonson describes his wife as 'a shrew yet honest' (*Drummond*, 208).

c.1596   Probably a strolling player in a troupe without a London base.

1597   *The Case Is Altered* staged by unknown actors.
        (28 July) Lent £4 by Philip Henslowe.
        Imprisoned (*c*.August–October) as co-author and ac-
        tor in *The Isle of Dogs*, performed by Pembroke's Men
        at the new Swan playhouse.
        (3 December) First record of employment by Henslowe,
        as the deviser of a play-plot.

1598   (September) *Every Man In His Humour* performed by
        the Lord Chamberlain's Men (with William Shakespeare
        and Richard Burbage among the actors) at the Curtain.
        Francis Meres names him among the 'best for tragedy'
        in *Palladis Tamia*.
        Kills fellow actor Gabriel Spencer in a duel (22 Sep-
        tember), pleads self-defence, escapes gallows by claim-
        ing benefit of clergy (i.e. demonstrating ability to read
        from the Bible), branded on the thumb and all goods
        confiscated. 'Then took he his religion by trust of a
        priest who visited him in prison. Thereafter he was
        twelve years a papist' (*Drummond*, 204–5).

1599   Collaborates with Dekker and others for Henslowe and
        the Lord Admiral's Men on the lost tragedies, *Page of
        Plymouth* and *Robert II, King of Scots*.
        Every Man Out of His Humour performed by the Cham-
        berlain's Men at their new Globe theatre in the winter,
        presented at court around Christmas.

1600   (January) Prosecuted for debt, imprisoned in the
        Marshalsea.[2]
        (? December) *Cynthia's Revels* acted by the Children of
        the Chapel at the indoor Blackfriars playhouse.
        Quarto of *Every Man Out of His Humour* published.

1601   (6 January) *Cynthia's Revels* performed at court; pub-
        lished same year.
        Quarto of *Every Man In His Humour* published.
        Poetaster acted by Children of the Chapel (? spring);
        examined for it by the Lord Chief Justice, Sir John
        Popham; published 1602, but 'Apologetical Dialogue'
        suppressed.

Satiromastix, a full-scale satire on Jonson by Dekker (? and Marston) performed both by the Chamberlain's Men and Paul's Children: last shot in the 'War of the Theatres', 1600–1.
Henslowe pays £2 for additions to Kyd's *The Spanish Tragedy*.
? Birth and death of daughter Mary (see *Ep* XXII).

1602   Henslowe pays £10 for further additions to *The Spanish Tragedy*, and in earnest of the lost *Richard Crookback*.

1603   Eldest son Benjamin dies of the plague, aged seven (see *Ep* XLV).
(February 12) John Manningham's *Diary*: 'Ben Jonson the poet now lives upon one Townshend [i.e. Sir Robert Townshend], and scorns the world.'
Queen Elizabeth dies, 24 March; succeeded by James I (James VI of Scotland).
Entertainment at Althorp for Queen Anne and Prince Henry progressing south from Edinburgh.
Sejanus performed by the King's Men at the Globe (the Chamberlain's Men, now under royal patronage: Shakespeare's last recorded acting assignment). Play a failure with the audience; Jonson quizzed about it for 'popery and treason' by the Privy Council (*Drummond*, 273), either now or, more likely, after publication in 1605.

1604   (15 March) *The Magnificent Entertainment*, with Dekker; published text later that year first uses the form 'Ben: Jonson', used exclusively thereafter by the poet.
(19 March) *A Panegyre* on the King's opening of Parliament.
(1 May) *The Entertainment at Highgate*.
Paid by Haberdashers' Company for a 'device, and speech' presented before James at the 'Lord Mayor's triumphs'; Jonson did not preserve this or any other of his many civic commissions.

1605   (6 January) *The Masque of Blackness*, first of Jonson's court masques; most, like this, staged by Inigo Jones.

(8 January) *Every Man Out of His Humour* revived at court by the King's Men.

(2 February) *Every Man In His Humour* revived at court by the King's Men, possibly in the revised (1616 folio) version.

Eastward Ho co-authored by Chapman, Marston and Jonson for the Children of the Queen's Revels at the Blackfriars; Chapman and Jonson imprisoned for satire on the Scots (Marston apparently fled): 'The report was that they should then had their ears cut and noses' (*Drummond*, 228–9). Jonson writes a series of letters asking for help to, among others, the Earl of Salisbury (the king's chief minister), Lord Chamberlain Suffolk, and Esmé Stuart, Seigneur D'Aubigny, cousin of King James, with whom Jonson stayed (?) 1604–6, and again (?) 1613–18.

(After August) Publication of *Sejanus*, which 'in all numbers, is not the same with that which was acted on the public stage, wherein a second pen had good share' ('To the Readers', Appendix, p. 173).

(October) Present at a Catholic supper party given by Robert Catesby, leader of the Gunpowder Plotters.

(November) Employed by the Privy Council in its enquiries following the foiling of the Gunpowder Plot to blow up the king and Parliament.

1606   (5 January) *Hymenaei* (masque) presented for the wedding of the Earl of Essex and Lady Frances Howard, daughter of the Earl of Suffolk.

(9 January) Indicted as a recusant at the London Sessions and cited on the same charge before the Consistory Court (January and April).

(? March) *Volpone* acted by the King's Men at the Globe and later at both universities.

(24 July) *The Entertainment of the Two Kings at Theobalds*.

1607   (11 February) Epistle dedicating *Volpone* to the Universities of Oxford and Cambridge signed 'From my house in the Blackfriars' and published with the play later in the year.

(22 May) *An Entertainment of the King and Queen at Theobalds.*

1608   (January) *The Masque of Beauty.*
          (Shrove Tuesday) *The Haddington Masque.*

1609   (2 February) *The Masque of Queens.*
          (? or early 1610) *Epicoene, or The Silent Woman* acted by the Children of the Whitefriars.

1610   (January) *Speeches at Prince Henry's Barriers.*
          (? before July) *The Alchemist* acted by the King's Men. Returned to Church of England.

1611   (1 January) *Oberon, The Fairy Prince*, masque for Prince Henry: first certified use of proscenium arch staging in England.
          (3 February) *Love Freed from Ignorance and Folly*, masque.
          (before 29 August) *Catiline* acted by the King's Men at the Globe: hissed off the stage after the second act. Publication of the King James Authorised Version of the Bible.

1612   (6 January) *Love Restored*, masque.
          (May) *Epigrams* entered in Stationers' Register, but either not published then or all copies lost.
          (c.August–June 1613) Accompanies Ralegh's son Wat to the Continent as tutor (*Drummond*, 245–53).

1613   *The Alchemist* revived at court, amid celebrations of the wedding of Princess Elizabeth to the Elector Palatine.
          (29 June) The Globe burns down during a performance of Shakespeare's *All Is True* (*Henry VIII*); Jonson eyewitness.
          (29 December and 3 January 1614) *The Irish Masque at Court.*

1614   (1 January) *A Challenge at Tilt*, for the marriage of the Earl of Somerset to Lady Frances Howard (divorced from the Earl of Essex).
          Bartholomew Fair acted by Lady Elizabeth's Men at the

Hope (31 October) and at court (1 November).

1615   (6 and 8 January) *Mercury Vindicated from the Alche-mists at Court*, masque.[3]

1616   (1 and 6 January) *The Golden Age Restored*, masque.
(6 February) Granted annual pension of 100 marks by
King James (= £66 13s 4d).
Publication of *The Workes* of Benjamin Jonson (the 1616
folio): contains all *preserved* plays to this date entirely
his own work (except *The Case Is Altered* and *Bar-tholomew Fair*), plus *Epigrams* and *The Forest*, and all
royal masques and entertainments.
(November–December) *The Devil is an Ass* acted by the
King's Men at the Blackfriars. Abandons the public stage.
Christmas His Masque.
Deaths of William Shakespeare, Francis Beaumont.

1617   (6 and 19 January) *The Vision of Delight*, masque.
(22 February) *Lovers Made Men*, masque, at the house
of Lord Hay.

1618   (6 January) *Pleasure Reconciled to Virtue*, masque, re-vised as *For the Honour of Wales* (Shrove Tuesday) af-ter the king's dissatisfaction.
Walks on foot to Scotland; reaches Edinburgh *c*.August
and received with great honour; returns end of Jan-uary 1619. Conversations with the poet William Drum-mond of Hawthornden.

1619   (17 July) Awarded honorary degree of Master of Arts
at Oxford, at the suggestion of the Chancellor, the Earl
of Pembroke.

1620   (17 January and 29 February) *News from the New World*,
masque.
An Entertainment at the Blackfriars for the christening
of Charles (b. 20 May), son of William Cavendish, later
Earl of Newcastle and an important late patron for
Jonson.
(? 19 June) *Pan's Anniversary*, masque.

1621   *The Gypsies Metamorphosed*, celebrating the king's greatest
            favourite, Buckingham, presented at Burley-on-the-Hill
            (3 August), Belvoir (5 August), Windsor (September).
            (21 October) Awarded the reversion of the Mastership
            of the Revels.

1622   (6 January) *The Masque of Augurs*, with additions (early
            May).

1623   (1 January) *The Alchemist* revived at court.
            (19 January) *Time Vindicated*, masque, presented in Inigo
            Jones's new Banqueting House at Whitehall.
            (20 October) Named in lawsuit as residing at Gresham
            College: possibly deputy Professor of Rhetoric there –
            parts of *Discoveries* and *The English Grammar* could be
            lecture notes.
            Publication of the first folio of Shakespeare's plays,
            with Jonson's commendatory poem (see Appendix,
            p. 194).
            Fire destroys Jonson's library (see 'An Execration upon
            Vulcan', *Und* XLIII).

1624   *Neptune's Triumph*, masque, prepared for 6 January but
            not performed.
            (19 August) *The Masque of Owls* presented before Prince
            Charles at Kenilworth.
            (27 December) Court performance of *Volpone*.

1625   (9 January) *The Fortunate Isles*, masque.
            (March) Deaths of King James, John Fletcher, (?) John
            Webster; accession of Charles I.

1626   Without assured court masque commissions, returns
            to public stage: *The Staple of News* acted by the King's
            Men at the Blackfriars and at court.

1628   (September) Appointed City Chronologer of London
            in succession to Thomas Middleton.
            (26 October) Interrogated about verses on the assassi-
            nation of Buckingham.
            Late in year suffers stroke, leaving him paralysed.[4]

1629   (?19 January) *The New Inn* acted at the Blackfriars by the King's Men: reportedly 'cried down the first day'.

1630   Gift of £100 from King Charles; royal pension increased to £100 yearly and supplemented with a tierce (42 gallons) of Canary wine.
         (19 November) *Volpone* revived by the King's Men.

1631   (9 January) *Love's Triumph through Callipolis*, masque. Public antagonism with Inigo Jones over the value of their respective roles in the creation of masques (see 'An Expostulation with Inigo Jones', UV XXXIV).
         (22 February) *Chloridia*, final court masque.
         Every Man In His Humour (18 February) and *The Alchemist* (1 December) revived by the King's Men.
         (November) Salary as City Chronologer (50 marks) withdrawn, following failure to perform duties.
         Death of John Donne, Dean of St Paul's.
         Abortive attempt to create a second folio of works, including *Bartholomew Fair*, *The Devil is an Ass* and *The Staple of News*: only individual copies of these works printed.

1632   *The Magnetic Lady* acted by the King's Men at the Blackfriars. Jonson and Sir Henry Herbert (Master of the Revels) examined before the Court of High Commission; the Court finally accepted that offensive material had been inserted into the play by the actors, after it had been licensed.[5]

1633   (7 May) *A Tale of a Tub* licensed to Queen Henrietta's Men, on condition satirical gibes at Vitruvius Hoop (= Inigo Jones) be deleted; acted at the Cockpit.
         (21 May) *The King's Entertainment at Wellbeck*.

1634   *A Tale of a Tub* acted at court; 'not liked'.
         (30 July) *Love's Welcome at Bolsover*, final entertainment, commissioned by Earl of Newcastle; incorporates Vitruvius Hoop satire on Inigo Jones.
         (18 September) At king's request salary as City Chronologer restored.

1637   (August) Death of Jonson; buried in Westminster Abbey. Different accounts record his death on 6 August and burial 9 August, or death on 16 August and burial next day.

1638   Publication of *Jonsonus Virbius,* memorial tributes.

1640   Surreptitious publication by John Benson of various unpublished Jonson works, including *The Gypsies Metamorphosed* and translation of Horace's *Ars Poetica.* Publication of 2-volume second folio of Jonson's *Works,* supervised by Sir Kenelm Digby, using sheets from the abortive 1631 folio; previously unpublished works include *The Underwood,* a different version of the *Ars Poetica, Discoveries, An English Grammar,* and fragments of *The Sad Shepherd,* a pastoral, and *Mortimer His Fall,* a chronicle history.

A Note on Texts

Jonson's criticism emerged in any number of different contexts, in prologues and epistles, addresses to the reader, apologies, choruses, commonplace books, poems, interludes between the acts of his plays, and in the dialogue of his plays and masques themselves. To grasp the significance of any particular item we need to relate it to the form and context in which it appeared, and sometimes also to the different contexts in which it *re*-appeared, subtly transmuted.

All of this poses problems when it comes to referring readers to the texts of Jonson's criticism. It is so widely dispersed among his works that nothing short of a complete edition of his writings is adequate. There is, however, still no complete modern-spelling version of Jonson's works. Something like one might be compiled *ad hoc* from G. A. Wilkes's edition of the *Complete Plays* (Oxford, 1981–2), Stephen Orgel's edition of *Ben Jonson: The Complete Masques* (New Haven, Conn., 1969) and Ian Donaldson's *Ben Jonson* in the 'Oxford Authors' series (Oxford, 1985), which contains all of the non-dramatic verse, together with his commonplace book *Timber, or Discoveries*, and the *Conversations with Drummond*. But even this would not be complete (it would lack some of his royal entertainments, for example), and would not be editorially consistent; it would, moreover, be a clumsy expedient to refer readers to such an array of works.

Since this book is about Jonson as a critic, one way of cutting the Gordian knot would be to refer to the edition of *Ben Jonson's Literary Criticism* by James D. Redwine, Jr, in the *Regents Critics Series* (Lincoln, Nebraska, 1970). This is a helpful compilation, and Redwine's introduction is the best general survey of Jonson's criticism and its philosophical premises. But his volume is resolutely *unhistorical*, in the sense that it treats Jonson's critical classicism as, in effect, part of a disinterested debate about timeless literary values – the very antithesis of this book, in which I argue that it is a pragmatic response to the problematic status of authorship in Jonson's lifetime. The organisation of his volume very much suggests the coherence of and continuities in Jonson's criticism, minimising the extent to which individual documents were adventitious responses to specific conditions and problems. This is reflected in a preference for versions of documents, like the revised texts of *Cynthia's Revels* and of the Epistle to *Volpone*, given in the 1616 folio of Jonson's *Works* (where he himself affected the status of a timeless 'classic' writer), rather than in their original form and context. It would, therefore, be quite inappropriate for me to align my book too closely with Redwine's, which is, moreover, not universally accessible.

Which leaves us (a mixed blessing, familiar to all Jonson scholars) with the magisterial eleven-volume *Ben Jonson*, edited by C. H. Herford, and Percy and Evelyn Simpson (Oxford, 1925–52). This is, however, in old-spelling and normally only available in reference libraries. And even here the choice of copy-text can be problematic: they too, for example, print the folio Epistle to *Volpone*, and while it is possible to reconstruct the quarto original from their scrupulous editorial apparatus, this is not a task for untrained eyes. Given all these problems, I have concluded that the logical solution is to reproduce as an appendix those parts of Jonson's criticism to which I refer most often, in all cases in their *original* versions (though in modernised spelling). Considerations of space make it impossible to reproduce Jonson's criticism comprehensively: a glance at Redwine's selection will confirm that this is so. I particularly regret not being able to include the absorbing *Conversations with William Drummond* or the single most substantial item, *Discoveries*.

Where I refer in my text to *Drummond* and *Discoveries*, the reference will be to Ian Donaldson's 'Oxford Authors' *Ben Jonson*, mentioned above, pp. 595–611, and 521–94, respectively, citing the line numbers only. For all other texts not in my Appendix, the reference will be to the Herford and Simpson edition (*H&S*), though silently substituting modern spelling, typography etc., and expanding elisions (I have, incidentally, modernised *all* quotations in this way, where necessary). Quotations from the plays will be identified simply by act, scene and line; from masques (*H&S*, VII) by line numbering; from the non-dramatic verse (virtually all in *H&S*, VIII) by its Roman numbering in the relevant collection: that is, *Epigrams* (hereafter *Ep*), *The Forest* (*For*), *The Underwood* (*Und*) and *Ungathered Verse* (*UV*), with line numbering where appropriate; from all other works, including prefaces, prologues, inductions etc., by volume and page numbers, and line numbering if necessary. Once a context is established, I give lineation alone.

References to works other than by Jonson are to the editions specified in the Notes, modernised as I say, if necessary.

This note will have served its primary purpose if it alerts readers to the fact that Jonson's critical views were not a settled quantity when he formulated them, nor should they be allowed to seem so now. The Prologue to *Every Man In His Humour* did not appear – indeed, could not have appeared – with the original 1598 version of the play; the prefatory addresses to the reader in the quartos of *Sejanus* and *The Alchemist* do not appear in the 1616 folio at all, while the Epistle to *Volpone* is subtly changed there, and the 'Apologetical Dialogue' to *Poetaster* appeared in print there for the first time, as did various dedications. The Induction to *Bartholomew Fair* was for its performance at the Hope theatre on 31 October 1614; for the performance the following day at court it was replaced by a prologue addressed to King James. More so than with many critics, it is vital to remember that nothing Jonson wrote is set in amber, all the more so because he himself often sought to pretend it might be so, and because many people since have sought to collude with that pretence.

1
The Lone Wolf

But thou hast squared thy rules, by what is good;
And art, three ages yet, from understood:
And (I dare say) in it there lies much wit
Lost, till thy readers can grow up to it.

Francis Beaumont, 'Upon [Jonson's] Catiline'

Ben Johnson [sic], I think, had all the critical learning to
himself; and till of late years England was as free from critics,
as it is from wolves

Thomas Rymer, preface to Rapin's *Reflections on*
Aristotle's Treatise of Poesie, 1674

In a world where the canonical status of writers cannot be taken for granted, David Riggs, a recent biographer, makes out one of the most compelling cases for Ben Jonson's continuing significance: 'Since his career coincides with the rise of the literary profession in England, his personal success story takes on the characteristics of a cultural phenomenon: in following his rise we are also witnessing the emergence of authorship as a full-time vocation.'[1] And, as I shall argue, it is in his criticism that we can best trace Jonson's own thinking about this 'cultural phenomenon', to which he was so integral. Alvin Kernan suggests some of the specific conditions within which this unfolded: 'An older system of polite or courtly letters – primarily oral, aristocratic, amateur, authoritarian, court-centered – was swept away at this time and gradually replaced by a new print-based, market-centered democratic literary system'.[2] As a matter of fact, Kernan is here describing the era of Dr Johnson in the mid-eighteenth century rather than that of his namesake a century and more before. But there was a real continuity between the two periods.

1

Jonson was at the beginning (as Johnson was at the mid-point) of a faltering process in which the practice of criticism shadowed the growth of the modern world of letters. Patrick Parrinder has argued that 'Samuel Johnson was the first Englishman to practise criticism as a major literary genre', which is true, and many recent accounts of literary criticism (such as those of Terry Eagleton) focus on it as the product of eighteenth-century bourgeois social structures.[3] But Ben Jonson was the first Englishman to practise literary criticism with any system and consistency, laying the groundwork which made the idea of criticism as 'a major literary genre' in our culture possible. And so, with some changes of emphasis, Kernan's summary remains valid. The 'older system of polite or courtly letters' (to which, for example, Philip Sidney unequivocally belonged, and John Donne essentially did) was *not* 'swept away' during Jonson's lifetime;[4] his practice as an author was very largely shaped by the dominance of the court, as the principal source of both patronage and authority. But it *was* paralleled, and to a degree challenged, 'by a new print-based, market-centred . . . literary system', even if that could hardly yet be described as democratic. There *was*, however, a totally unprecedented, quasi-democratic dimension to Elizabethan and early Stuart literary culture, that of the public playhouses of London. 'Democratic' is, of course, a relative term, and we must not minimise the extent to which the playhouses were only allowed to operate under licence from the court.[5] Nevertheless they were open to a more broadly-based 'readership' than any previous form of literary production. Only sermons, of the type preached publicly at Charing Cross or by John Donne in St Paul's Cathedral, had a comparable size and social mix of audience.[6]

Men like Robert Greene and Thomas Nashe had made a living of sorts by their writing in the 1580s and 1590s, and William Shakespeare had compounded the income from writing plays with the profits from being a shareholder in various theatrical enterprises. But Jonson may lay reasonable claim to have been the first Englishman to build a sustained career solely on his skill with a pen. He did this, perhaps fortuitously, not by siding with either the old or the new literary systems, but by exploiting the potential of both, as they existed (not always harmoniously) side by side. He was involved, often simultaneously, in the old system of courtly, aristocratic and civic patronage (to that extent remaining locked into the expectations and practices of earlier ages), in the commercial world of the playhouses, and in the print culture where the future was to lie (in those spheres anticipating many of the changes that were to overtake authorship in succeeding generations). No one else in his time had such a wide and various experience of the possibilities of authorship. His criticism is a response to that experience, an attempt to make sense of it and impose some shape on it: it demands attention because it is a unique record of the opening up of literature into what it would become in the modern world.

Jonson's career, that is, coincided with a key turning point in early modern culture, one that set the course for the profession of letters essentially as it has unfolded over the last four centuries. It is the moment to which Michel Foucault refers when he writes that the 'coming into being of the notion of the "author" constitutes the privileged moment of *individualization* in the history of ideas, knowledge, literature, philosophy, and the sciences'.[7] As I observed in the Preface – the coincidence is hardly accidental – this is also the moment when the modern sense of 'critic' emerged. In the context of English literature, Jonson embodies that moment as no other writer does, and at no small personal cost, given the turbulence that these changes involved. As his career unfolded, the status of the written word, and with it that of the 'author', was in an unprecedented state of flux, and their relationship to other forms of political, social and religious 'authority' was radically unstable. The challenge of Jonson's criticism is that it captures that flux, that sense of instability, as no other document does, a first attempt to articulate the forces that shaped the modern literary world.

Barely thirty years ago this would have seemed an extraordinary claim to make. George Watson in *The Literary Critics* (revised edition, 1964), for example, briefly admires the 'authentic' Jonson captured by William Drummond of Hawthornden in his *Conversations*, but passes over the rest in his conviction that 'descriptive' criticism outfaces 'legislative' or 'theoretical' criticism and is 'the only one [of the three] which today possesses any life and vigour of its own'. And 'descriptive criticism' really starts in England, not with Jonson himself but – almost as if to point up the omission – with Dryden's critique of one of Jonson's own plays, his 'examen' of *The Silent Woman* in *Of Dramatic Poesie*.[8] Jonson, by contrast, is far too ready with assertions of what literature is or should be, far too light on the critical exegesis of texts.

But Watson's 'today' is the early 1960s, still in the grip of the New Criticism instigated by T. S. Eliot and his successors, before waves of structuralist, Marxist, feminist, deconstructive, psychoanalytic, cultural materialist and post-structuralist criticism broke on Anglo-Saxon shores. His tri-partite division of criticism into 'descriptive', 'legislative' and 'theoretical' modes no longer seems as natural as it did then, nor is it now remotely arguable that the first of these has totally supplanted the other two.[9] It is now abundantly clear that the business of criticism is not restricted to the analysis of literary texts, out of time and context, but involves – like so much modern 'Theory' – an investigation of the ways language operates, of the reading process itself and of the culture(s) to which texts relate, issues which Jonson certainly recognised as central to his own concerns.

The fact that Jonson wrote so much of his criticism in open defence of his own practice as a writer is another point which troubled the New Critics. Such a degree of self-regard does not square easily with notions of criticism in its purest form being an *objective* exercise, being what Eliot described as 'the common pursuit of true judgement'.[10] This, of course, needs to be confronted as the myth it is. Eliot himself, for example, was nowhere near as disinterested as he purported to be in his criticism. In an earlier formulation he argued that 'The important critic is the person who is absorbed in the present problems of art, and who wishes to bring the forces of the past to bear upon the solution of these problems', where 'the present problems of art' essentially (but discreetly) means the issues addressed in his own poetry.[11] The tacit agenda of Eliot's criticism (and indeed that of so many writer/critics, including Dryden, Pope, Wordsworth, James and Lawrence) is to provide a descriptive vocabulary, and an informed readership, for his own creative writing, which is self-consciously at odds with current modes and tastes. The same is true of Jonson. But Jonson did not have a tradition of such self-promotion behind him, to demonstrate how the personal agenda of criticism might be veiled in a show of disinterested or universal application. Nor did he share a Modernist aesthetic, which made the 'disinterested' or 'impersonal' author such a necessary fiction. Jonson is, in fact, engagingly open about advancing his own agenda, in promoting new definitions of his own authority as a writer. To that extent he does exactly what Eliot or any other worthwhile author/critic does, but with a minimum of hypocrisy.

Broadly speaking, there are two other commonly voiced reservations about Jonson's criticism which need to be outfaced before I
can proceed to give it the attention I have argued it deserves.
Neither of these can be ascribed to the prejudices of former ages,
though they have certainly been compounded by them. I am referring to the substance of the critical legacy Jonson left behind,
in both its omissions and its commissions. On the one hand, Jonson
(or, more precisely, his transcribers and editors) bequeathed us
two major repositories of his critical thinking – the *Conversations
with Drummond* and *Timber, or Discoveries* – both of which are
highly problematic, often in antithetic or even flatly contradictory ways. On the other, he has left us with no single treatise as
coherent, sustained and engaging as Sidney's *Defence of Poesy* or
Dryden's *Of Dramatic Poesie*.

Since I shall often be quoting from *Conversations* and *Discoveries*,
I need to establish from the outset what kinds of documents they
are and the reservations we should properly entertain about their
contents. On the absence of a more authoritative central statement from Jonson, I must first echo David Klein's ironised frus-
trations from the beginning of the twentieth century: 'The trouble
is that Jonson's ideas are not set down for us by him in a book,
to be conned by rote'.[12] What is even more frustrating is that
Jonson did, apparently, write such a treatise, but it has not survived. The fact that he never put it into print tells us a number
of things (or, at least, raises a number of pointed questions) about
the place of criticism in his career. So I shall address that, too,
before continuing.

CONVERSATIONS WITH DRUMMOND

The *Conversations* are a record kept by William Drummond of
Hawthornden of 'Informations be Ben Jonston to W. D. when he
came to Scotland upon foot 1619'. That is, Drummond's account
of Jonson's conversation when he stayed with him at Hawthornden
in the winter of 1618/19, having walked all the way to Edinburgh. The survival of this unique record is so fortuitous that the
possibility of forgery cannot be entirely discounted. The original
manuscript has not survived, but a version said to be based on it
(rearranged and edited by Sage and Ruddiman) was published
in Edinburgh in 1711; what appears to be a more accurate and

authentic copy of the original was made by Sir Robert Sibbald (1641–1722), and that is now the basis for all modern versions. Even if we accept Sibbald's probity (there is, in fact, no good reason not to do so), there is no way of vouching for his accuracy, except where his version can be compared with the unsatisfactory Sage and Ruddiman one. In the end, we have to make do with what we have and (perhaps) conclude, with Herford and Simpson, that 'the desultory character of the jottings, the repetitions and even the errors are a convincing proof of their authenticity' (H&S, I, p. 219).

But even if we accept that they are, in that sense, authentic, what do we make of what they contain? They carry a colloquial and uninhibited conviction, which it is difficult to believe does not embody Jonson's own words; this is as true of his comments on poets and poetry as much as on other matters: 'that Markham . . . was not of the number of the faithful [i.e. poets], and but a base fellow. That such were Day and Middleton'; 'Samuel Daniel was a good honest man, had no children, but no poet'; 'Drayton feared him, and he esteemed not of him'; 'that Donne, for not keeping of accent, deserved hanging'; 'that Shakespeare wanted art'; 'that Sharpham, Day, Dekker were all rogues, and that Minsheu was one'; 'He had many quarrels with Marston: beat him, and took his pistol from him; wrote his *Poetaster* on him'; and so on (*Drummond*, 131–3, 17, 119, 36, 37, 38–9, 235–6). Perversely, however, the unbuttoned vigour of all this reflects badly in some eyes on the more considered (some have said laboured and pedantic) criticism Jonson saw fit to preserve himself.[13] Some of the opinions recorded so pithily here even seem at odds with his published comments on the same authors. His observation 'That Francis Beaumont loved too much himself and his own verses' (*Drummond*, 120) does not readily square with the compliments in the poem 'To Francis Beaumont' (*Ep* LV), while the near-prophetic judgement 'That Donne himself, for not being understood, would perish' (*Drummond*, 158) rather detracts from the exaggerated deference he pays him in *Ep* XXIII and XCVI. It is only too easy to conclude from this that Jonson was either an inconsistent or a hypocritical critic, and perhaps to regret that he did not always write as racily as he spoke under the influence of Drummond's wine: 'drink', his host tartly recorded, 'is one of the elements in which he liveth' (607–8).

This raises yet another level of hermeneutic difficulty. What exactly was the relationship between Drummond and Jonson, and to what extent do we need to deconstruct what the former transcribed of the latter? To put it another way, can we differentiate between 'pure' Jonson, and a Jonson highly coloured by Drummond's view of him? For example, the *Conversations* conclude with what appear to be Drummond's considered opinions of his guest: 'He is a great lover and praiser of himself, a contemner and scorner of others, given rather to lose a friend than a jest . . . He is passionately kind and angry, careless either to gain or keep, vindicative, but if he be well answered, at himself. For any religion, as being versed in both' (605–13). How much of this is Drummond's private conclusion, and how much is prompted by Jonson's own claims about himself? Is the comment 'For any religion . . .' his own wry joke or Drummond's tart conclusion? By the same token, what are we to make of Drummond's closing comment: 'When his play of a *Silent Woman* was first acted, there was found verses after on the stage against him, concluding that that play was well named *The Silent Woman*: there was never one man to say *plaudite* to it' (617–19). Did Jonson himself feed Drummond this anecdote, and if he did so, did he do it bitterly, ruefully, or even with a grin? Or was Drummond privately getting his own back, after what was clearly a very wearing visit?

A few lines earlier Drummond describes Jonson as 'oppressed with fantasy, which hath ever mastered his reason, a general disease in many poets' (614–15) – 'hath ever mastered' suggests that this was, in origin, a 'confession' on Jonson's own part, and other passages bear out this possibility: 'he hath consumed a whole night in lying looking to his great toe, about which he hath seen Tartars and Turks, Romans and Carthaginians, fight in his imagination' (268–70). But was Jonson straight-faced when he said this, and was Drummond entirely unironic in recording it? Compare it, for example, with the account of Jonson's premonition of his eldest son's death, when William Camden temporarily 'persuaded him it was but an apprehension of his fantasy, at which he should not be disjected' (220–1). There is, presumably, no element of joking or irony here. Yet it is difficult not to believe that, for at least some of the time, Jonson was amusing himself at Drummond's own expense, the famous 'poet' performing larger than life before the rather prim and bookish Scottish laird. This might well have led him, for example, to embroider tales of his swordsmanship and of his brushes with authority as a young man.

At one point Jonson delivered his 'censure' of Drummond's own verses: 'that they were all good, especially my epitaph of the prince, save that they smelled too much of the schools, and were not after the fancy of the time' (81–3); but he had already 'recommended to my reading Quintilian (who, he said, would tell me all the faults of my verses as if he had lived with me), and Horace, Plinius secundus *Epistles*, Tacitus, Juvenal, Martial' (9–11) – apparently sending him back to the very 'schools' of which he felt the verses 'smelled too much', and so on. To take one final example of the indeterminacies of the text: we are told early on 'that Sidney did not keep a decorum in making every one speak as well as himself' (13–14), while 'Guarini in his *Pastor Fido* kept not decorum in making his shepherds speak as well as himself could', and 'that Lucan, taken in parts, was good divided; read altogether, merited not the name of a poet' (47–8, 49–50). Towards the end we seem to have a recapitulation of all this: 'Lucan, Sidney, Guarini, make every man speak as well as themselves, forgetting decorum; for Dametas sometimes speaks grave sentences. Lucan, taken in parts, excellent; altogether, naught' (537–9). Is this Jonson repeating himself rather tediously, possibly wandering in his cups? Or is it Drummond making an attempt to reduce his notes to order of sorts, or simply forgetting that he had already jotted them down – the process of transcription was presumably haphazard, and there is no indication (another point to bear in mind) that Jonson knew that it was going on.

For these reasons, at no point can we vouch for the absolute authenticity of tone of anything that Jonson 'says' in the 'Conversations'. But that does not render them worthless. On the contrary, as we shall see, nothing of Jonson's criticism can be wrenched from its context and offered as his 'definitive' view on any matter. The complexity of his position in the intellectual and literary marketplace, which I began this chapter by outlining, rendered such categorical positioning impossible: every document is a strategic intervention in an argument with history, never the final word. And therein lies its value. The *Conversations* are merely a particularly problematic demonstration of that fact. They offer us a refracted image of the man at a specific point in his career: a literary celebrity at the height of his powers, who had published a folio of his *Works*, had a pension and a secure position at court, whose very journey to Edinburgh (where he was fêted by the Town Council and other worthies, not just Drummond) signified his standing as – in all but title – poet laureate to the King of Great Britain.

In such a context perhaps the single most revealing entry in them is 'In his merry humour he was wont to name himself The Poet' (560). Again we may ask whether this is Jonson's reflection on his own habits or simply Drummond's observation of them, but either way there is a wry acknowledgement here of a role to be played, the role of a particular kind of author, of an identity that does not come naturally and has to be invented or sustained. It is a game of sorts, a game which is responsible for everything that Drummond records – the cantankerous, bawdy, irreverent know-it-all, who continually re-invents himself in relation to his contemporaries and his classical predecessors, more often than not at their expense – and a game we shall explore further. Seen in such a light, the *Conversations* are a fascinating and revealing document, though one to be treated with circumspection. There will be occasions in this book when it is helpful to draw on them in relation to Jonson's other criticism – but never without a proper recognition of their problematic nature.

TIMBER: OR DISCOVERIES

The *Discoveries* pose difficulties of a kind that seem at first antithetic to those posed by the *Conversations*; in the end, however, they prove to be strikingly analogous. The text is, in appearance, a commonplace book, of a kind frequently compiled in the Renaissance. It contains highly miscellaneous observations, relatively brief and on disparate subjects at the beginning, but with more sustained essays on literary style and practice towards the end. It is not clear whether the organisation, or the annotation, of the treatise are Jonson's own work or that of the editor of the 1640 second folio (where it first appeared), Sir Kenelm Digby. The provenance of these observations is very mixed, but only a small portion is original to Jonson himself. As Paul Sellin observes, 'The passages touching on poetry and rhetoric are culled from Seneca, Plutarch, Quintilian, Vives, Lipsius, Buchler, Scaliger, and Hoskyns, to say nothing of Heinsius, and little can be ascribed to the pen of Jonson himself'.[14] This poses a different version of the question we confronted in the *Conversations*: who precisely is speaking at any particular point in the volume?

To take one example: a casual reading of the *Discoveries* would suggest that Bacon became one of Jonson's cultural heroes, a writer, philosopher and statesman whose works he not only quotes from (2109–44) but whom he singles out for exceptional praise: 'He, who hath filled up all numbers; and performed that in our tongue, which may be compared, or preferred, either to insolent Greece, or haughty Rome' (924–6). These opening compliments turn out, however, to be drawn from the preface to Seneca's *Epistles*, Book 1. A further paragraph that seems to square up confidently to the fact of Bacon's political disgrace, 'My conceit of his person was never increased toward him by his place or honours . . .' (948–9), turns out to be a close paraphrase of a letter from Father Fulgenzio Micanza to the first Earl of Devonshire. As Ian Donaldson observes, 'Jonson's act of transcription may perhaps be presumed to imply endorsement of its sentiments, but the statement is not quite so self-revealing or so sturdily independent as it at first appears'.[15]

To a modern way of thinking this is simply plagiarism, but it is in fact deeply symptomatic of a situation in which a professional writer like Jonson literally had no precedent for speaking his own mind, at least not in public. The fact that there may also have been prudential considerations, that Jonson may have felt the need to draw lines (however notional) between himself and a man with many political enemies, only dramatises something he must have felt in making all his critical statements: his exposure, his lack of ready authority. As a 'critic' in the sense partly opened up by Bacon himself, Jonson purports to have special authority for *what he says*, but in fact it is one he has to create for himself as he goes along. Hence what seems to us an awkward compromise: the 'originality' of his praise of Bacon lies in the ingenious application of Seneca to the subject, in the public utterance of what had been private sentiments (though presumably not so private that they had not circulated in manuscript), and indeed in the marriage of these two 'sources'. In this way Jonson forges an identity, or a speaking voice, for himself out of pre-existing materials. And this in turn is given a different status by its publication in a prestigious two-volume collection of Jonson's writing, clearly devised to establish (or, strictly, re-establish, given his fate in the literary marketplace after the first folio) his canonical standing.

Once we appreciate this, it is easier to see that *Discoveries* is not quite the haphazard collection of conservative, humanist commonplaces (with occasional nuggets of 'essential' Jonson) which it has often been assumed to be. As Timothy Murray observes,

> 'Sorting', 'cutting out', 'woods' and in this case *Timber: or, Discoveries* are metaphors used in the Renaissance to suggest the dual process of selection and grouping together passages for contemplation. Similar to the printing of plays, the common placing of variant texts unites them in one spatially apprehensible image through which its compiler becomes trained in visually maintaining identities and differences – what is done manually in transcribing the commonplace book.[16]

The fact of assembling what are known to be passages derived from other authors, and presenting them in a printed format which calls attention to the fact (often with running glosses), creates an inherently new text which calls attention both to 'the compiler's' breadth of reading and to his discrimination. The fact that Digby may have contributed to the process does not alter the essential nature of the text, or the way it subtly implicates the reader in questioning why the passages have been selected, why in that order, why in that context. Even the title page gives us reason to expect something more sophisticated than random selection: 'Discoveries: Made upon men and matter: as they have flowed out of his daily readings, or had their reflux to his peculiar notion of the times'. 'As they have flowed out of his daily readings' does suggest something casual and haphazard, but 'had their reflux ["a flowing back, return, refluence", OED] to his peculiar notion of the times' implies something more personal and purposeful, a reaction to contemporary events and ideas: not Olympian reflections, but specific engagements with issues and pressures that assailed Jonson elsewhere.

Unlike so many items of Jonson's criticism, it is impossible to date most of *Discoveries* precisely. In his reflections on rhyme he is thinking back as far as 1603–4 and quarrels he had then with Daniel and Campion on the question, though he may not be reproducing the words he used then. For the most part, what *can* be dated seems to be late: the observations on Shakespeare seem to post-date the Shakespeare first folio of 1623; the major passage on Bacon refers to 'the late Lord St Albans' (he died in 1626); many of the borrowings from Daniel Heinsius are specifically from the commentary to his 1629 edition of Horace, while there are references to incidents in 1630 and to a book published in 1633.[17] This is not surprising when we consider that the 'Execration upon Vulcan' (*Und* XLIII) tells us that one item he lost in the 1623 fire which destroyed his library was 'twice twelve years' stored-up humanity, / With humble gleanings in divinity', which may well have been one or more earlier commonplace books. Unless Jonson deliberately attempted to reconstruct some of what was lost, the *Discoveries* as we have them would necessarily be post-1623, much of it after he had lost his central place at court, when the gloss of the 1616 folio would be wearing thin, and he had returned to the public stage (most probably because he needed the money) and to public print; some of it clearly dates from after he had been disabled by a stroke in 1628, but all when he had adopted a new persona as a 'father' to a 'tribe', the 'sons of Ben'. These are the pressures of contextual identity that we are likely to find in that complex volume and, as with the *Conversations* though for different reasons, we must beware of treating anything in it as Jonson's definitive word on any subject.

Paul Sellin is thus correct in the following observation, though I think wrong to advance it as a criticism: 'the material assembled in the *Discoveries* cannot be regarded as focused into an integrated doctrine of poetry which Jonson "made his own" out of the snippets gathered from his reading. . . . The *Discoveries* does not present a system of ideas on poetry, and the treatise seems to be little more than a mere collection of ideas, a common-place book . . . he is not a Heinsian critic'.[18] He is right to conclude that Jonson is not theoretically or methodologically consistent, in the way that one would expect of a scholar–critic like Heinsius (who is, in fact, the main focus of Sellin's attention). But he is wrong to dismiss the result as a 'mere' collection of ideas, for reasons I have already suggested. As he also observes – thinking specifically of passages of Heinsius, but it would apply to any of Jonson's 'sources' – 'it is obvious . . . that he has not tried to preserve the assumptions of his original'. This is not, as he implies, laziness or indifference on Jonson's part; it occurs precisely because the passages he draws upon 'had their reflux to his peculiar notion of the times' (that is why he draws upon *them*, and not others) and it is the perceived timely relevance – rather than 'the assumptions of his original' – which engages him and which he enhances and preserves.

That the results did not cohere into a 'system of ideas' is my point. Jonson did not have a scholar's regard for consistency; he had a writer's regard for the problems of language, of communication and of representation in a world where the concept of free speech was unknown, and the passage on Bacon demonstrates exactly the kind of pragmatic accommodations he was prepared to make to overcome them. Dryden was thus very much to the point when he concluded his main comments on Jonson in the *Essay of Dramatic Poesie* with the observation: 'as he has given us the most correct plays, so in the precepts which he has laid down in his *Discoveries*, we have as many and profitable rules for perfecting the stage, as any wherewith the French can furnish us'.[19] Precepts – in the sense of 'practical rules of art' – are just what Jonson's method in the *Discoveries* generates; not a coherent poetics, but an assemblage of pragmatic advice, discrimination and demonstration, keyed to the practicalities of addressing peculiar notion[s] of the times. They may be unsystematic and even inconsistent, but they are not lazily random in the sense that Sellin's 'common-place book' implies. And, even at their most magisterial, the elements he assembles in this way are more circumspect and psychologically fraught than a modern reading may readily suggest; to recycle the authority of earlier writers is not always complacent conservatism, but can betray the fragility of your own authority, exposing foundations of sand.

THE LOST 'OBSERVATIONS ON HORACE'S ART OF POETRY' OR 'APOLOGY FOR BARTHOLOMEW FAIR'

Naturally, what we should most like to know about this missing treatise is what it said, and indeed how it changed between what must have been at least two distinct versions. The earliest we hear of it is in the 'To the Readers' (*Sejanus*, 1605), where he mentions 'my observations upon Horace his *Art of Poetry*, which (with the text translated) I intend shortly to publish' (Appendix, p. 173). It is probably the same document to which he refers in the Epistle to *Volpone* (quarto, 1607), where he seems to allude to his earlier promise: 'To which, upon my next opportunity toward the examining and digesting of my notes, I shall speak more wealthily, and pay the world a debt' (Appendix, p. 178). By the 1616 folio this enthusiasm has been reduced to a much more perfunctory: 'To which I shall take the occasion elsewhere to speak'.

Then, in the *Conversations*, we find that he read the treatise to Drummond, though clearly not in its original form: 'To me he read the preface of his *Art of Poesy*, upon Horace['s] *Art of Poesy*, where he hath an apology of a play of his, *St Bartholomew's Fair*. By Criticus is understood Donne. There is an epigram of Sir Edward Herbert's before it. The [translation], he said, he had done in my Lord Aubigny's house ten years since, anno 1604' (61–5). The bracketed 'translation' is an editorial conjecture, since Sibbald appears to have missed a word out at the end of a line; it could equally be the (original) preface. Either way, the date of 1604 (even though it was more than 'ten years since' when Drummond wrote – one of the minor conundrums in the *Conversations*) exactly chimes with the original promise made in *Sejanus*.

The last we hear of the preface is in the 'Execration upon Vulcan', where he laments the loss of 'All the old Venusine in poetry, / And lighted by the Stagirite' (ll. 89–90). Ian Donaldson glosses these lines: 'Horace's *Ars Poetica*, translated and commented upon in the light of the *Poetics*, from which it was thought to derive. (Venusia was Horace's birthplace, Stagira Aristotle's)'.[20] Jonson, or his editors, were able in fact to recover *two* versions of the translation of Horace, both published in 1640. But neither version had the preface attached. The only sustained attempt to reconstruct what it might have said is that by Freda L. Townshend in *Apologie for Bartholomew Fayre*, a slightly misleading title since she only devotes five pages to the missing treatise itself.[21] She in fact assumes that the preface would have been a distillation of Jonson's opinions from throughout his career, without distinction as to their timing and context, with a bias towards those which were most 'modern', least restrictive and law-bound. She imagines, for example, that Giraldi Cinthio's defence of *Orlando Furioso*, which champions the 'laws of mother Nature' over those of critical prescription, might have been a suitable precedent: 'Certainly the basis for a similar vigorous pronouncement by Jonson lies already before us in the *Sejanus* preface, in the Grexes to *Every Man Out of His Humour*, and in the *Discoveries*, where he, too, stoutly opposes Aristotelian dictatorship and urges the superiority of poesy to poetic laws, the necessity of adaptation to "these our Times"' (pp. 92–3). Quite apart from the question of whether Jonson would have described anything so indifferent to critical 'laws' as 'lighted by the Stagirite', this entirely ignores the fact that he was *not* consistent about the status of 'poetic laws'; to take only a couple of (equally widely-spread) examples of him taking a less relaxed attitude to such matters, the Prologue to *Volpone* offers

> quick comedy, refined,
>   As best critics have designed;
> The laws of time, place, persons he observeth,
> From no needful rule he swerveth
>
> (ll. 29–32)

while the commendatory poem to Richard Brome's *The Northern Lass* (1632) speaks without apparent irony of 'observation of those comic laws / Which I, your master, first did teach the age' (*UV* 38, ll. 7–8).

Given such disparities, it is pointless to try to reconstruct what he actually said in this preface. But it is instructive to consider an equally unanswerable question, that of why he never lived up to the promise to publish it – though part of the answer might well be that he never felt he had sufficiently reconciled his own conflicting instincts on the question of 'poetic laws' to go into substantial print on the question. One very practical considera-tion must have been the publication in 1610 of 'Daniel Heinsius's edition of Horace's works, which contains a rearranged version of the *Ars Poetica* that won Jonson's acceptance'.[22] This is what generated the second translation, the one published in Digby's second folio, though it may well have been completed before Jonson visited Drummond, as the revision of the preface certainly was. Jonson met Heinsius in person on his visit to the continent in 1613, and this may also have affected these revisions.

But these factors would only explain a delay, not a final failure to publish. The translation itself (the differences are not so great that we need to discuss the versions separately) may suggest some of the difficulties Jonson would have had to confront in the pref-ace. As Michael McCanles points out,

> Jonson's translation yields up aspects of Horace's argument . . . which suggest that Jonson read it as a treatise concerned less with rhetorical effect and poetic decorum than with the ethical discriminations of the poet that underlie and are reflected in his artistic choices. Horace domesticated in Jonson's poetic *oeuvre* comes, not unexpectedly, to the defence of the poet as humanist

scholar. . . . Jonson here gives us a lesson in humanist imitation
of classical texts; specifically in how meanings latent in the original emerge in new contexts, or meanings already obvious expand in new directions.[23]

That is, in exactly the same way as the borrowings in *Discoveries*
'had their reflux to his peculiar notion of the times', translation
for Jonson is always a process of emphasising or elaborating upon
those elements of the original which directly address immediate
concerns (here, his own self-definition as a poet).

So in the translation, as in more open appropriations (e.g. in
Discoveries), Jonson showed a cavalier disregard for what Paul
Sellin called 'the assumptions of his original': his own agenda,
'his peculiar notion of the times', always came first, something
which would have become uncomfortably apparent in a preface.
His treatise would, in effect, have to be a defence, not of Horace
in the abstract, but of *his* Horace – one with the emphases which
McCanles observes, in which Jonson was to an extent flying in
the face of (continental) formalist critical theory in his own time,
a fact apparently not appreciated by formalist critics in ours.[24]
Jonson was never one to duck a quarrel with the fashionable view,
and that in itself would not have prevented him from publishing
the preface. But the extent to which any argument would have
betrayed the lengths of his own self-serving might have given
him pause. The charged relationship between 'the assumptions
of his original' and Jonson's 'peculiar notion of the times' tacitly
surfaces in relation to every translation and imitation. For him to
invoke an authoritative predecessor is always to appropriate him
in a very particular sense, to shape that authority to his own requirements. Dryden said of his borrowings that 'he invades authors
like a monarch; and what would be theft in other poets, is only
victory in him'.[25] He makes it sound both easy and arrogant; in
fact it is one of the surest signs of Jonson's insecurity, a tacit
admission of the limits of his own independence, and to ignore
this (as Dryden does) seriously distorts the tone and status of
Jonson's humanist practice as an invasive borrower and translator.

   There is a further dimension to this insecurity, in so far as the
missing preface is concerned. It is striking that Drummond, following a second mention of both the translation and the preface,
immediately adds: 'The old book th[a]t goes about, *The Art of
English Poesy* [almost certainly by George Puttenham, but pub-

lished anonymously], was done twenty years since, and kept long in writ as a secret' (357–9). The issue here is partly the stigma which, for a gentleman, attached to public print, an issue we shall consider shortly; but deliberate secrecy is another matter. On the one hand literary theory was proper matter for coterie debate among Renaissance gentlemen, who were educated to be interested in the power and effect of language; on the other, it was always potentially indiscreet, in explaining too much about how their private understandings might be encoded and shared. As Annabel Patterson has argued, self-censorship, writing (and reading) within known, decodable but largely unvoiced constraints, was an endemic feature of English Renaissance literature.[26] So discussions of literary theory – however formal, technical or abstract – inevitably trespassed on such potentially dangerous territory. Puttenham, for example, spelled out a feature of pastoral eclogue which everyone doubtless knew, but which some readers/writers may have preferred left unvoiced: 'The Poet devised the Eclogue . . . not of purpose to counterfeit or represent the rustical manner of loves and communication; but under the veil of homely persons, and in rude speeches to insinuate and glance at greater matters, and such as perchance had not been safe to have been disclosed in any other sort' – citing Virgil's *Eclogues* as a definite example. Jonson himself had a copy of Puttenham's book, with four of its pages cancelled by the censor.[27]

Jonson was doubtless conscious of the risk of being similarly unguarded, but also of the danger of even more intimate indiscretions. By the time he read his treatise to Drummond, it was in dialogue form and 'By Criticus is understood Donne'. What other private understandings were encoded in the text? The fact that Sir Edward Herbert had written an introductory epigram further suggests that the preface had circulated in certain circles, and it may eventually have seemed to Jonson indiscreet or unmannerly to break the circle of confederacy and confidentiality. Sidney's *Defence of Poesy*, though not a dialogue, offered Jonson a precedent of sorts, but an awkward one. Here, as elsewhere, Sidney projected himself not as a professional writer, but as an aristocrat 'provoked to say something unto you in the defence of that my unelected vocation' – the 'you' clearly addressing a circle of friends and social peers among whom the *Defence* was meant to circulate in manuscript, rather than indiscriminately among the reading public at large.[28] The work only emerged in print in 1595, nine years after Sidney's death, and then in two unauthorised versions, the differences between which suggest the ways in which a manuscript of that sort remained to a degree both personal and *provisional* or on-going, a statement which the writer might adapt or develop in the light of his readers' responses. Jonson presumably shared something of this sense of provisionality, since he altered his own 'observations' after 1614, to relate them in some way to *Bartholomew Fair*, and this is what he read to Drummond.

The equation of Donne with 'Criticus' (at whatever stage in the composition) underlines the 'private' nature of the document, and this may well have given Jonson second thoughts about giving it the public and definitive status of print – even in the 1616 folio, where the promise to publish the preface is downgraded to a half-hearted 'To which, I shall take occasion elsewhere to speak'. Given that he printed neither the translation of Horace nor *Bartholomew Fair* in the folio (it is clear that there was simply no space for the latter), there was no ready context for the preface. In the folio Jonson seems to identify himself implicitly with the new print culture and the quasi-independence it conferred on the author.[29] Yet the *Works* is an equivocal milepost in his career. No sooner was it published than, as David Riggs puts it, 'Jonson withdrew from the literary market-place'.[30] Secure in an annual royal pension (granted February 1616), Jonson not only abandoned the commercial stage – after *The Devil is an Ass* later that year – but also lost the habit of putting his works into public print. Neither *Bartholomew Fair* nor *The Devil is An Ass* was printed until the 1630s, when a shortage of money seems to have been the main motivation; no further selection of his poetry (after *Epigrams* and *The Forest* in the folio) was published in his lifetime, though at some stage he reduced to order of a kind what posthumously emerged as *The Underwood*. Most of the remaining Jacobean masques were *privately* printed and circulated at court, but were not put on sale to the public. Possibly some work in progress (and the long-promised preface) would eventually have seen print, had it not been for the 1623 fire that destroyed his library. But by then, to all intents and purposes, the first great professional champion of print had retreated (as it may seem to us) into the world of private patronage and coterie manuscripts – of which the preface remained an example, if it survived at all. It is not impossible that, secure in the authority of the 1616 *Works*, Jonson was taking the long view and simply not contemplating print again until he could match that volume with one of similar substance. But if so he miscalculated his capacities, and either way we can only really speak of the effect of his actions, not his intentions.

So, in the wider view, Jonson's career was not one of linear progress from the old world of courtly letters to the modern one of moveable-print technology, but a journey fraught with internal contradictions, which are all highlighted by the failure to publish the 'Apology for Bartholomew Fair'. David Klein's comment: 'I wish that commentary on Horace had not been destroyed in that confounded conflagration' is heartfelt but, in a sense, misses the point.[31] Of course we would rather have it, but a single coherent treatise – which gave the *appearance* of being a definitive statement – might well have obscured the fact that Jonson's most lasting achievement was his whole career, with its tensions and internal contradictions, a unique 'document' which transcends all the individual documents that record it, and absolutely central to the development of the profession of letters in England. As we go on to consider that 'document', and the criticism Jonson (and others) *did* preserve, we should, however, bear in mind the 'absence' which the preface represents – as revealing in its way as any published item, and as much a part of the evidence.

Speaking of absences, it will be salutary to try to retain a sense of Jonson as he might have seemed to contemporaries who knew nothing of the *Conversations with Drummond* or of *Discoveries*. Whether by accident or design, these are part only of the posthumous record, not of his public engagement with the life of his time. We cannot now expunge them from our own sense of Jonson as a critic, nor should we want to. But this book will continually stress the important differences between the resonance of his criticism as it first made an impact on the world, and the very different weights it has carried (at various times) with hindsight. If we look at the two epigraphs at the head of this chapter, for example, we should bear in mind that Beaumont's commendatory poem was written by someone who probably did know the lost preface, had probably experienced something of the flavour (though not the precise substance) of the *Conversations with Drummond*, but knew nothing of *Discoveries*. The supercilious Rymer, by contrast, knew nothing of the *Conversations*, had not read (or probably even known of) the lost preface, but certainly knew *Discoveries*. We are different again, and the difference is what I want to stress.

We are now in a position to begin to substantiate the large claims I made earlier for Jonson's criticism. If we review those three key documents, the *Conversations with Drummond, Discoveries* and the lost preface to the *Art of Poetry*, what emerges consistently is a curious mixture of assurance bordering on arrogance, and deep insecurity. It is a mixture we shall encounter repeatedly. The sense of assurance is reinforced by the fact that Jonson inherited a coherent intellectual tradition of Christian humanism from scholar/writers of the sixteenth century including Sir Thomas More, Erasmus, Juan Luis Vives, Joseph Scaliger, Sir Thomas Chaloner, Sir Thomas Elyot, Roger Ascham and Richard Mulcaster. This gave him a vocabulary for the discussion of literature which was inherently positivist, informed by a sense that writing could play a constructive role in human affairs, and reinforced by a deeply engaged study of the classical past, where writers (Aristotle, Cicero, Seneca, for example) had contributed significantly to the public affairs of their day. Much of this must have been instilled into Jonson by his master at Westminster School, the distinguished historian William Camden, whom he credited with 'All that I am in arts, all that I know' (*Ep* XIV) and to whom he dedicated the folio *Every Man In His Humour*.

But the conditions in which humanism had flourished in England for a century were already changing by the time that Jonson was born; in his own lifetime Bacon, Galileo and Descartes would promote more sceptical philosophies, more firmly based on empirical observation, less enthusiastic about the role of the liberal arts in furthering the human condition. Social and economic changes too – the growth of London and a competitive urban culture, the growth of trade and its distortion of traditional assumptions about the relationship between wealth, virtue and status – all of these made the fundamentally optimistic agenda of humanism more difficult to sustain and advance. So that there is always a sense that Jonson's humanist vocabulary is under strain, fighting a rearguard action in a world (and the Stuart court, dominated first by Salisbury and the Howards and then by Buckingham, was just such a world) where its assumptions are increasingly alien. The aggression with which he sometimes deploys it speaks as much of desperation as of assurance.

There are times when he almost admits as much, as when, in his set-piece praise of Bacon, he lists those predecessors and contemporaries whose achievements Bacon may be said to crown:

'In short, within his view, and about his times, were all the wits born that could honour a language or help study. Now things daily fall: wits grow downward, and eloquence grows backward' (*Discoveries*, 928–31; see also 303–8). In the main, however, he resists the elegiac strain (which in this instance actually derives from Seneca's reflections on Cicero – again, not *exactly* Jonson's own sentiments). More characteristically he insists (in a passage based on Vives): 'I cannot think nature is so spent and decayed that she can bring forth nothing worth her former years. She is always the same, like herself; and when she collects her strength, is abler yet. Men are decayed, and studies: she is not' (126–30) – an admission that things are bad, though not irredeemable: but an admission, too, of the pressure this places him under.

Yet the anxiety at the heart of Jonson's career, which gave rise to the evasions and internal contradictions in his criticism, concerned his new and indeterminate status as a professional author – an issue which had never faced earlier humanist writers, thus seriously qualifying his use of their characteristic vocabulary, even if other circumstances had not done so. He was strung between at least three distinct forms of publication – the theatre (even here, there are distinctions to be drawn between what we may loosely label public, private and court performances), coterie circulation of manuscripts, and commercial print – each with a different audience, each implying a different relationship between the writer and the reader/audience, each with its own subtle social encoding. Jonson would seek on occasion to elide these differences, to assert that his own integrity as an author over-rode the lesser distinctions of the manner and circumstance of publication, but the effort involved in such assertions – the extent to which their claims cannot be taken at face value – is always apparent.

AUTHOR, AUTHORITY, AUTHORSHIP

These complexities are perhaps most clearly illustrated in the different senses of 'author', 'authority' and 'authorship' that Jonson and his contemporaries used in relation to that most distinctive of Jacobean forms, the court masque. We may begin with the printed text of *The Masque of Queens* (1609), where he describes how he chose as his 'argument' or theme for presentation by Queen Anne and her ladies

a celebration of honourable and true fame bred out of virtue. . . .
And because her majesty (best knowing that a principal part of
life in these spectacles lay in their variety) had commanded me
to think on some dance or show that might precede hers and
have the place of a foil or false masque, I . . . therefore now
devised that twelve women in the habit of hags or witches,
sustaining the persons of Ignorance, Suspicion, Credulity, etc.,
the opposites to good Fame, should fill that part, not as a masque
but a spectacle of strangeness, producing multiplicity of gesture, and not unaptly sorting with the current and whole fall
of the device.   (Appendix, p. 181)

The anti-masque is not itself a masque, but 'a spectacle of strangeness', yet its figures are not entirely arbitrary or heterogeneous
to the masque itself ('not unaptly sorting') and they function as
'a foil, or false masque', setting off the true one. The anti-masque
is Jonson's most important technical and structural contribution
to these elaborate disguisings, and a good example of the way in
which throughout his career he had a genius for adapting pre-
existing forms, rather than devising entirely new ones, and bringing
them to a new level of perfection. Yet Jonson is careful to acknowledge, or perhaps to invoke, the Queen as the originator of
the anti-masque. This is in part simple deference to a patron whom
Jonson would hope to serve again. But it also provides him with
a sanction – an authority of sorts – for an innovation which would
not necessarily meet with universal approval. In this way it touches
on a delicate and complex perception of the 'authorship' of a work
such as this. Writing home about *The Masque of Beauty* (1608),
which Jonson had written for Queen Anne the year before, the
Venetian ambassador Guistinian reported: 'So well composed and
ordered was it all that it is evident the mind of her Majesty, the
authoress of the whole, is gifted no less highly than her person.'[32]
This was not for public consumption, and the ambassador had
no reason to flatter the queen. He knew full well that a team of
writers, designers and musicians had collaborated in devising this
entertainment, but he subsumes their achievements under that of
Queen Anne, 'the authoress of the whole'. The word Guistinian
uses is 'autrice', glossed by John Florio in his dictionary (see below) as 'a she author or doer'.[33]
    He may in this be reflecting his knowledge that Anne took a
particular delight in theatricals, and was perhaps more personally

involved in the preparations of these masques than most royalty would be.[34] He had earlier reported, of this particular masque, that 'at the King's request the Queen and Principal Ladies of the Court are preparing to give a magnificent masque' and 'at her own charges'.[35] But he was certainly also articulating the common Renaissance perception that *patrons*, rather than the artisans they employed, were the true 'authors/esses' of any work produced in their service. However distinguished the workman employed – be it a Leonardo da Vinci, a Ben Jonson or an Inigo Jones – the work of art was in some essentials the creation of the patron, its 'author' or originator. John Florio, in the work I have just cited, ingeniously manipulates this understanding in dedicating the revised version of *A World of Words* (1598, and unequivocally his own work) to Queen Anne: 'entitled *Queen Anna's New World of Words*, as under your protection and patronage sent forth. It shall be my guard against the worst, if not grace with the best, if . . . with heart I may say, This is *Queen Anna's*, as the author is, and shall ever be'.[36] Her patronage tacitly appropriates the text as it validates and so protects it, subsuming the self-effacing 'author' in the process: as she 'owns' him, she authorises his writing. Jonson himself invokes all these nuances when, in the jointly-published texts of the *Queen's Masques of Blackness and of Beauty* (1608), he acknowledges his duty 'to that Majesty who gave them their authority and grace' (Appendix, p. 180).

In the case of a court masque, a collaborative piece commissioned for a specific occasion and performance both by and for its patrons, this conception of the relationship between patron and artist is readily intelligible: Jonson's use of 'authority' here could equally apply to the queen's patronage of the entire event, or specifically her gracious performance within it. But with printed texts a different dynamic is inevitably at work: the name of the person responsible for the final choice of words and their imprint (the two principal signifiers in this medium) carries an unmistakable force, even if that person makes a show of deferring to the authority of a patron. So it is in the printed texts of Jonson's masques, and in particular the earliest ones published – *Hymenaei* (1606), *The Haddington Masque* (1608), *Queen's Masques of Blackness and of Beauty* (1608) and *The Masque of Queens* – where he defers very properly to the patrons who had 'graced' and paid for these events: and yet asserts his own particular authority over the published record of them. The written words, which had served as functional frameworks for exclusive events, are translated into a re-creation of them in different terms, a re-presentation of them for different consumers. And Jonson signifies his own authorial control over these 'translations' by investing them with a complex commentary of classical and other sources which flaunts simultaneously their intellectual authenticity and his guiding spirit behind these evanescent spectacles. Yet even here there are wheels within wheels, at least in the case of *The Masque of Queens*, of which Jonson produced an elaborate holograph copy, dedicated to the young Prince Henry, and presented to Queen Anne. In this Jonson explains to the queen that it was the prince who asked him to 'add this second labour of annotation to my first invention', thus conferring upon it 'life, and authority' (H&S, VII, p. 279). In this private interchange between the artist and the royal patron Jonson both defends himself against the derision of those who mock his ostentatious learning, and is content to subsume that learning under a form of royal authority. In the printed text, however, the role of the prince is not mentioned, and the annotations are all Jonson's own; as Evelyn B. Tribble observes: 'the authorities [i.e. the literary, historical and mythological authorities] will shield the work from ignorance and censure once it leaves the protective space of the court and enters the published realm.'[37]

Even in Jonson's deference over the 'invention' of the antimasque, the precise dynamics of authority are more complex than I have so far suggested because, having credited the queen with the idea, he goes on to explain: 'I was careful to decline not only from others', but mine own steps in that kind, since the last year I had an anti-masque of boys . . .' (Appendix, p. 181). That is, he publicly registers his knowledge that others have done *something* of this sort before, and that it was his responsibility to consult the precedents; and quietly observes that among these precedents was his own masque of the previous year, *The Haddington Masque*. The patron's authority and that of the poet stand in elegant complementarity.

The 'carcass' is all that remains after the performance of a masque (see Appendix, p. 180), but the printed text creates (or arguably preserves) for it a 'spirit' which will live on: and it does so by Jonson's authority, not that of his patrons. The quarto of *Hymenaei* is squarely 'by Ben. Jonson' on its title-page, *The Haddington Masque* 'devised by Ben. Jonson', *Blackness and Beauty* 'invented by Ben. Jonson', *Queens* 'written by Ben Jonson', even as their patrons are properly acknowledged. In the 1616 folio the 'Masques at Court' are credited collectively and magisterially to 'The Author B.J.' Jonson, that is, pursues the opposite tack from that of Florio, respectfully distinguishing himself from his patrons, not subsuming himself in their aura.[38] There is a parallel here with his treatment of his plays, the printed texts of which often carefully distinguish his authority as a writer from that of his patrons, the actors who commissioned his work and staged *a version* of it: the quartos of *Every Man Out of His Humour*, *Sejanus* and *The New Inn* are particularly marked examples.

This self-assertion in respect of the texts of his masques lay at the heart of Jonson's protracted quarrel with Inigo Jones over their relative 'authority' in the creation of these shows.[39] In the quarto of *The Masque of Queens* Jones is carefully credited 'with the invention, and architecture of the whole scene, and machine' (ll. 37–8), but this is in the spirit of a historical record; it allows him no authority in creating anything significant, anything that could or should be preserved. Jonson's spirit of self-assertion also underlay his earlier disagreements with Samuel Daniel about masques (as it did a dispute with Thomas Dekker over the publication of their respective parts in *The Magnificent Entertainment*, 1604).[40] When Daniel had published the first of the Jacobean court masques, his *The Vision of the Twelve Goddesses* (1604), he had done so with some diffidence, explaining in a preface to the Countess of Bedford that he had only been prompted to do it by the 'unmannerly presumption of an indiscreet printer', who had foisted an unsatisfactory text on the world – an excuse commonly deployed by gentlemen amateurs, who wished to avoid the stigma attached to professional print. As Richard Helgerson observes of courtier-poets like Daniel, seeking for office or advancement rather than a strictly literary career: 'they rarely began without an apology or ended without a palinode. They thus enclosed and rejected the self-as-poet in order to reveal the dutiful and employable self-as-civil-servant'.[41] While print represented the technology of the future, and an independence of sorts to those who submitted themselves to it, it also represented (in some quarters at least) manual labour, questionable self-advertisement, unfortunate associations, from all of which anyone with social aspirations would naturally wish to distance himself.

In his preface to *Tethys' Festival* (1610) Daniel explicitly dissociates himself from pretensions to the kind of authority to which

Jonson had by then laid extensive claim. In putting his words into print he disavows any personal ambition or desire to assert himself ('having my name already wider in this kind than I desire, and more in the wind than I would'), claiming merely that 'it is expected (according now to the custom) that I, being employed in the business, should publish a description and form of the late masque' (*ed. cit.*, vol. III, p. 305). This is subtler than it looks: the matter-of-factness concedes a peripheral role for himself in these events (he describes himself and his fellow artists as 'the poor engineers for shadows') but instantly defers to the primacy of his royal patrons, subsuming his identity in theirs rather than asserting a separate one for himself. It is an even more self-effacing variant on the Florio formula, and particularly appropriate to someone styling himself on the title-page 'one of the Grooms of her Majesty's most Honourable Privy Chamber': *just* within the hallowed circle of power but properly sensible of his lowly status there. He is, and acknowledges himself to be, a very small cog in a very big wheel; masques are properly the business of those much grander than himself, persons he serves on occasion with his pen, then publishing the product as no more than a journalistic record, 'a description and form', with no pretension to literary status. The gentleman escapes the stigma of the artisan by sheer diffidence.

These differences between Jonson and Daniel are exactly mirrored in the attitude of the two poets to the historical and mythological subject-matter of their masques. Jonson had published *Hymenaei* (1606) with a preface and annotation which proclaimed it to be 'grounded upon antiquity and solid learnings', relating such qualities to the lasting 'sense' of works which were otherwise splendid but evanescent; in doing this he defiantly outfaces anyone who 'may squeamishly cry out that all endeavour of learning and sharpness in these transitory devices . . . is superfluous' (Appendix, p. 174). This is a direct response to Daniel's comments in *The Vision of the Twelve Goddesses* on 'all these curious and superfluous observations' by other writers, in turn almost certainly glancing at Jonson himself in even earlier texts such as *The Magnificent Entertainment* of 1604 (see note 40). Scorning the false certainties of 'mytheologers' and therefore 'owing no homage to their intricate observations, we were left at liberty to take no other knowledge of them, than fitted our present purpose, nor were tied by any laws of heraldry . . . than they fell out to stand with the nature of the matter in hand' (III, pp. 188–9). Note that Daniel is happy to represent himself as part of a team, not as an individuated author. In *Tethys' Festival* he stands his ground with studied nonchalance: 'these figures of mine, if they come not drawn in all proportions to the life of antiquity (from whose tyranny, I see no reason why we may not emancipate our inventions) yet I know them such as were proper to the business' (*ed. cit.*, vol. III, p. 307). In all this, he is affecting the *sprezzatura* of the courtly amateur, for whom all writing is (or should seem to be) a matter of casual inspiration rather than serious labour; he is echoing the likes of Sir Philip Sidney when he describes the *Arcadia* as 'this idle work of mine', containing 'no better stuff than as in a haberdasher's shop, glasses or feathers'.[42] Jonson's insistence, by contrast, on the integrity and solidity of his own scholarship (drawn 'out of the authority of ancient and late writers' as he puts it in the preface to *The Masque of Queens*) puts masques, and his part in their creation, on a different footing. He proudly admits to intellectual labour, while insisting it is *not* the labour of an artisan.[43] His citation of classical and other precedents thus helps to define his status as a writer, conjuring up an 'authority' for himself as he discreetly distances himself from that of his patrons, though one which the readership of the time would not readily acknowledge.

The nuances of going into print were extremely subtle, and are not always readily decodable at this distance. Spenser, for example, had submitted many of his works to the press – notably *The Faerie Queene* (1590, 1596) – without in any obvious sense demeaning himself. A scholar like John Florio seems to have had no compunction about it, though one like Francis Bacon (who never gave up hope of advancement in the political sphere) was much more ambivalent and circumspect about it.[44] Despite his reservations over masques, even Daniel was not against print in principle. Indeed, he was the first English author to bring out a collection of his own writing under the classically-inspired title of *Works* (*opera*), as early as 1601; much less imposing than Jonson's 1616 monument, and containing far fewer pieces though still in folio format, the principal difference was that it contained nothing which had been written for the public stage: that was what fuelled the derision which greeted Jonson's volume.[45] Even a writer like George Chapman (a collaborator and, for many years, friend of Jonson), who much of the time deliberately wrote for a select and educated coterie, in what he himself called 'my far-fetched and, as it were, beyond-sea manner of writing' (introduction to *Achilles Shield*, 1598), nevertheless saw fit to publish the most arcane items. Donne's practice in respect of print seems perplexingly mixed: he published the *Anniversaries*, but not the 'Songs and Sonets', *Pseudo-Martyr* but not *Biathanatos*, the sermons but not the 'Divine Poems'. In some cases, the likelihood of pleasing patrons (e.g. *Anniversaries*) or attracting them (*Pseudo-Martyr*) seems to have swayed him towards publication. Some of the omissions may, however, have been due to chance rather than to deliberation: he seems to have contemplated a volume of shorter pieces around 1611 and again in 1614, but on both occasions it fell through, perhaps preserving the impression of a stonger aversion to print (at least for some works) than he actually felt.[46] Wherever Jonson looked, in short, he would be confronted by mixed and contradictory prejudices about print and its place in the self-definition of an author.

I have observed how ironic it is that Jonson defers to Queen Anne as the originator of the anti-masque. His career in most forms – as a writer of comedies, tragedies, epigrams, verse epistles, odes, songs, and virtually every other species of writing – is based on a process of creative adaptation or imitation.[47] In the court masque, where he had no classical precedent to follow, but a good number of recent examples to compare with his own – including reports of continental ones, which Inigo Jones and others would have furnished him with – the anti-masque is his most strikingly *original* contribution to the form.[48] Yet he cedes the honour to his royal patron, and for all we know its adoption and structural development in *The Masque of Queens* may indeed have been at Queen Anne's instigation (even if Jonson had tried something of the sort earlier, in *The Haddington Masque*).

It is, however, indisputable that the anti-masque is completely typical of Jonson as a writer, a perfect embodiment of his most characteristic rhetorical strategy: a 'foil or false masque', setting off the true one. The spelling 'anti-masque' – implying this contrastive quality – is his own, facing down usages such as 'ante-masque' preferred by Daniel and others (neutrally implying something that comes before a masque) and 'antic- (or antique-) masque', which highlights grotesqueries in the supposed style of the ancients, the staple fare of courtly interludes (see the 'stew' supposedly served up by the Cook as the antimasque for *Neptune's Triumph for the Return of Albion*, Appendix, pp. 203–5). In the non-dramatic verse, too, Jonson repeatedly locates himself by contrast or comparison. 'Thou art *not*, Penshurst . . .' (my emphasis) is how he begins the famous poem in praise of the Sidney family estate, expending six lines in the negative before he picks up his positive theme; he also concludes the poem in comparative mode – 'they that will proportion thee / With other edifices . . .'. 'To draw no envy (Shakespeare) on thy name' is how he starts the prefatory poem in the Shakespeare first folio, taking fully sixteen lines to contemplate the false praises he might have bestowed, before resolving: 'I therefore will begin' (Appendix, p. 194).[49]

'Understanding' – a key term in Jonson's critical vocabulary – is to be found by an exploration of disparate information, sometimes even of binary opposites, leading to a discrimination between different, possibly antithetic registers. As he jokingly allows the Cook to put it in *Neptune's Triumph for the Return of Albion*: 'there is a palate of the understanding as well as of the senses. The taste is taken with good relishes, the sight with fair objects, the hearing with delicate sounds, the smelling with pure scents, the feeling with soft and plump bodies, but the understanding with all these, for all which you must begin at the kitchen. There the art of poetry was learned and found out, or nowhere, and the same day with the art of cookery' (Appendix, p. 202). Much of Jonson's writing is in this cumulative, *comparative* mode, chary of absolutes and superlatives, at least until antithetic voices have been disempowered. We may see in this a similarity with the self-effacing strategies we observed in *Discoveries*.

Another characteristic trope is one in which his own role as poet, and even that of language itself, is marginalised to the point of insignificance: 'What need hast thou of me, or of my muse, / Whose actions so themselves do celebrate?' (*Ep* XLII, 'To Robert, Earl of Salisbury'); 'I do but name thee, Pembroke, and I find / It is an epigram on all mankind' (*Ep* CII, 'To William, Earl of Pembroke').[50] These are, in fact, some of the marks of insecurity in a man often accused of arrogant certainties, one of the clearest traces of the fact that he wrote not from an establishment complacency but as a self-made man with no *given* status, constantly under pressure to justify himself. The methods he employs in this are neither arrogant nor pedantic, but rather careful and defensive, aware that nothing he says carries *inherent* authority. As Jonas Barish observes: 'The presence of tension in Jonson reveals itself most obviously in his insistent claim to be without tension'.[51] This is a shrewd insight, but one often overlooked in modern estimates of Jonson, not least as a critic.

As we have seen with the masques, even within the narrow context of direct court patronage, the option of translating his writing from that intimate and privileged mode of exchange to one of public and commercially available print placed him in a very ambiguous position. There must have been a similar ambiguity about the printed publication of verse addressed to aristocratic patrons (and even to fellow artists and friends): private compliments once reserved at most for a small coterie become part of the public face of those to whom they were addressed, while that enhanced status reflects in turn on the authority of the writer who (in however small a way) shares in making them what they are. This must have been particularly marked in the 1616 *Works*; note, for example, the complex reciprocities established in print between Jonson and the Earl of Pembroke, the dedicatee of both *Catiline* and the *Epigrams*, addressee of one poem (*Ep* CII) and tacit sponsor of another (*For* VII).[52] In such a context Jonson claims for himself the independence of print, the superiority of 'the author' whose conspicuous and prestigious productivity speaks for itself. Yet, at the same time, he depends in critical ways on an array of sponsoring 'authorities', among whom the pre-eminence of Pembroke is at least partially in response to his recent advancement in court circles, becoming Lord Chamberlain in succession to the disgraced favourite, Somerset.[53] So Jonson simultaneously denotes for himself the timelessness of the author of a volume of *Works* and a continuing involvement (however discreetly distanced) in the factional politics of the Jacobean court.

In such a context, the nature of the 'authority' of a writer over his text could not but remain problematic. Elsewhere it was even less clear-cut. In as much as a concept of copyright was acknowledged, it lay with the licence-holding publisher rather than with the writer, a commodity jealously guarded on his behalf by the Stationers' Company, who registered it and exercised a legally-imposed cartel of the printing industry.[54] Work written for the theatre was the property of the acting company that commissioned it, and to whom it was licensed by the Master of the Revels; then, in performance, it became in a sense the property of the audiences who paid money and 'consumed' it.[55] These were two very different patrons from those for whom Jonson wrote his masques and poems, and he was to conduct a heated public debate with them about the nature of *his* 'authority' and how it differed from *theirs*. The instability of the 'authority' of the writer, and the indeterminate status of the texts he produced, lie at the heart of all of Jonson's critical writings. They are attempts primarily to define himself and his writings in a context where no adequate definitions pre-existed. Anyone predisposed to dismiss his apparently servile dependence on classical precedents, on the 'rules' of the ancients, should bear in mind that no one – least of all the classical authors he cites – had ever experienced the conditions of professional authorship to which he himself was subject. As Richard Burt puts it: 'Unable to resolve the contradictions and paradoxes of criticism either by identifying with one authority or submitting to another, Jonson oscillated in neurotic fashion between them, setting one against the other, sometimes unwittingly setting himself to be censored or censured by both'.[56]

If Jonson is at times inconsistent, or over-pedantic, or brusquely dismissive of others, it is hardly surprising: he was in a sense making up the rules as he went along (rules which others might well not even acknowledge, much less endorse), and placed in the almost existential situation of having repeatedly to create new identities for himself in his various literary endeavours. In a revealing remark, he told Drummond, 'of all styles he loved most to be named honest, and hath of that an hundred letters so naming him' (555–6). 'Honest' was a term in flux, just like 'author' and 'critic'. In an older sense it meant something like 'honourable', relating to the medieval warrior-culture, in which allegiance to the clan and actions that promoted its reputation were primary virtues. In the late sixteenth century there was an intense debate in and around the aristocracy as to whether such status, like nobility itself, was inherent in aristocratic blood ('native') or emanated only from the monarch ('dative'), who might bestow it wherever he saw fit.[57] At a time when people of relatively undistinguished birth were being granted peerages and knighthoods (the Cecils and Sidneys were examples), and under James virtually any title could be bought, such distinctions generated a lot of heat; they help to explain many of the tensions in Jonson's panegyric verse – so inflected with the ethics of public status – since to praise any form of 'nobility', 'honour' or 'honesty' required fine discriminations and tact.[58]

At the same time, however, more modern inflections of 'honest' were also gaining currency: 'of good moral character, virtuous, upright, well-disposed' and 'sincere, truthful, candid, that will not lie, cheat, or steal' (*OED*, v.3 'of persons', a. and c.). The earlier usage rests heavily on an external perception of the individual and his actions, the latter incorporates a stronger consideration of private self-esteem and personal motivation (though neither entirely precludes the other). Jonson seems torn between the two, cultivating a private integrity, but vulnerably dependent on its public recognition – the 'hundred letters so naming him', which Ian Donaldson has speculated may relate to his prosecution for recusancy in 1606, a classic instance where public conformity and private integrity might be in conflict. Note also Jonson's blunt summation of the wife from whom he lived apart for so long as 'a shrew yet honest' (*Drummond*, 208),[59] probably in the specific sense of 'chaste', usually reserved for women: that too is ambiguously a matter either of public reputation or of inner virtue. Jonson's criticism often seems fraught with analogous tensions between the self-creation of a public figure ('the poet') and the private convictions of an intensely sensitive man.

CRITIC

Such conflicting notions of personal identity and integrity were symptomatic of the cultural contradictions of the period. The emergence during Jonson's career of the sense of the term 'critic' now operative in the formal study of literature and the arts – 'one skilful in judging of the qualities and merits of literary or artistic works' (which I mentioned in the Preface) – is a parallel symptom. It reflects changes affecting not only the literary profession but the fine arts as a whole, signalling a point where the consumption of their products – now largely divorced from functional origins in the service of the Church – had reached a level of such complexity that there was a need for new terms to register their qualities and for new forms of expertise to discriminate between them. The marketplace had become so diverse in terms of consumers, and so specialised in terms of products, that knowledgeable mediators were a logical necessity.

This sense of 'critic' is first seen in print in 1605, a year in which (as we shall see) some of the crucial determinants of Jonson's career were established. The passage from *The Advancement of*

Learning cited by the *OED* is: 'as certain critics are used to say hyperbolically, *That if all sciences were lost, they might be found in Virgil'*.[60] Bacon, like Jonson, instinctively associates a need for such skills with an appeal to classical precedent for 'authority'. *The Advancement of Learning* is a radical critique of current epistemologies, and, as such, a straw in the wind, a mark of residual medieval, dominant Renaissance and emergent modern worlds rubbing up against one another like continental plates, as they did to such disconcerting effect on contemporary minds like those of Donne and Sir Thomas Browne. Although, as we have seen, we have to be circumspect about Jonson's precise view of Bacon, it is clear that the two of them have much in common in these developments. In particular they share 'a linguistic doctrine which emphasised the proper order of words based on an assumed correspondence between words, ideas and things'. Or, as Martin Elsky puts it, 'Both Bacon and Jonson were searching for an ideal language in which mind, language, and reality, would each mirror the other perfectly in the "congruous" relationship between sign and referent'.[61] They also share many of the fundamental assumptions – positivist and empiricist – which R. S. Crane discerns in Augustan 'neoclassicism', and Michel Foucault associates with what he calls Classicism and identifies as the dominant ideological mode of the seventeenth and eighteenth centuries.[62]

In drawing such parallels, however, we should bear in mind Elsky's observation:

> It is, of course, ironic that a poet so widely associated with humanism should invoke the authority of the philosopher most associated with the attack on the humanist attitude toward language. But whatever their obvious differences, both Bacon and Jonson were deeply interested in a similar issue. Each in his own way was responding to a cultural and linguistic malaise – what Timothy Murray and others characterize as the crisis of signification.[63]

This offers a different perspective for looking at the oblique comments on Bacon in the *Discoveries*, and their significance within that volume as a whole. Jonson does not want to *identify* with Bacon, but he respects a fellow spirit responding with massive intelligence to what both perceive as a problem. *Discoveries*, however, does not offer a philosophically coherent response to that

problem, as the works of Bacon do: it offers incomplete, and sometimes conflicting, reflections upon it, in ways that mirror Murray's
'crisis' rather than resolving it. Like so much of Jonson's criticism (a point this book will explore), *Discoveries* could be described
as a rearguard action to defend humanism from its ever more
palpable inadequacies.

So, for all the apparent certainties of Jonson's criticism, there is
a tentative and oblique quality to it that reveals an underlying
struggle for the independent authority of a professional writer,
in a culture where such a notion was unprecedented. This is something later writers (like Dryden and Eliot) have disguised better
in their criticism, their art having acquired self-confidence as a
semi-autonomous discipline, as the status of the professional writer
has become at least familiar if not exactly assured. But they have
never in fact eradicated it: nor could they, since the most challenging criticism is always concerned with re-drawing the cultural map and redesignating its hierarchies. Jonson does himself
sometimes use 'critic' in the sense in which Bacon had used it, as
in the poem 'To the Learnèd Critic' (*Ep* XVII), whom he implicitly
contrasts with the subject of the next poem in the sequence, 'To
My Mere English Censurer' (*Ep* XVIII). Again, in the Prologue to
Volpone, Jonson defends the play as one which 'presents quick
comedy, refined, / As best critics have designed' (29–30). And he
may even be credited with antedating Bacon in the creation of
the character Criticus in the original version of *Cynthia's Revels*,
published in 1601 (he changed the name to Crites in the 1616
folio version).

These are good examples, incidentally, of why it is impossible
to draw final distinctions between his 'creative' and his 'critical'
writings: the 'creative' works constantly police themselves in this
way, articulating the reading process by which they are to be
consumed. As Richard Burt puts it: 'If the legitimacy of literary
criticism was at issue in early modern England ... so too it was
not a clearly defined self-identical discourse separate from literature.'[64] Jonson does not use the term 'critic' of himself, nor (as far
as I am aware) do his contemporaries use it of him in this sense,
though there are examples of him being so labelled by his enemies in the older sense of 'a censurer, fault-finder, caviller' (*OED*).
The one who comes closest is Dekker, who – sceptical of all pre-
tentious claims to literary 'authority' – refers sarcastically to 'the
court of critists' in a passage in *The Magnificent Entertainment* which

clearly has Jonson in its sights (see note 40). But the terminology is secondary to the cultural reality which the new term(s) shadow, and which I have here briefly outlined: Jonson *had* to be a critic (as we understand the term) because, for practical purposes, he was the first English 'individualised' author and had to explain that fact to those (like Dekker) who did not understand what this meant, or possibly resented it. At times, these may even have included himself.

It may be helpful to gloss this proposition by reference to Roland Barthes's definitions of 'criticism', very different from those advanced by George Watson earlier in this chapter, though propounded at much the same time:

> criticism is discourse upon a discourse; it is a second language, or a *metalanguage* . . . which operates on a first language (or *language object*). . . . In itself, a language is not true or false, it is or is not valid: valid, i.e., constitutes a coherent system of signs. The rules of literary language do not concern the conformity of this language to reality . . . but only its submission to the system of signs the author has established (and we must, of course, give the word *system* a very strong sense here). . . . One can say that the critical task (and this is the sole guarantee of its universality) is purely formal . . . only to adjust the language [the critic's] period affords him . . . to the language, i.e., the formal system of logical constraints elaborated by the author according to his own period.[65]

Barthes is here addressing the forms of what he would call 'interpretive' or 'ideological' criticism in the France of 1963, and assuming that the author (of 'creative' works) and his critic will be different people, probably living in different historical eras. But in essence what he is saying exactly describes Jonson's self-formulation as a critic, deploying a metalanguage founded very largely in humanism and neoclassical formalism to explicate the 'system of signs' that he as an author has established (though it is arguable, counter-intuitively, that for Jonson the criticism actually precedes the creative act).

So, for Barthes, 'critical discourse . . . is never anything but tautological: it consists in saying ultimately, though placing its whole being within that delay, what thereby is not insignificant: Racine is Racine, Proust is Proust', and so being above all 'a construction of the intelligibility of our own time' (pp. 259, 260). By the same token, whatever the ostensible object of Jonson's criticism, it is always essentially saying 'Jonson is Jonson' and in so doing is 'a construction of the intelligibility of [his] own time'. Barthes envisages such a construction as 'the dialogue of two histories and two subjectivities, the author's and the critic's'. And so it is. Only in Jonson's case both histories and both subjectivities are subsumed in the same self-made signifier 'Jonson', a unique version of the name, without an 'h', to distinguish him from the myriad Johnsons before and since (see the Chronology, 1604). The pressures of this dual self-creation must have been enormous.

Jonson is often described as a 'conservative' writer, and there are obviously senses in which that was true.[66] But he was, in himself, a profoundly new phenomenon, and it is too easily overlooked that there was a fundamental irony in a man like Jonson justifying himself by appeals to the past. As Don E. Wayne observes,

> Conservative as he may have been in principle, Jonson demanded a certain status that was unacknowledged in the traditional social and cultural system from which England was then emerging. In using the theater as a space for negotiating that demand he provided his audiences with a model of the society which they themselves were already in the process of creating. Thus, despite his classicism and traditionalism, Jonson looked ahead as much as he did backward in time.[67]

This may be less apparent in other forms, such as the masque and the non-dramatic verse, where evocations of classical models of manhood and an array of idealising mythologies disguise the contradictions. But they are there none the less, and detectable in the characteristic contrastive modes – the omnipresent anti-masques and comparative judgements, the self-promotions and self-elisions – which we have already observed.

In these circumstances there could be nothing mechanical or unimaginative about the application of the past to the present, which was in every sense a creative and challenging act. Whatever we make of the tone of Jonson's describing to Drummond a whole night consumed imagining Tartars and Turks, Romans and Carthaginians, fighting in the vicinity of his big toe, it suggests not only a very intense imagination, but also one in which the past could be vividly, even disturbingly alive. *Sejanus* is, in both substance and form, very nearly a model classical tragedy, carefully constructed from authoritative historical evidence, and observing 'truth of argument, dignity of persons, gravity and height of elocution, fullness and frequency of sentence [*sententiae*: pithy moral observations on the action]', though Jonson conscientiously observes that it 'is no true poem, in the strict laws of time . . . as also in the want of a proper chorus' ('To the Readers', Appendix, p. 173). But there is another side to this austere critical theory and meticulous historiography: 'he was called before the Council for his *Sejanus*, and accused both of popery and treason by [the Earl of Northampton]' (*Drummond*, 272–3).[68] So, for one important reader at least, Jonson's classical orthodoxy here was equated, not with pedantry, but with religious heresy and political sedition. When, therefore, we talk of Jonson as a conservative or a (neo)classicist, we should rid ourselves of the notion that this was a safe, conformist thing to be, merely reiterating the wisdom of the ages.

There is, however, one final twist in this tale. In the absence of Jonson's 'Apology for *Bartholomew Fair*', English letters had in fact to wait a further fifty years for Dryden's unabashed publication of *An Essay of Dramatic Poesie* (1668), a critical 'apology' in dialogue form, whose speakers invite identification with known individuals. One of these acknowledges Jonson (along with Beaumont and Fletcher) as 'only [i.e. alone] capable of bringing us to that degree of perfection which we have'.[69] This has all the conviction of complacent hindsight about it, as is even more evident in Dryden's 'Defence of an Essay' (also 1668) where he openly declares that his 'propositions' were 'derived from the Authority of Aristotle and Horace, and from the Rules and Examples of Ben. Johnson and Corneille' (*ibid.*, pp. 139–40). Dryden is writing from beyond the Civil War and the Commonwealth, from where he is able to observe the broad and complete example of a career – indeed parallel careers in England and France – which in many ways helped to make possible (to authorise) both what he himself wrote and the conditions in which it could be published. He could see in Jonson a man of the theatre who was also a man of the court, a poet rubbing shoulders with the aristocracy and who also confronted the quasi-democracy of print; he could consult an array of works of self-proclaimed 'classic' status, folios littered with triumphant prologues, choruses, grexes, inductions and other forms of self-justification.

As Richard C. Newton observes, 'Of this Ben Jonson, the (re-) inventor of the book, the first English classic author, virtually all subsequent English authors claim some degree of paternity.'[70] Dryden claimed more of that paternity than most, though it was a claim shot through with Oedipal tensions.[71] When it suited him, Jonson was a model to follow, an authority to invoke, as he was for many writers in the Restoration; John Oldham, for example, speaks of Jonson as 'being of so established an authority, that whatever he did is held as sacred'. Few were quite as fulsome as that and, as with Dryden, a number of serious reservations were registered. But what mattered most was that Jonson was inescapably *there*, a native English base line on which they could build, a position with which they could negotiate, an 'authority'. Edward Howard, for example, could depend upon Jonson's being so well known (both visually and by reputation) that he wrote for his play *The Women's Conquest* (1671) 'The Second Prologue personated like Ben Johnson rising from below':

> Did I instruct you (well near half an age)
> To understand the grandeur of the stage,
> With the exactest rules of comedy. . . .[72]

And, in constituting him as such, what Dryden and the others could not see, or chose to ignore, were the tensions and internal contradictions which ran through that achievement, making its outcome less than assured. (It is striking how often, for example, they ignored the unique spelling of the name.) Jonson's own example only *belatedly* resolved (or could be construed by his successors as resolving) the problematics of authorship with which he himself always had to wrestle.

By 1674 Thomas Rymer could facetiously write: 'many great wits flourished . . . but Ben Johnson, I think, had all the critical learning to himself; and till of late years England was as free from critics, as it is from wolves'. In his usual insensitive way he seems to have given no thought to what it might be like to be a lone wolf in such a context. Jeremy Collier, too, seems to treat Jonson (as he does most Elizabethan/Jacobean dramatists) with a degree of condescension in his *A Short View of the Immorality and Profaneness of the English Stage* (1698): 'Ben Johnson shall speak for himself afterwards in the character of a Critic.'[73] To be fair, we must acknowledge that Jonson wished some of this on himself. The two monumental folios that confronted the world as his legacy, after 1640, inevitably engendered resentment as well as respect. And his career after the 1616 folio was almost calculated to inspire filial loyalty and Oedipal resentment in equal measure; Jonson's eminence translated him (how willingly or deliberately is not clear) into the Father of a 'tribe' or 'sons' of Ben, who congregated in the Apollo Room of the Devil tavern, admonished by Jonson's own *Leges Convivales*, rules for tavern conduct. That father-figure role inspired not only 'sealed members' of the tribe but a younger generation as a whole to think in terms of 'our acknowledged master, learned Jonson' (James Shirley, dedication of *The Grateful Servant*, 1629), his longevity doubtless enhancing the effect. And there are moments when Jonson actively connives in his own myth, as in his commendatory poem to Brome's *The Northern Lass*, quoted earlier. As William Winstanley observed in 1687, 'he may be truly said to be the first reformer of the English stage, as he himself more truly than modestly writes in his commendatory verses of his servant's Richard Broom's comedy of *the Northern Lass*'.[74]

This is only one instance of something we shall observe again, Jonson's own words being refracted into a posthumous – and not always very attractive – reputation.[75] This may have been a price he was bound to pay for latterly acquiring what, despite his own pretence to the contrary, he never securely held in his own lifetime: the status of a classic author. Succeeding generations could not ignore that status, but appropriated or belittled it, as suited their own situations. In the process they elided into a single magisterial (and essentially *safe*) figure the complex, combative and shifting personalities which had built up the first lone wolf of English criticism.

2
Poet and Critic

One of the most striking features of Jonson's career, which has a direct bearing on the criticism he wrote, is the sheer variety of forms of writing to which he turned his hand, and the differing audiences and publishing contexts which these entailed. He was a writer of plays (among which he would distinguish the forms of comedy, comical satire, tragedy and pastoral), of masques and other entertainments commissioned by royal, aristocratic and civic patrons; he wrote poetry which, despite a marked statistical preference for iambic pentameter rhyming couplets ('he detesteth all other rhymes', *Drummond*, 3), is in a far wider range of forms than a casual reader might suppose – love lyrics and epigrams, verse epistles and odes, eulogies and mock-heroics – and some of these (notably the Pindaric ode) were only recent importations into English; he wrote a history of Henry V, lost in the 1623 fire, translated Horace's *Ars Poetica*, and planned 'an epic poem, entitled *Heroologia*, of the worthies of his country roused by fame' and '*A Discovery*' of his 'foot pilgrimage', which would have been a topographical poem about Scotland (*Drummond*, 1–3, 347–9), though neither of these seems to have come to fruition; he kept a commonplace book, *Timber, or Discoveries*, which there are signs that he was reworking for publication in the later part of his life, and compiled *An English Grammar*.

THEATRE AND PRINT

Some of these he published, others not. And, while certain kinds of writing predominate during particular phases of his career, this is never to the total exclusion of others. Economic or other pressures ensured that he was never able to settle into a comfortable groove, but had constantly to maintain a facility in more than one mode, to make himself available to a multiplicity of audiences. This is nowhere more marked than in the fraught first two decades of his career, and in the severely edited *version* of those decades which Jonson presented to his readers in the 1616 folio of his *Works*, which I shall review in some detail as the context from which his earliest critical manifestos emerged.[1]

The first writing with which we can associate Jonson is the play *The Case is Altered*, which was probably performed in the first half of 1597.[2] It is an intriguing and instructive anomaly in his career, in several senses. A romantic comedy, in the manner if not the style of Shakespeare's comedies, and unlike anything else by him that has survived from this period (though the late plays, *The New Inn* and *A Tale of a Tub*, have interesting affinities), it is the only one of his plays to have reached print without Jonson's own apparent sanction. Though we do not know who first staged the play, it met with favourable comment (from, among others, Thomas Nashe) and Jonson himself apparently thought it worth revising at a later date, since the satire on the playwright Anthony Munday (as 'Antonio Balladino') seems to be an afterthought. The later staging was probably by the Children of the Chapel Royal (Queen's Revels, as they became, and as they are described on the title-page of the 1609 quarto), possibly during the so-called 'War of the Theatres' of 1600–1, when Jonson was engaged in satiric battle with various rivals, including Dekker and Marston.[3] Every other Jonson play that was printed prior to 1616 (and one, *Epicoene*, that was not) was reprinted in the folio of his *Works* that year, but *The Case is Altered* was not. Unless he had lost control of the copyright (which is not impossible: as we shall see, it is remarkable that he retained the copyright of so many other plays) we must regard this as an act of self-censorship, possible reasons for which I shall review later.

The next we hear of Jonson as a writer was as co-author of a lost play by Pembroke's Men, *The Isle of Dogs* (1597), which was deemed by the Privy Council so offensive that it very nearly tipped the balance in favour of those, like the City of London authorities, who wished to eradicate the public playhouses altogether.[4] Shortly thereafter he was one of those paid by Philip Henslowe, the financier behind the Lord Admiral's Men and various other acting companies, for providing play 'plots' and authoring or co-authoring plays, of which only the titles, such as *Robert II of Scotland* and *Page of Plymouth*, have survived. Here he must have become well-versed in the quasi-democratic, but commercially driven, world of the public theatres. Henslowe employed teams of writers, in ways analogous to the practice of the Hollywood movie studios in the 1930s and 1940s. Even when a writer scripted a piece from start to finish there can have been little sense of the work *belonging* to him. Strictly speaking, in fact, it belonged to the acting company which commissioned it and to whom it was licensed, who in most circumstances jealously guarded their property.

As E. K. Chambers circumspectly puts it: 'It is generally supposed, and I think with justice, that the acting companies did not find it altogether to their advantage to have their plays printed' (*The Elizabethan Stage* [hereafter *ES*], III, p. 183), citing Thomas Heywood's comments in the Epistle to *The English Traveller* in support of this view. Heywood observes, as just one of the reasons why many of his own numerous plays were never published: 'Others of them are still retained in the hands of some actors, who think it against their peculiar profit to have them come in print' (quoted in *ES*, III, p. 339). Why exactly this should be so is something of a moot point: note that Heywood's wording suggests that only *some*, and not all, actors took this view of the matter. Chambers goes on to speculate: 'Presumably the danger was not so much that readers would not become spectators, as that other companies might buy the plays and act them.' But while certain instances of this do appear to have occurred (the most notorious is the King's Men's performance of the Children of the Queen's Revels' *The Malcontent*), these generally seem to have been special circumstances, and there were normally safeguards against it, in as much as most plays were only licensed *for performance* to the company owning the copy 'allowed' by the Master of the Revels.[5] Publication in print ought not to affect that licence.

This is, therefore, something of a grey area, and it is rarely possible to identify why certain plays were allowed into print and others not. Often, it seems, plays were only sold to printers if the company had no further use for them, or when adverse financial circumstances made it a necessary sacrifice. The author(s) would have no say in the matter and almost certainly would not share in any profit. It is entirely possible that this is why nothing Jonson is known to have written for Henslowe's companies ever found its way into print.[6] It is commonly supposed that Jonson himself deliberately disowned these plays as beneath the dignity of those he chose to preserve in print. But it is at least possible that he was simply never *allowed* to print them. If so, however, during the period when Henslowe was recording their dealings (late 1597 to June 1602, when Jonson was paid a joint fee for *Richard Crookback* and further additions to Kyd's *The Spanish Tragedy*) he must have been able to negotiate different contractual arrangements with other companies for whom he also wrote.

The Lord Chamberlain's Men, the premier acting troupe of the time, staged the original version of his *Every Man In His Humour* in 1598 and *Every Man Out of His Humour* the following year. Jonson somehow contrived to publish the latter in 1600; his own involvement in the careful text can hardly be doubted. Contrary to the usual practice, the title-page mentions nothing of the acting company involved, but proclaims it to be 'As It Was First Composed by the Author B. J. Containing more than hath been publicly spoken or acted'.[7] (Jonson was to be less coy thereafter: most of his subsequent publications give his name in full.) The success of the published *Every Man Out of His Humour* – it went through three editions within the year – may have prompted the publication of the earlier work the year after that. By then Jonson was writing for yet another company, the Children of the Chapel, who performed in the Blackfriars theatre. *Cynthia's Revels* (1600) and *Poetaster* (1601) were both in print within a year of their first performances. So Jonson's writing for the stage between 1597 and 1602 was done for at least four companies (Pembroke's, Henslowe/ Lord Admiral's, Lord Chamberlain's and Children of the Chapel), though only that written for the latter two found its way into print. While most dramatists were free to sell their products to any company that would take them, Jonson spread his wares at this time more diversely than anyone else.

In this respect, as in so many others, the most marked contrast is with Shakespeare who, after 1594, was the 'ordinary poet' of his company, the Lord Chamberlain's (latterly King's) Men.[8] That is, Shakespeare wrote all his plays for them, and was probably contractually engaged to deliver two a year (the terms may have changed around 1608, when the company took over the Blackfriars theatre in addition to the Globe, since his output seems to have dropped off markedly after this time).[9] And the plays he wrote for them remained their property. There is no evidence that Shakespeare had any hand in the publication of those that got into print during his lifetime, or indeed that he had any ambition to see such works preserved for posterity – unlike his poems *Venus*

and Adonis and *The Rape of Lucrece,* both published with dedications to the Earl of Southampton and clearly related to the earl's
actual or potential patronage. Shakespeare's apparent indifference
to the fate of his plays must have been partly a matter of contractual arrangements, but equally also a reflection of the low
esteem accorded to 'playbooks' at the outset of his career in the
late 1580s. They were not seen as what later ages would call 'literature': such texts as got into print were offered either as memen-
toes of performances, or possibly as acting copies, but no effort
was made to make them suitable for private reading in their own
right. Nor, significantly, did anyone seem to think it particularly
important to mention the name of the author. None of the earliest
quartos of Shakespeare's plays, such as *The Taming of the Shrew,*
Titus Andronicus (both 1594), *Richard III* (1597) or *Romeo and Juliet*
(1597, revised 1599), bears his name at all. William Drummond
had to write Shakespeare's name into his own copy of the 1599
Romeo and Juliet.[10] These were all matters that Jonson's own example was largely responsible for changing; the title-page of *Every*
Man Out of His Humour sets the tone. The immediate issue, however, is that Jonson never did become 'ordinary poet' to one of
the acting companies, nor shows any sign of wanting such a position, though it must have accorded an unusual degree of security for a writer at the time. John Heywood with Queen Anne's
Men, for example, and John Fletcher (who was Shakespeare's
successor with the King's Men and of whom Jonson always spoke
with respect) seem to have regarded it as a desirable niche.[11]

We cannot here review the possible reasons for Jonson's rest-
less transfers from company to company and back again, though
alternate sheer necessity and a search for the most sympathetic
audiences are amongst the likeliest causes. What we should observe is that, in the process of all this, Jonson rapidly acquired a
unique first-hand experience of virtually every facet of the professional theatre of his day, from a troupe of 'incomers' like
Pembroke's Men who had no permanent London base but hoped
to make their mark (not, of course, in the way they actually managed), to both members of the cartel of Lord Admiral's and Lord
Chamberlain's Men, who had the only regular London bases –
and so the only entrée to court – between 1594 and 1600 (reinforced in 1598 by Privy Council orders that no rival companies
were to be permitted), to the company of boys at the Blackfriars
who, secure in their privileges as supposed adjuncts of the royal

choir school, were probably revived at this time to meet a demand for live entertainment, which was increasing just when the Privy Council were trying to limit the number of its outlets: the population of London had virtually doubled to 200,000 since the start of Elizabeth's reign.

The linked factors of state control and of quasi-monopoly conditions may well also have had a bearing on Jonson's restlessness. Pembroke's Men, as 'incomers', were not subject to the authority of the Master of the Revels, the court official who licensed plays for the regular London companies; they would have been licensed by the Surrey magistrates responsible for the Bankside, where the Swan was situated. Whether or not Jonson and Pembroke's Men *banked* on the relative inexperience of the county magistrates in these matters, compared with that of the Master of the Revels (Edmund Tilney, who had been licensing plays since 1581), it is entirely likely that this was a factor in a play as scandalous as *The Isle of Dogs* actually reaching the stage. In *Poetaster*, written for the Children of the Chapel, Jonson has one of his characters mutter dark promises to the actors, Histrio and Aesop (linked with 'your Globes, and your Triumphs' and so inevitably with the Lord Chamberlain's Men, who performed at the Globe), of 'a monopoly of playing, confirm'd to thee and thy covey, under the Emperor's broad seal'.[12] The boy companies also came under Tilney's authority, but their situation was unique and anomalous. It was the favoured adult companies who really comprised a court-licensed cartel, and there are signs that Jonson resented this. Presumably one reason for his resentment was the practical constraints it actually imposed on him as a writer: he was notionally free to sell what he wrote to whom he chose, but, in an artificially restricted market, the buyers rather than the sellers must have called the shots. Without the kind of competition that 'incomers' like Pembroke's Men might bring, Jonson's own freedom to write what he wanted must have been materially circumscribed. For a time the reappearance of the Blackfriars boys perhaps offered him the scope he sought, though it did not preclude the apparent necessity of also having to work for Henslowe more or less simultaneously.

A further factor behind Jonson's restlessness as a writer of plays may well have been his decided ambivalence about the medium of drama itself. There is ample evidence that he was not comfortable writing for the theatre and receiving the kind of instant, communal judgement its audiences would render on his work.[13] Once Jonson started receiving commissions for masques at court (1605) and entertainments elsewhere, his output of plays dropped markedly; in the decade between *Volpone* and *The Devil is an Ass* (1606–16) he wrote only six plays, which may seem reasonable by modern standards but is negligible in Jacobean terms, where a thorough-going man of the theatre like Thomas Heywood could claim in a forty-year career to have had 'an entire hand, or at least a main finger' in the composition of 220 plays.[14] Either by temperament or by training Jonson rarely had the kind of facility that this required and which, in the case of Shakespeare, he would equate with a degree of intellectual carelessness.[15] In the *Apologetical Dialogue* to *Poetaster* he portrays himself as 'I, that spend half my nights, and all my days, / Here in a cell, to get a dark, pale face' (ll. 233–4), a boast of sorts. Others, however, taunted him for the slowness of his writing, a taunt he turned back on his detractors in the case of *Volpone*:

> And when his plays come forth, think they can flout them,
>   With saying, he was a year about them.
> To these there needs no lie, but this his creature,
>   Which was, two months since, no feature;
> And though he dares give them five lives to mend it,
>   'Tis known, five weeks fully he penned it.
>
> (Prologue, ll. 11–16)

Once they reached the stage, his plays were quite likely to meet a rough reception. *Sejanus*, *Catiline* and latterly *The New Inn* appear not to have survived their first performances. Even what we now think of as his comic masterpieces were not met with unmixed approval. Although there is much contemporary comment in its praise, Robert Herrick felt moved to reprove those 'who once hissed / At thy unequalled play, *The Alchemist*'.[16] And the *Conversations with Drummond* end on this sour note: 'When his play of a *Silent Woman* was first acted, there was found verses after on the stage against him, concluding that that play was well named *The Silent Woman*: there was never one man to say *plaudite* to it' (617–19). As I have observed, we do not know if this is Jonson's voice or Drummond's. But it would not be surprising if it were the dramatist's own.

Given all this, it is not surprising that Jonson withdrew from the public stage altogether in 1616, after he was granted his royal pension. The financial rewards of the theatre, while they might provide an adequate living for someone like Heywood, were not so impressive for anyone not tied to its treadmill; Jonson told Drummond 'Of all his plays he never gained two hundred pounds' (493). The pension (£66 13s 4d) combined with the fee that he received almost yearly for his masques at court (usually £40) relieved him of the necessity of confronting public audiences even intermittently. It was only when, with the death of King James, he lost the assurance of regular masque commissions that he was virtually forced back to the stage, despite his resolution in 'An Ode. To Himself' (for which unfortunately we have no date): 'Make not thyself a page / To that strumpet, the stage' (*Und* XXIII). Following the failure of *The New Inn* he vented all his rage on both the actors and the audience, introducing it on the title-page of the 1631 edition 'As it was never acted, but most negligently played by some, the King's Servants. And more squeamishly beheld, and censured by others, the King's subjects'. He also wrote the much more bilious 'Ode to Himself', which begins 'Come, leave the loathèd stage' (Appendix, p. 206).

It is not difficult to construe Jonson's antagonism towards the theatre as priggishly anti-democratic, resisting the pressure to stoop to the lowest common denominators of taste in a public forum. Quite apart from his formal complaints about the practice of his rivals in writing preposterous romantic comedies, shapeless and inaccurate chronicle histories and indecorous tragedies, he repeatedly attacks those features of the theatre purely there to divert a public that knows no better. The prologue to the folio *Every Man In His Humour* invites the audience to a play:

> Where neither Chorus wafts you o'er the seas;
> Nor creaking throne comes down, the boys to please;
> Nor nimble squib [firework] is seen, to make afear'd
> The gentlewomen; nor roll'd bullet [cannonball] heard
> To say, it thunders.
>
> (ll. 15–19)

The prologue to *Volpone* carefully advertises:

> no eggs are broken;
> Nor quaking custards with fierce teeth affrighted,

Wherewith your rout are so delighted;
Nor hales he in a gull, old ends reciting,
To stop gaps in his loose writing;
With such a deal of monstrous and forced action
As might make Bedlam [madhouse] a faction
(ll. 20–6)

In 'To the Reader', prefaced to *The Alchemist* he complains about 'the concupiscence of dances and antics [i.e. grotesques]', and describes the times, in his dedication of *Catiline* to the Earl of Pembroke, as 'jig-given' – references to the indiscriminate use of song, outlandish dances and 'jigs', which were (often obscene) mixtures of dance and extempore versifying, the stock-in-trade of comedians such as Will Kempe.[17]

It is easy to represent all of this in terms of social snobbery, as aimed at the 'groundlings' or 'the understanding gentlemen o'the ground' (his own paradoxical pun, Induction to *Bartholomew Fair* (Appendix, p. 197), the people who stood in the pit in the public theatres, paid least to get in, and by inference were likely to be the least well educated and therefore might well be deficient in real 'understanding'. But the issue was more fundamental than that, as we see in the fact that Jonson appears to have been no more at ease writing for the boy companies in their private theatres than he was in writing for their adult rivals in the public auditoria, even though the audience was entirely seated there and the actors eschewed some of the cruder devices which Jonson deplored. There was a marked difference between the cost of a place in one of the 'public' theatres, like the Swan and the Globe, where it cost a penny to stand in the pit around the turn of the century, and a 'private' indoor house like the Blackfriars, where even the cheapest seat cost sixpence. Jonson probably therefore had some sense of addressing a more socially élite and better educated audience in the latter than he did in the former. But in fact the constitution of the two audiences overlapped to such an extent (members of the Inns of Court, for example, figured prominently in both contexts) that this can only ever have been a relative and not an absolute distinction.[18] And, of the plays he wrote for the boy companies, we have seen one report of the reception of *The Silent Woman*, which stirred Jonson to write a second prologue 'Occasioned by some persons' impertinent exception', while *Poetaster* elicited not just hissing or verses thrown upon the stage, but apparently a formal examination: Jonson later dedicated it to Richard Martin, a Middle Temple lawyer, as a piece 'for whose innocence, as for the author's, you were once a noble and timely undertaker to the greatest justice of this kingdom [i.e. the Lord Chief Justice, Sir John Popham]' (*H&S*, IV, p. 201). Nothing is known of the circumstances of this, though the play is fairly indiscriminate in its satiric attacks on lawyers, soldiers and indeed the adult actors, and any aggrieved individual might well have taken Jonson to law.[19]

Even, then, in what *might* have been the more congenial context of the private theatres, Jonson was not able to relax. It was not just a matter of the social mix of the audiences, or of their education, but something as fundamental as a distrust of the kind of communal experience involved. The fluidity of the moment when a large crowd gathered and confronted the unpredictable skills of the actors, in a rendition of a work over which the author no longer had any rights or control (though there is evidence that Jonson, like other dramatists, acted as a director of sorts for at least some of his later plays), was anathema to him. The Induction to *Bartholomew Fair* is his most sustained commentary on the problem, the tensions only just hidden in a display of joviality. The mock-solemn 'Articles of Agreement' allow that 'it shall be lawful for any man to judge his six pen'orth, his twelve pen'orth, so to his eighteen pence, two shillings, half a crown, to the value of his place' – but only 'provided always his place get not above his wit' (Appendix, p. 198). Money might not be the final determinant of intelligence or judgement, and an audience in one context was not *inherently* superior to one in another: *all* audiences are suspect. 'It is also agreed that every man here exercise his own judgement, and not censure by contagion, or upon trust, from another's voice, or face, that sits by him, be he never so first in the commission of wit' (p. 198). As he puts it in 'To the Reader in Ordinary', which prefaced the 1611 quarto of *Catiline* after its failure on the stage: 'most commend out of affection, self-tickling, an easiness, or imitation', adding 'but men judge only out of knowledge. That is the trying faculty' (Appendix, p. 184). We shall have occasion again (at the end of Chapter 4) to observe Jonson's special use of the term 'knowledge' and its centrality to his concept of what criticism is. For the moment, let us observe that it is not a quality which he expects to find in the charged and volatile context of the theatre, where (he implies) people surrender to all their fundamental weaknesses and in a crucial sense cease to be 'men'.

Doubtless there is something here of Jonson's personal touchiness about the reception of his own plays, but we also hear in it something of a newly emerging culture irritated with the one it is replacing. Early Elizabethan drama was still very much in touch with an agrarian society that marked its seasonal and religious cycles with 'timeless' festivities, in which the community renewed and re-asserted itself, acknowledging its place in the cycles of nature. Comedy, in particular, 'is structured by the paradigms of festival: the alternation of order and disorder, urban world and green world, Carnival and Lent'.[20] Plays like *Love's Labour's Lost, As You Like It* and *Twelfth Night*, for all their sophistication, clearly draw on such festive rhythms, and play-watching at the courts of Elizabeth and James was largely confined to the period of midwinter festival. As Peter Burke observes, looking at Carnival as 'the example *par excellence* of festival', it 'was a favourite time for the performance of plays, and many of these plays cannot be properly understood without some knowledge of Carnival rituals, to which they often allude'. However such festivities were reiterated or stage-managed in the context of the theatre, there was no more than a minimal sense of an author or a script, any more than there was a clear dividing line between participants and audience: the experience was one of what Clifford Geertz calls 'a collective text'.[21]

By the end of the sixteenth century, acting in London had perhaps established itself as a distinct profession, but it still retained something of these roots (as it still retained the lingering stigma of vagrancy and needed the 'cover' of liveried service in a noble household). The 'author', in some of the ways we have reviewed, remained an indeterminate quantity, while the audience were as much participants in a formulaic experience (which included onstage dancing at the end even of the most sombre tragedy) as they were detached observers.[22] Jonson, as a Londoner from birth and the product of an urban culture to which these conventions were essentially alien, challenged them at every point: he insisted increasingly on his own autonomous identity as an author (a key turning point seems to have been in 1604 when he settled on the distinctive form, 'Ben Jonson', of his own name[23]) and insisted that the audience too had a distinctive identity and role. They were not participants, but 'judging spectators' (prologue to *The*

Alchemist), in some essential ways detached from the experience to which they were party. The 'Articles of Agreement' in the Induction to *Bartholomew Fair* may be a comic fiction, but the contractual relationship they spell out belies a fundamental truth about the author/audience polarity, and the nature of the 'exchange' between them, which underlies the concept of 'literature' as the modern world has known it.

The distinctions we are here observing are paralleled in the transition from a culture dominated by the spoken word to one dominated by the written. The spoken word has a specific, local force which is eventually lost; the written word can at least masquerade as permanent, immutable. The spoken word can be publicly shared by a community; the written word is essentially for the private reading of an individual. In all of Jonson's plays (or, more precisely, all of those he preserved), and despite their effectiveness on the stage, their status as *written* words is unmistakable. The very first play he published, *Every Man Out of His Humour*, appeared in 1600 'Containing more than hath been Publicly spoken or Acted', indeed untouched by the exigencies of performance, 'As It Was First Composed by the Author' (*H&S*, III; see Plates). The 1605 quarto of *Sejanus* is introduced bluntly as a 'book', and one which 'in all numbers, is not the same with that which was acted on the public stage, wherein a second pen had good share', so doubly translated from the stage event which had provoked the audience's violent response. One of the commendatory verses to the volume, signed 'Ev. B.', speaks of 'the people's beastly rage' in the Globe as 'that doubtful Hell. / From whence, this Publication sets thee free'. In the book, all of Jonson's historical sources are carefully cited in the margins, a monument to the on-going power of the written word, a bravura display of intertextuality in which the author (unlike his 'dead' postmodern counterpart) proudly asserts himself and his role in the re-creation of that power. The texts of *Cynthia's Revels* and *Poetaster* were revised for the 1616 folio in ways that make them less satisfactory for performance, but fuller and more engaging for the private reader. This is not, however, just a matter of how the texts appeared in print – though, as we have already observed, the very fact that they got into print as they did, and with the clear direction of Jonson himself behind them, is significant in itself.

There is also a very clear sense in which Jonson's plays, even in performance, address themselves not to the audience as a

corporate entity, but rather to the separate individuals assembled
there. The folio text of *Sejanus* contains a dedication to Lord
Aubigny, who had been in the original theatre audience but (so
Jonson implies) is one of those who has stood out against the
popular verdict: 'It is a poem that (if I well remember) in your
Lordship's sight, suffered no less violence from our people here,
than the subject of it did from the rage of the people of Rome;
but . . . this hath . . . begot itself a greater favour than he lost, the
love of good men. Amongst whom . . . I make your Lordship the
first it thanks' (Appendix, p. 192). This is analogous to the role
he confers on the Earl of Pembroke as dedicatee of both *Catiline*
and the *Epigrams*, and on King James himself in the Epilogue to
Bartholomew Fair, where he claims:

> This is your power to judge (great Sir) and not
>   the envy of a few. Which if we have got,
> We value less what their dislike can bring,
>   if it so happy be, to have pleased the King.
>   (ll. 9–12)

Of course, Jonson is vicariously sharing here in royal and aristocratic authority, which he invokes to complement his own, and
there is an element of flattery in singling out these great men as
the ideal 'judging spectators'. But there is a wider issue of principle, behind the conventional deferral to such patrons. That is
the sense in which those sturdily independent dedicatees offer a
model for every member of the audience that Jonson envisages
for his plays: in their inward judgements, unswayed by opinion
or the distractions of the crowd, they are essentially private *readers*
of an event, not participants within it.

Jonson had, in fact, anticipated what Aubigny represented, even
before he summoned him by name. Following the reaction to
Poetaster, he composed an *Apologetical Dialogue* which 'was only
once spoken upon the stage' and was indeed not allowed into
print in the 1602 quarto (it was first published in the 1616 folio).
Here he looks forward to his next work, which was to be *Sejanus*:

> And since the comic muse
> Hath prov'd so ominous to me, I will try
> If tragedy have a more kind aspect.
> Her favours in my next I will pursue,

Where, if I prove the pleasure but of one,
So he judicious be; he shall b'alone
A theatre unto me.

(Appendix, p. 191)

In one sense this is arrogant, and it is not hard to see why Jonson
met with such resistance, and so much personal abuse for what
was perceived as pretentiousness. But in all of this Jonson was
carrying the flag for a new perception not merely of theatre, but
of the relationship between authors and readers in general. And
this is what *most* of his criticism is ultimately about.

NON-DRAMATIC VERSE

Given the tensions he faced in the theatrical world it is not surprising that, long before he was financially free to abandon the
stage for a time, Jonson also sought other outlets for his talents.
At least as early as 1599 he was also writing verse for a very
different audience, of a kind that was to form the bulk of his
non-dramatic writing. *Epigram* XL, 'On Margaret Ratcliffe', is an
elegy for one of Queen Elizabeth's maids of honour, who died
that year. This is the earliest item we can date that directly links
Jonson with the court and aristocratic circles, where commendatory poems might elicit a fee from the subject (or, as perhaps
here, the subject's family) but more generally where poetry was
a means of self-promotion in the pervasive patronage system, a
way of displaying one's talents that might lead to employment,
possibly as a tutor in a noble household (a route followed, for
example, by Samuel Daniel) or to something more elevated at
court.[24] The latter course was John Donne's ambition, and he got
as far as becoming secretary to the Lord Keeper of the Great Seal,
Sir Thomas Egerton. But an indiscreet secret marriage to his em-
ployer's niece cost him that post and all further civil employment, and he eventually ended up in the Church.

Again, the contrast with Shakespeare is instructive. *Venus and
Adonis* and *The Rape of Lucrece* both belong to the plague years of
1593/94, when Shakespeare's income from the theatre must have
dried up entirely for a precariously long period. In the circumstances the pursuit of aristocratic patronage may be seen as a
necessary expedient. But the evidence suggests that, once the

theatres re-opened, he returned to them almost exclusively for his living. We cannot date the sonnets with any certainty, or reliably ascribe them to a patronage relationship with Southampton or anyone else (though it is not unlikely). But they too may well also be products of the 1593/94 lay-off, and at all events would seem to be a side-issue in Shakespeare's career as a whole. In Jonson's case, he wrote verse for aristocratic patrons virtually throughout his career, alongside his activities in the theatre and later as a writer of court entertainments. Of his contemporaries only George Chapman (with whom he was on friendly terms for most of his life, though there was bitterness in later years) maintained anything like a similar footing in both the 'professional' world of the theatre and the 'amateur' world of the poet seeking advancement through patronage.[25] Chapman had the misfortune to invest too much of his hopes and energy in pursuing patrons, including Ralegh, Essex, Somerset and Prince Henry who, through no fault of his own, were unable to be of long-term help to him.

Jonson was perhaps luckier in this regard, but his precise ambitions in writing poetry of this sort, beyond the fees he might expect in return for such 'presents', are less clear than we might suppose. He addressed complimentary verses to a wide range of the aristocracy of the day. For example, he addressed an Epistle to the Countess of Rutland as a New Year's gift for 1600 (*For* XII); she was the daughter of Sir Philip Sidney, and this is the first indication of his best-remembered connections, those with the Sidneys and their collateral families, the Wroths and the Herbert Earls of Pembroke. But it is too simplistic to construe from this Jonson's personal affiliation with a family famous for its literary associations, a high-minded identification with the best traditions of humanist scholarship.[26] He also wrote poems for less immediately attractive figures, such as the Earls of Salisbury, Suffolk and Somerset, and did not scruple to write *The Gypsies Metamorphos'd* at the behest of Buckingham at a time (1621) when Pembroke was openly antagonistic to the royal favourite. There are, perhaps, moments in Jonson's career when something like factional or principled affiliations are discernible. David Riggs, for example, makes a case for the organisation of the *Epigrams* in 1616 reflecting the new ascendancy of the Pembroke circle at court, and I would add that the centrality of the Sidneys (a family above all associated with militant Protestantism) to *The Forest* may reflect a particular enthusiasm in the wake of his conversion back from

Catholicism in 1610.[27] But looking at his career overall, he never seems tied to one set of interests to the exclusion of others. So, while he was thoroughly engaged in the patronage system as a whole, and the old literary system that related to it, it is not clear if he sought through it specific advancement by attachment to a particular faction, or indeed an escape from the profession of letters by more sustained employment in an aristocratic household.[28]

Jonson spent more than one prolonged period attached to a noble household, that of Esmé Stuart, Lord D'Aubigny, cousin to King James, in about 1604–6 and again from 1613 to 1618.[29] He wrote one of his *Epigrams* for Aubigny (CXXVII) and an Epistle to his wife, Lady Katherine (*For* XIII), and dedicated *Sejanus* to him. But we do not know on what basis he 'remained w[i]t[h] my lord Aubigny' (*Drummond*, 208), or whether Jonson was ever formally in his service. It is a simple fact that the documentary record of a figure like Aubigny, who probably wielded significant influence though little direct power, is much smaller than that of men like Salisbury, Pembroke and Buckingham; if we knew more about him, Jonson's relationship with him might loom larger than it does in most estimates. Jonson did act for a time as tutor to Sir Walter Ralegh's son Wat, in 1613, but this was clearly a role for which he was not cut out (*Drummond*, 245–53). In 1621 he even received the reversion to a significant post at court, that of Master of the Revels, among whose responsibilities was the censorship of plays for the public stage. It is reasonable to suppose that, had he actually taken on that post, his literary career would largely have ended, or at least taken a very different form from that it actually followed. But a reversion could only take effect on the death of the incumbent and of anyone with a prior reversion, and the man ahead of Jonson in the queue – Sir John Astley – in fact outlived him.

Whether by accident or design, Jonson remained a professional man of letters. And in one particular sense he distanced himself from courtly 'amateurs' like Donne, in that he committed a good deal of his poetry to public print. The Renaissance had made the acquisition of literary skills a necessary part of the education of the privileged classes – not as an end in themselves, but as an adjunct of their newly emerging roles in the power-structure of the day. Their predecessors had been feudal soldiers, serving themselves and their overlords primarily on the battlefield. Latterly, their skills as administrators, diplomats and magistrates had come to be valued at least as highly, and a basic facility with language and a grasp of its expressive force was essential for all these roles. So even the most prosaic of politicians, such as Burghley, could turn their hands to a poem when the occasion demanded, while more dashing courtiers like Ralegh and Essex naturally used poetic facility to advertise their other talents. Philip Sidney had merely carried this tendency further than any other English courtier of the day. But none of these would have stooped to the stigma of print, which was the mark of an artisan and not of a gentleman. They affected to write for their own entertainment and that of a select circle, among whom their works would circulate in manuscript, in which context (as we have seen) even such a complex and voluminous romance as the *Arcadia* could be brushed over as 'but a trifle, and that triflingly handled'.

Jonson in fact never affected such *sprezzatura* nonchalance. He was openly proud of his learning and of the care that went into producing the pithy, plain-style lucidity of his verse.[30] He did, however, write most of his verse in the first instance for specific dedicatees and often also for manuscript circulation among a select circle. We see this process reflected in *Ep* XCIV, 'To Lucy, Countess of Bedford, with Mr Donne's Satires', where his own compliments to the poets' mutual patron are passed on with his friend's satires. 'Rare poems ask rare friends' he observes there (l. 6), introducing the most delicate of competition into these polite exchanges, and asserting his own identity even while he defers to the countess's request for Donne's works. Such matters were one thing within the circle that frequented Lucy Harington's estate at Twickenham Park, rather another when the poem appeared in print as one of the *Epigrams*. Semi-private compliments become very public ones, and are threaded into a much wider network of compliment and condemnation which intermittently takes on a narrative life of its own.[31] The particular circumstances and pressures that occasioned the poem are lost in the formal timelessness of print and the author/editor's tacit but commanding presence. Moreover, Jonson's status as a suitor for patronage is overshadowed by the palpable 'authority' of the folio *Works*, in which the collection finally appeared. What in isolation must always have carried with it an implicit acknowledgement of the poet's need of the countess and her influence has tacitly become part of an assertion that he has to a degree transcended such considerations: the plays and the *Epigrams* each have their dedicatees in the *Works*, while the masques and entertainments continue to celebrate the subjects who commissioned them, but the volume itself is Jonson's own monument to himself.[32]

Much of the derision which greeted Jonson's *Works* on its publication focused on its presumption in giving plays the status of folio publication. One writer turned Jonson's own epigrammatic wit against himself:

> Pray tell me Ben, where doth the mystery lurk,
> What others call a play, you call a work.

Henry Fitzgeoffry more bluntly derided 'books made of ballads; works, of plays' and John Boys was simply indignant that 'the very plays of a modern poet are called in print his *Works*'. As late as 1633 Thomas Heywood thought it worth observing: 'My plays are not exposed unto the world in volumes, to bear the title of *Works* (as others), in numerous sheets and a large volume; but singly, as thou seest, with great modesty and small noise' (Preface to *The English Traveller*).[33] But if Jonson was thought unduly to have elevated his plays in this publication, he may also be said to have demeaned his non-dramatic verse by associating it with them, even if this side of the equation elicited less comment. The fact is that the *Works* is in one sense a compromise, an attempt to blend different strands of Jonson's career which in the eyes of many people were discrete and very nearly contradictory.

This was a contradiction which Jonson himself never acknowledged. He circumvented it by insisting that all his writings (all, at least, that he chose to preserve) were 'poems' and that he himself was always a 'poet'. This is very different from the primary modern sense of a writer in verse but focuses on the creative force of the imagination itself. In *Discoveries* (which *may* have been partly lecture notes for Gresham College, and so affect an impartial authority, distinct from his own creative works: see Chronology for 1623) Jonson poses the question 'What is a poet?' and answers himself:

> A poet is that which by the Greeks is called κατ εξοχην, ο ποιητηζ [*the maker par excellence*], a maker or a feigner; his art, an art of imitation or feigning, expressing the life of man in fit measure, numbers, and harmony, according to Aristotle: from the word ποιειν, which signifies to make or feign. Hence, he is

called a poet, not he which writeth in measure only; but that feigneth and formeth a fable, and writes things like the truth. For, fable and fiction is (as it were) the form and soul of any poetical work, or poem.   (ll. 2368–78)

This immediately begs a further question: 'What mean you by a poem?', which he answers rather cryptically: 'A poem is not alone any work, or composition of the poet's in many, or few verses; but even one alone verse sometimes makes a perfect poem' (2379–82). He cites Virgil's own description of a single-line inscription within the Aeneid as 'a poem, or carmen [song]', gives two pithy epigrams by Martial as examples of similarly brief 'poems', then invokes Horace's odes, 'his lyric songs' as more substantial 'Carmina', concluding with a whole book of De Rerum Natura which Lucretius himself had described as a song. 'And anciently, all the oracles were called carmina; or, whatever sentence [idea, statement] was expressed, were it much, or little, it was called, an epic, dramatic, lyric, elegiac, or epigrammatic poem' (2382–96). In essence, then, a poem is any coherent idea or fable expressed by a poet: its categorisation into a particular form of literature is a secondary consideration, primarily dictated by the magnitude of the idea.

This is the nub of much of Jonson's defence of himself and self-definition, in whatever context it arises. 'In all his poems . . .' he says in the Prologue to Volpone (l. 7), incorporating that work and its predecessors for the stage in the larger circle of his writing. All the plays he prints are 'poems', even those like Epicoene and Bartholomew Fair which are written in prose. Verse itself is no guarantee whatever of 'poetry': 'The common rhymers pour forth verses, such as they are, extempore, but there never come[s] from them one sense worth the life of a day. A rhymer, and a poet, are two things. . . . I have met many of these rattles that made a noise, and buzzed. They had their hum, and no more' (Discoveries, 2469–72, 2486–8). Rhyming, like any other formal feature of a work, is an empty embellishment unless it is in the service of a poet's idea or conception. And, if the idea is sound, it can survive inadequacies in the author's execution of the work. In dedicating Sejanus to Aubigny, he calls it a 'poem', but acknowledges in 'To the Readers' that it 'is no true poem, in the strict laws of time . . . as also in the want of a proper chorus' (Appendix, p. 173). So he admits to some formal deficiencies, but not to essential, disabling ones. The questions of forms, of 'rules', and of their relation to classical precedent, are ones that we shall examine in due course. For now, we should observe that they are less constricting in Jonson's thinking than is often supposed and always secondary to the creative imagination of the poet, which is the key determinant. It is that, for example, which allows Jonson to claim his masques as 'poems', even though there is no classical precedent for such a form whatever.

There is nothing here that is inherently new. All the ideas can be traced back to the ancients, notably Aristotle, Horace and Seneca, and indeed to more recent reformulations, such as Sidney's *Defence of Poesy*. What is different is that Jonson is not writing as a detached theorist, but as a writer who needs to sell and justify himself in the marketplace. There may be a relationship between Sidney's engagement with literature and his political career, but in many ways writing is on the margins of his central concerns as an aristocrat and courtier; it is likely that he would have written far less if his talents had been better appreciated and employed by the queen or his uncle, Leicester.[34] In Jonson's case, these matters are crucial to his whole identity and career as a writer. He deploys notions of the poet as maker not in a selfless perpetuation of accepted wisdom, but in order to establish spaces and shapes for himself in a world where none pre-exists and to which he has no given right. These spaces and shapes are found in the prefaces and prologues of his plays and masques, and in the images of himself in his non-dramatic verse – as a dutiful subject of a king who is also a 'poet' (*Ep* IV and LI, both entitled 'To King James'); as a humble student of the great scholar Camden (*Ep* XIV, 'To William Camden'); as a respectful friend of other poets (*Ep* LV, XXIII, XCVI, 'To Francis Beaumont', and two poems 'To John Donne'); as an admiring equal of historians and musicians (*Ep* CX, CXIII, 'To Clement Edmondes, on His *Caesar's Commentaries Observed and Translated*' and 'To the Same, on the Same', and CXXX, CXXXI, 'To Alphonso Ferrabosco, on His Book', 'To the Same'); as a grieving father (*Ep* XXII, XLV, 'On My First Daughter', 'On my First Son' – the latter remembered as 'Ben Jonson his best piece of poetry', line 10); as the surrogate father of his poetic 'sons' (*Und* XLVII, 'An Epistle Answering to One that Asked to be Sealed of the Tribe of Ben'); as the grateful but never subservient recipient of so much aristocratic patronage in so many contexts, and so on.

Every address to another person, be it a named individual or
an anonymous reader (even 'To All to Whom I Write', where he
carefully distinguishes a 'poet' from a 'herald', *Ep* IX), implicitly
'places' Jonson himself. So in every work he redefines himself,
comparing and associating, or contrasting and dissociating, with
all around him (a process which is fundamental to the entire structure of the play *Poetaster*). Poems such as those on 'Old-End Gath-
erer', 'Poet-Ape' and 'To a Weak Gamester in Poetry' create negative
self-images, from which Jonson carefully distances himself (*Ep*
LIII, LVI, CXII). This is most strikingly the case with a sequence
of poems on 'Playwright' (*Ep* XLIX, LXVIII, C). The *OED* does
not record this term before the Restoration, and it is entirely possible that Jonson coined it himself; it clearly denotes a manual
craft, on the analogy of cartwright or wheelwright. Jonson always
applies it to other people, never to himself, and it is always a
term of abuse. He consistently advocates careful application to
the 'art' of poetry, stressing the need for learning, judgement and
instructive imitation, distrusting casual inspiration, as he distrusted
the 'inspired' rantings of Puritan divines like Zeal-of-the-Land
Busy in *Bartholomew Fair*, and indeed as he avoided associations
with notions of the *divinus furor* of poetry, its visionary rapture,
a concept given currency by the neoplatonist Marsilio Ficino and
espoused to an extent by his friend Chapman. (Cordatus recognises it in Asper in the preliminaries to *Every Man Out of His
Humour*, one of the warning signs in that play that its satiric voice
and Jonson's own vision are not identical: 'Why this is right *Furor
Poeticus!*', Appendix, p. 167). Nevertheless, Jonson will not compare the work of the poet to that of a manual craftsman, which
lacks the 'soul' of the creative imagination. The poems on 'Playwright' thus draw a clear distinction between his own dramatic
'poems' and so many of the other plays being written at that
time – just as, in the printed versions of his own contribution to
The Magnificent Entertainment which belatedly greeted James I's
ceremonial entry into London, Jonson distinguished his own artful devices from the work of Dekker, whom he seeks to characterise as a journey-man pageant-maker.

SELF-CENSORSHIP AND SELF-CONSTRUCTION

We must presume that Jonson was observing this distinction himself in his decisions over which of his plays to include in the 1616 *Works*. While, as I have observed, it is quite possible that he simply did not have the copyright of all his earliest pieces, the sheer number of items he omitted (compared with what he included) suggests that it was more a matter of choice than of necessity. By 1598 Francis Meres (though not the most discriminating of judges) already thought him among our 'best for tragedy' but none of the works on which that judgement was based has survived; even the titles are lost to us. Jonson himself told Drummond 'That the half of his comedies were not in print' (336).[35] 'Comedies' might here be synonymous with plays (as 'comedians' was synonymous with 'players') so this could include all his work for Henslowe, which seems mainly to have been on histories and tragedies; *Bartholomew Fair* and *The Devil is an Ass* are his only two comedies, formally speaking, which we know about and were not in print by 1619, there being room for neither in the *Works*. The one comedy which *was* in print, but which was not in the *Works*, was *The Case is Altered*. Here again we cannot speak with certainty, but it seems that Jonson was deliberately disowning the play, presumably as the work of a 'playwright' and not of a 'poet'. This is mildly surprising since, although the play is no masterpiece, it is not inconsiderable either. It is certainly not unlearned, being based on two works by Plautus which were not available in English translation when he wrote. Most of his fellow writers for Henslowe in the 1590s, with the notable exception of Chapman, had no more than the 'small Latin, and less Greek' that Jonson himself conceded to Shakespeare (Appendix), so the achievement of *The Case is Altered* was no mean one. Yet he chose to overlook it.

While the decision not to reproduce *The Case is Altered* and his writings for Henslowe is very likely to be an attempt to protect what he came to regard as his work as 'poet' from contamination by what he tacitly acknowledged as his own employments as a 'playwright', we should observe that this was not the only self-censorship. In compiling the *Epigrams* and *The Forest* he certainly set aside some poems, either because they did not suit the idiosyncratic arrangement of those selections or because he wished to disown them. These included two that finally appeared posthumously in *The Underwood*, both with intriguingly detailed epigraphs: XXV, 'An Ode to James, Earl of Desmond, Writ in Queen Elizabeth's Time, Since Lost and Recovered', and XXX, 'An Epigram on William, Lord Burghley, Lord High Treasurer of England (Presented Upon a Plate of Gold to His Son Robert, Earl of Salisbury, when he was also Treasurer)'. James Fitzgerald was an odd choice of patron to court; the 'Tower Earl' was kept a royal prisoner from childhood because of his father's rebellion, and was only confirmed in his earldom and provisionally released from the Tower of London in the autumn of 1600 because the English felt he might be useful in their efforts to put down Tyrone's rebellion. Jonson probably wrote the poem for him at this sudden turn in his fortunes, since a portion of it appeared in an anthology, *England's Parnassus*, that October. This, of course, partly gives the lie to Jonson's later claim that the poem was 'lost', since he could have recovered the published part of it if he had really wanted to. But Desmond died in 1601; by 1616 Jonson's brief attempt to cultivate his patronage may have seemed an irrelevance, or even possibly a real embarrassment.

The latter would certainly seem to be the case with the epigram for Burghley/Salisbury. Two poems to Salisbury are in fact included in the *Epigrams* (LXIII, LXIV) but they are followed there very pointedly by LXV, 'To My Muse', which begins

Away, and leave me, thou thing most abhorred
That hast betrayed me to a worthless lord.

Jonson's relations with Salisbury, which went back at least to 1597 and the *Isle of Dogs* affair, seem to have been complex and sometimes stormy. It was to Salisbury that Jonson wrote the most detailed and revealing of the letters he wrote during his imprisonment over *Eastward Ho*, parts of which reappeared in the Epistle to *Volpone* (see Appendix, p. 213). It was Salisbury who called in Jonson to help find a certain Catholic priest in the wake of the Gunpowder Plot. But it was also Salisbury who managed to offend Jonson's prickly sense of his own dignity: 'Being at the end of my Lord Salisbury's table with Inigo Jones, and demanded by my Lord why he was not glad, "My Lord", said he, "You promised I should dine with you, but I do not", for he had none of his meat. He esteemed only th[a]t his meat which was of his own dish' (*Drummond*, 264–7). And Jonson told Drummond: 'Salisbury

never cared for any man longer nor he could make use of him'
(297–8). The decision to drop the epigram with all its memories
of ceremonial presentation on a golden plate, and its attempt to
construct a genuine aristocratic lineage out of the mere fact that
Salisbury had succeeded to the high office previously held by his
father, probably reflects Jonson's more considered opinion of Salisbury (who was dead by 1616), which is hinted at in the location
of 'To My Muse' (see above, p. 31, and note 58).

We can also trace one other category of self-censorship. In 1604
the Haberdashers' Company paid Jonson twelve pounds for a 'device, and speech' that were part of the 'Lord Mayor's Triumphs',
the show that accompanied the annual installation of the Lord
Mayor of London. This was the first such show in James's reign,
since the plague had ruled it out the previous year; the king himself
was present and the Haberdashers obviously wanted to make an
impression in honour of their own member, who had been elected
to office that year. Jonson's part in the 'Magnificent Entertainment' that greeted James when he made his plague-delayed ceremonial entry into London in March 1604 had obviously been
judged a success.[36] Twelve pounds was as much as Jonson might
expect to make from a play, between the basic fee and a share in
the second-performance profits, so the Haberdashers were paying him well in the hope of making a similar impression. Yet
Jonson never saw fit to publish what he wrote for them, either at
the time or in the 1616 folio. Anthony Munday certainly rushed
out copies of his *Triumphs of Reunited Britannia* for the Lord Mayor's
Show the following year, and it became usual thereafter for their
authors to print them.[37] Although Jonson did not apparently con-
tribute to any Lord Mayor's Shows after 1604, it seems very likely
that he was employed by the livery companies and civic dignitaries on numerous occasions: a proven track-record of writing
what royalty wanted to hear was a qualification they could hardly
overlook.[38] Yet Jonson sought to preserve none of these. The 1616
folio did print for the first time several relatively minor pieces,
such as 'The Entertainment at Althorp' and 'An Entertainment of
the King and Queen at Theobalds', but none for civic patrons.
Those included were all either commissioned by royalty or for
occasions celebrating royalty.

In as much as these acts of self-censorship relate to the 1616
folio of his *Works*, they must be connected with the exceptional
nature of that volume itself. Jonson was not here merely preserving

his writing for posterity: apart from the non-dramatic verse and some royal entertainments, most of what was in it was already in print. He was making a further statement about himself and the status of his own writings, beyond that they deserved preservation. He was presenting himself to the world as a 'classic', an author who deserved the same serious attention as those Latin and Greek writers to whose precedents and opinions he so often deferred. He had sowed the seeds for this in earlier publications of his plays, where his division of the texts into acts and scenes imitated conventions used for the printing of classical drama, rather than contemporary stage practice (where scenes were determined simply by the entrance or exit of principal characters, and there were no formal act divisions); details like the acrostic 'argument' to *Volpone* were also deliberate allusions to similar features in the plays of Plautus. But the folio made a much larger claim, a comprehensive and indeed unignorable one. Of existing English authors, only Chaucer (and, to a lesser extent, Gower and Lydgate) securely held such classic status, and that owed something to their antiquity.[39]

Of more recent figures, Spenser came closest, largely on the strength of *The Faerie Queene*. Jonson was characteristically mixed in his response to Spenser, who had died in poverty after fleeing Ireland just as his own career was opening up. While he briefly invoked him as a model of a genuine poet in *Discoveries* (628), and admitted to Drummond that he had memorised some of *The Shepheardes Calendar* (95–6), he had reservations about the versification, the obscurity and the subject-matter of *The Faerie Queene* itself: 'Spenser's stanzas pleased him not, nor his matter, the meaning of which allegory he had delivered in papers to Sir Walter Raleigh' (*Drummond*, 15–16: see also 142–4). The rediscovery by James Riddell and Stanley Stewart of Jonson's own copy of the 1617 folio of Spenser's works, heavily annotated by him, does demonstrate the close attention he paid to his predecessor, though it was an attention that was rarely translated into imitation or other forms of public recognition. Spenser never registers as an influence on Jonson as he does, for example, on Milton, except perhaps negatively.[40]

Philip Sidney's reputation as a poet was also growing following the posthumous publication of his major works in the 1590s, culminating in a 1598 folio, in effect an 'authorised' edition, probably overseen by his sister, the Countess of Pembroke.[41] But it was still not entirely possible to divorce his standing as a writer from that as a national and Protestant martyr. Jonson was invariably respectful about him in public, but aired one particular reservation to Drummond: 'Sidney did not keep a decorum in making everyone speak as well as himself' and more specifically that 'Dametas [a clown in the *Arcadia*] sometimes speaks grave sentences' (13–14, 537–8).[42] We should bear in mind Jonson's precise definition of poetry in weighing his assertion that 'The Countess of Rutland was nothing inferior to her father, S[ir] P. Sidney, in poesy', while we may deduce from the context that he disagreed with the king when he 'said Sir P. Sidney was no poet' (*Drummond*, 172–3, 315).[43]

While Jonson would argue that it was a matter of his own integrity that he should retain the right to pass judgement on such august figures, it was an act of considerable self-conviction, not to say self-conceit, to publish, in the *Works*, a carefully edited version of his own achievement as bearing comparison with theirs. The fact that the bulk of his volume was taken up with what many people still saw as mere 'playbooks' only compounded the arrogance. More than arrogance, however, what is perhaps most striking is the element of wish-fulfilment in the *Works*. Here Jonson presents himself as 'the poet' par excellence. The acts of self-censorship we have observed divorce Jonson from his own identity as a 'playwright', from some of the wrong turnings in his pursuit of aristocratic patronage, and from all of his civic commissions (except that of 'The King's Coronation Entertainment', as it is here somewhat misleadingly described). These, and other editorial decisions, promote a view of Jonson not merely as a fine writer but (the ultimate qualification for a 'classic') as a *timeless* one, floating free of the contingent pressures that shaped him. All the evidence suggests that it is Jonson himself, rather than popular or critical acclaim, that settled on *Every Man In His Humour* as *the* beginning of his career. The publication sequence, and pressure of early comment, make *Every Man Out of His Humour* a more likely starting point if one were looking for an objective moment when he could really be said to have distinguished himself from his co-workers with Henslowe. But Jonson glosses that over in printing the earlier play first in the folio, very possibly revising the text – and translating the action from Florence to London – to give the play a *retrospective* pre-eminence there, the subsequent currency of which is summed up in John Aubrey's typically facile comment that it 'was his first good one'.[44]

The motive for this piece of self-construction would appear to be related to a desire to impose on his career a clear and purposeful shape, one that ignored accidents and the vicissitudes of audience reaction, standing out in its own hermetic perfection against the ravages of time itself. Much later, Jonson was openly to articulate such a sense of coherence in his (dramatic) career, in the Induction to *The Magnetic Lady, or Humours Reconciled*: 'The Author, beginning his studies of this kind, with *Every Man In His Humour*; and after *Every Man Out of His Humour*: and since, continuing in all his plays, especially those of the comic thread, whereof the *New-Inn* was the last, some recent humours still, or manners of men, that went along with the times, finding himself now near the close, or shutting up of his circle, hath fantasied to himself, in *Idea*, this *Magnetic Mistress*. . . . And this he hath called *Humours Reconciled* (*H&S*, VI, pp. 508–15, ll. 99–111). The 1616 folio is more subtle in its self-presentation, but its underlying claims of consistency and coherence are even more pronounced: the non-dramatic verse is not allowed to appear as a random collection of pieces arising from any number of accidental occasions, but appears as two enigmatically structured selections more authoritative than any of their constituent parts. It was perhaps because he could never hope to impose more than a specious coherence on his civic commissions, which could never entirely sever their ties with the circumstances of their presentation, that he omitted them altogether.

Royalty, however, mirrored poetry in its pretence to timelessness, so the masques and other royal entertainments posed no such problems. The identities of the principal celebrants of *Hymenaei* and *A Challenge at Tilt* had to be suppressed, as we shall observe at the end of the next chapter. But the final passage of the latest masque, *The Golden Age Restored* (1616), concludes on the triumphant note of Astraea, goddess of justice who fled the earth in the Age of Iron, choosing to return in the balmy days of King James.[45] It is, of course, a compliment to the king, and so, like all the masques, intimately tied to the Jacobean court and its perceptions of its own power; indeed, it implicitly celebrates James's insistence on standing firm as an impartial judge, even though his favourite, the Earl of Somerset, was implicated in the murder of Sir Thomas Overbury. But as Jonson prints it here, it is also an assertion of the timeless power of his own pen, celebrating the essential victory of poetry itself over the vicissitudes of life. Within the masque, the Golden Age is actually restored by the 'classic' English poets, Chaucer, Gower, Lydgate and Spenser. Alongside whom Jonson tacitly stands himself, a living 'classic'.

All this had subtle but serious implications for the literary criticism actually embedded in the folio. The Prologue to *Every Man In His Humour*, for example, was written specifically for the revised version of the play and is thus, after the preliminaries (and a dedication to Camden), the first document the reader confronts in the book, a preface in effect for all the plays and to some extent for the volume as a whole. The *Apologetical Dialogue*, originally meant to be appended to *Poetaster*, but suppressed in 1601/2, finally appeared here; where once it was intended to represent the defiance of a man embattled, it now speaks for a man who has proved his detractors wrong. Even the Epistle to *Volpone*, Jonson's first substantial critical document to see print, enjoys a quietly different status. In the 1607 quarto it is signed 'From my house in the Black-Friars this 11 of February. 1607', which is partly a quiet piece of boasting (the Blackfriars was a prosperous neighbourhood: the felon stripped of his goods after killing Gabriel Spencer has done well for himself) but is also a very specific locus: the thinking that goes into the Epistle (as we shall see) has a discernible history, which can be traced back to the *Isle of Dogs* affair and to more recent traumas over *Eastward Ho* and Jonson's recusancy. In the folio, those details are omitted: the Epistle presents itself as a (literally) timeless document. Like the much larger document in which it is now embedded, it speaks 'classic' truths, not tied to particular histories.

But all of this remains, in a sense, wish-fulfilment, except to the extent that subsequent readers (either by choice or out of ignorance) have taken Jonson at his word. The *Works* is itself a product of its moment: the 'timeless' structure of the *Epigrams* does not obscure the ascendancy of the Pembroke faction which to an extent they endorse, and the ending of the Cecil and Howard influences which made that possible. *The Golden Age Restored* may be an elaborate literary conceit, but it was also the occasion for an early participation in a masque by George Villiers, a handsome young man promoted by Pembroke and his allies to counteract the influence of other royal favourites, notably the Earl of Somerset. Villiers succeeded so spectacularly as to outface his makers and become Duke of Buckingham, the first non-royal duke in

England since Norfolk went to the block in 1572. In Jonson's own career, the *Works* also marked a crossroads, in ways that he himself may not fully have understood. The royal pension (6 February) that gave Jonson a significant degree of financial independence actually preceded the book and was not in any direct sense a reward for the eminence which its publication (summer) proclaimed, though the book had been long in the press and may to an extent have been anticipated. The royal patent only cites 'divers good considerations us at this present especially moving', and it may have been more in recognition of his services in entertaining the court (and anticipation that these would continue) than of his 'classic' status.[46]

Strikingly, despite the pension and the appearance of the *Works*, Jonson did not *immediately* abandon the stage: *The Devil is an Ass* followed both of these, in the second half of 1616. However strong his anti-theatrical prejudice, he either experienced some difficulty in tearing himself away or had difficulty re-directing his energies. More perplexingly still, having so resoundingly identified himself with the emerging print culture, he now effectively abandoned it in favour of the private circulation of what he wrote, the hallmark of the courtly amateur. Although printed copies survive of some of his later Jacobean masques, such as *Time Vindicated* (1623) and *The Fortunate Isles* (published 1625), they do not bear the name of a bookseller on their title-pages, as was usual, and it is apparent that these were run off as presentation copies for favoured friends and patrons, and were not commercially available. Jonson did not resort to *public* print again until 1630, when he published the text of *Love's Triumph through Callipolis*, and that – like his return to the stage somewhat earlier – may well be a reflection of financial need rather than principled conviction. Jonson, however, contrived to introduce an issue of principle into it, by publishing the masque as by 'Ben Jonson, Inigo Jones' – his own name as poet before that of the stage-designer. This brought to a head differences between the two men over what was really important in a masque.

In some ways, therefore, the *Works* represents a dead-end rather than a definitive statement; its Olympian posture might disguise the tensions inherent in Jonson's career, but it could not eradicate them. Possibly he recognised this himself. When Drummond records how 'In his merry humour he was wont to name himself The Poet' (560), it is as if Jonson could see the incongruity in this portentous public pose. Being 'The Poet' was at bottom only a stratagem for dealing with the pressures of being a professional man of letters at this time. The literary criticism with which he sought to underpin the title was a series of tactical feints, formulations to meet particular challenges. If at times he sought to translate it into something else, into 'classic' truths, that too was a matter of tactical necessity. We must treat each piece, therefore, as an adventitious intervention in the cultural marketplace of the early seventeenth century.

3

Poet and State

Following his imprisonment for *The Isle of Dogs*, the next controversy over one of Jonson's plays concerned the ending of *Every Man Out of His Humour*. It was a relatively minor business, but instructive because it concerned – literally – the representation of authority. The play is dominated by Asper, whose 'character' is defined in the printed text: 'He is of an ingenious and free spirit, eager and constant in reproof, without fear controlling the world's abuses. One, whom no servile hope of gain, or frosty apprehension of danger, can make to be a parasite, either to time, place, or opinion' (*H&S*, III, p. 423). Within the action proper, however, Asper takes the role of Macilente or envy, which adds a malicious and almost pathological edge to his exposure of the grotesque 'humours' he confronts. This leaves him as the last, and in some ways most disturbing, of all the 'humours' in the play. In Jonson's original staging he was cured of this, and restored to his 'character' of Asper, by the sight of the Queen: that is, a boy disguised as Queen Elizabeth actually appeared on stage, and 'her' appearance shocked Macilente back to his senses. Someone, however, objected to this (Jonson implies that it was the public, but it may have been someone in authority) and he changed it.

As he explained in the quarto text: 'It had another catastrophe, or conclusion, at the first playing: which (διὰ τὸ τὴν βασιλισσαν προσωποποιεισθαι [*because of the impersonation of the Queen*]) many seem'd not to relish it'; and therefore, 'twas since alter'd' : in the revised version Macilente rather lamely runs out of people to be envious of. Jonson goes on, however, to justify the original, arguing that there were precedents for such impersonations of the monarch (possibly thinking of the plays of Lyly, where there are several thinly-veiled versions of the Virgin Queen) and that they were a feature of the Lord Mayors' Shows. Besides, the intensity of Macilente's 'humorous' obsession required the most intense of correctives, and 'there was nothing (in his examined opinion) that could more near or truly exemplify [the Queen's] power and strength of her invaluable virtues, than the working of so perfect a miracle on so opposed a spirit' (*H&S*, III, Appendix, pp. 602–3). So in Jonson's view there was nothing offensive in co-opting the image and authority of the monarch to complement that of himself as poet. Apparently, when the play was performed at court, he reverted to the original ending, except that the character was overcome by the sight of Elizabeth herself rather than by a boy in disguise.

The relationship between the writer and the state lies at the heart of Jonson's self-definitions and so of his criticism. 'Author' (or 'auctor') and 'authority' have a long intertwined etymology, in which questions of state power, moral leadership, the force of words, their credibility, and who takes responsibility for them, all overlap. In the sixteenth century these issues became particularly fraught, since the wider dissemination of writing through printing coincided with the Reformation, where the ultimate question of the authority of 'the word' – the word of God – became an issue over which states went to war and dynasties rose and fell. Broadly speaking, under the Tudors the assumption in law was that the monarch was the ultimate authority behind everything written and so, in a sense, author of all. His or her subjects (another etymologically fascinating term) might commit words to paper, but only by the monarch's leave, and even then they were in a sense using the monarch's own language, parroting words that depended for their validity on his or her sanction (see the Epilogue to *Bartholomew Fair*, Appendix, pp. 200–1). When Mistress Quickly in *The Merry Wives of Windsor* fears that 'here will be an old abusing of God's patience and the King's English', the phrase is rather more than a pat formula.[1] And, given the Elizabethan settlement, which made the Queen not only head of state but also Supreme Governor of the Church of England, God's patience and the Queen's English might properly be arrayed together, since the crown claimed sovereignty in matters of religion, dictating forms of worship, limiting the freedom to preach, imposing the use of ultra-orthodox sermons or 'homilies' and controlling the language both of the Book of Common Prayer and of the Bible itself: the King James Authorised Version of 1611 is only the best-known legacy of this fusion of royal authority, the English language and the word of God.

Martin Elsky pursues these matters in *Authorizing Words: Speech, Writing and Print in the English Renaissance*, linking Jonson's views

on them with those of such sixteenth-century humanists as Roger
Ascham, Sir Thomas Elyot and Richard Mulcaster. For them
'language is primarily speech, historically and culturally determined, embodying the consensus of the social community from
which it arises and expressing the community's ability to represent reality with moral astuteness' (p. 6). As such, language itself
(like the community it serves) is ultimately authorised by the monarch, who is its fountainhead and literally represents the consensus of the community. So, for these early humanists, it was not
only their *ideas* which were ultimately validated by the existence
of the monarch (who is often explicitly invoked in their works,
in a gesture which is more than conventional); it is the whole
process of linguistic exchange and representation in which they
are engaged, and the relationship of their discourse to events in
the external world – reciprocities far more confidently taken as
axiomatic than anyone brought up in a world of post-Saussurean
linguistics could imagine.

Jonson inherited much of this sense of the place and function
of language, though in a more sceptical framework. The earlier
humanists largely shared a sense of the perfectibility of society –
however long and drawn out the project might be – and of the
efficacy of language in that process. Jonson is characteristically
more guarded and embattled, much less optimistic that the conditions for positive change exist, which in turn raises serious doubts
about the inherent powers of language itself: I shall discuss later
perhaps the single most telling instance of this, the disappear-
ance of Lorenzo Jr's enthusiastic celebration of poetry in the revision of *Every Man In His Humour*. Elsky argues:

> The larger social conditions of language are as important to
> Jonson as the moral condition of the individual speaker's mind.
> For him, as for Ascham and Mulcaster, the state of language
> depends on the state of the commonwealth. . . . The link be-
> tween the moral and the social context of poetry is fast: as words
> do not exist apart from speakers, speakers do not exist apart
> from society. Jonson subscribed to the humanist idea that, *at
> least ideally*, good societies produce good speakers, as good
> speakers produce good societies. This view of language is re-
> flected in Jonson's poetry, which frequently probes the inter-
> relationship of moral, social and linguistic orders. In so doing,
> it translates a referential theory of language into a theory of
> poetic diction and poetic authorship.   (p. 84, my emphasis)

In this view, Jonson's frequent invocation of his monarchs, from the impersonation of Elizabeth in *Every Man Out*, which 'many seemed not to relish', to the fulsome and often frankly mendicant poems he addressed to King Charles and Queen Henrietta Maria (see *Und* LXII–LXVII, LXXII, LXXVI, LXXIX, LXXXII), which many since have seemed not to relish, but most signally those in the *Epigrams* (IV, XXXV, LI), masques, entertainments, and perhaps above all in that unique royal diversion, *Bartholomew Fair*, are a constant reminder 'that his authority to comment on social matters stems from the King. . . . Like Ascham and Elyot, Jonson points to the monarch as the guarantor of his word, though he does not go to the extreme of seeing his entire poetic as being constituted by the authority of the king.' This extreme was a particular danger in respect of King James, in as much as James himself had been a poet in his youth and had printed (another sidelight on the supposed 'stigma' attaching to print) *The Essays of a Prentise* (1584) and *His Majesties Poetical Exercises* (1591), along with a number of books on statecraft: James's 'authority', in matters both poetical and political, was a matter of public record and seemed to leave little scope for the independence of his subjects. Jonson neatly sidesteps this, however, by emphasising that the king's poetry was a product of his youth ('such a poet, while thy days were green, / Thou wert', *Ep* 4), leaving scope for the counsel of Jonson's own poetry in the maturity of his kingship.[2] Jonson's position as a writer, that is, is not an absolute and self-justifying one, but always relative to the community he addresses, which, both symbolically and practically, is constituted in the person of his monarch. This is a consistent condition, or philosophical proposition, throughout his career; what does change, however, is his interpretation of that relationship, his definition of his own place within it (the instability of which we have commented on repeatedly), and on that hang such questions as the degree of licence the relationship affords him in his writing, or the level of respect required of him towards others vested with honour and authority by the monarch, or the nature of his obligation to audiences of all kinds (including the audience of former ages). These are the sub-texts of much of his literary criticism.

In the post-Reformation context I have outlined, it was inevitable that there would be restrictions on people's freedom to publish what they wrote. From 1529 there were royal proclamations against heretical and seditious works, while in 1538 it was required for the first time that all books must be licensed by the Privy Council or by other persons authorised by the king. Under Queen Mary (1555) there was an edict to prevent the importation of Protestant literature from the continent: and the international context continued to be an important consideration, whatever religious orthodoxy held sway. An important development occurred in 1557, when the Stationers' Company was incorporated by royal charter and the right to print books of any description was limited to its freemen. One advantage of a cartel of this kind, from the point of view of the government, was that it was clearly in the Stationers' own corporate interest not to offend the powers that be, and it seems likely that their wardens would normally have required to see a properly executed royal licence before granting a book (especially a potentially contentious one) an entry in their Register, the procedure which established its copyright. In 1586, at the immediate instigation of the Archbishop of Canterbury (though largely prompted by the Stationers desire for even more exclusive control of the book trade), the Star Chamber ordered that, except for one press each in the university towns of Oxford and Cambridge, printing presses were only to be allowed in London and that there should be a strict limit on the number of these. Two years later Archbishop Whitgift appointed an ecclesiastical commission of twelve members, appointed by himself and the Bishop of London, to license all printed books.[3]

Parallel to these developments, efforts were also made to limit and control the activities of the acting profession. Successively more stringent measures were introduced throughout the second half of the sixteenth century to make acting companies accountable to someone, mainly by requiring that they should formally be attached to a household of some substance; by the end of the century this had to be the household of a peer of the realm. Moreover they had to be licensed for public performances by the local Justices of the Peace or other civic magistrates. After 1581, in the London region, where theatrical activity was naturally most intense, the leading companies came under the control of the Master of the Revels, a royal official whose primary responsibility was the provision of entertainment at court but who, in order to facilitate that task, was given authority over the actors who might perform there; he made a steady income out of licensing their theatres, and censoring and licensing their plays for public performance.[4] As we have already seen, in 1598 the Privy Council tried to restrict the number of such privileged companies to two, both patronised by its own members, who were moreover both cousins of the queen. Commercial and other pressures finally expanded the number of companies allowed to operate in the London region during the period Jonson was writing for the stage to four or five, though the fact that they, like the Stationers, were a licensed cartel (and, moreover, stood to make a substantial income from performances at court, if invited) normally meant that they co-operated with the authorities rather than antagonising them.

These were the restrictions on publication and performance that Jonson faced when he began writing. He told Drummond: 'He hath a mind to be a churchman, and so he might have favour to make one sermon to the king. He careth not what thereafter should befall him; for he would not flatter though he saw death' (276–8). This is, of course, a highly romanticised notion. Elizabeth had not hesitated to rebuke preachers who strayed too far from what she took to be their business, and James 'selected clergymen to preach at court, provided them with texts and other material, and listened with close attention and with embarrassing signs of approval or dissent'.[5] But this was, for Jonson, the nearest he could imagine to something he never had, absolute freedom of speech: the right of the minister to speak his mind. He naturally envisaged the king as his audience, since he, above all, had the power to translate anything that was said into action, to affect the society of the day, and it is taken for granted that anyone who wished to speak or write at all would have some such ambition. Everything that Jonson has to say about language and literature is underpinned by the common Renaissance conviction that they are powerful social agents, able to affect what people think and do; it is precisely because this is so that it is important to weigh and quantify how language and literature actually work. Hence Jonson's concern with rhetoric and with the rules of composition. These may seem arcane or pedantic today, but for Jonson they were not only the tools of his trade but also the weapons of his armoury.

Now, the poesy is the habit or the art; nay, rather the queen of arts, which had her original from heaven, received thence from the Hebrews, and had in prime estimation with the Greeks, transmitted to the Latins and all nations that professed civility. The study of it (if we will trust Aristotle) offers to mankind a certain rule and pattern of living well and happily, disposing us to all civil offices of society. If we will believe Tully, it nourisheth and instructeth our youth, delights our age, adorns our prosperity, comforts our adversity, entertains us at home, keeps us company abroad, travels with us, watches, divides the times of our earnest and sports, shares in our country recesses and rec-- reations, insomuch as the wisest and best learned have thought her the absolute mistress of manners and nearest of kin to virtue. (*Discoveries*, 2404–19)

Literature, that is, informs us, shapes us: it is not something separate from the business of daily living, but concomitant with it. Aristotle and Cicero ('Tully', from Marcus Tullius Cicero) are two of the 'authorities' Jonson cites most often; in this instance he apparently has in mind passages from the *Poetics* and *Politics* of the former, the *Pro Archia* 16 of the latter. Notice that he does not assert these things to be true *because* the ideas are put forward by these figures from the classical past: 'if we will trust', 'if we will believe' – we are invited to compare notes, not to accept unconditionally.

If Jonson himself is inclined to second their opinion, it is not simply out of reverence for their antiquity. In a much-quoted earlier passage in the *Discoveries*, he says:

I know nothing can conduce more to letters than to examine the writings of the ancients, and not to rest in their sole authority, or take all upon trust from them. . . . For to all the observations of the ancients, we have our own experience; which, if we will use and apply, we have better means to pronounce. It is true they opened the gates and made the way, that went before us; but as guides not commanders: *non domini nostri, sed duces fuere.* Truth lies open to all; it is no man's several. (ll. 131–42)

This needs to be set against an equally well-known observation, in respect of Shakespeare, that 'a good poet's made, as well as born' (*UV* XXVI, l. 64). Jonson's criticism as a whole has more to say on what the poet 'is or should be . . . by exercise, by imitation, by study, and . . . through the disciplines of grammar, logic, rhetoric, and the ethics' than what he is 'by nature' (*Discoveries*, 2427–9). He was sceptical of poetic 'inspiration' that was not channelled by study and application, disdaining anyone who thinks 'he can leap forth suddenly a poet by dreaming he hath been in Parnassus, or having washed his lips (as they say) in Helicon' (2512–14).

Yet Jonson never circumscribed himself, or others, within a fixed circle of precedent or slavish imitation of what had gone before: 'I am not of that opinion to conclude a *Poet's* liberty within the narrow limits of laws which either the grammarians or philosophers prescribe' (2579–81), pointing out that there were good poets before there were critics ('amongst whom none more perfect than Sophocles, who lived a little before Aristotle', 2583–4). He has enormous respect for Aristotle as 'the first accurate critic and truest judge . . . because, he understood the causes of things; and what other men did by chance or custom, he doth by reason; and not only found out the way not to err, but the short way we should take, not to err' (2535–6, 2594–7). Yet he follows Bacon in condemning as ridiculous those Scholastics who made him their 'dictator': 'Let Aristotle and others have their dues, but if we can make farther discoveries of truth and fitness than they, why are we envied?' (2120–2). It is more a matter of building on the past than of simply aping or reconstructing it, and it must be done with a proper sense of addressing the modern world and its requirements, which is why Jonson argued that 'Spenser, in affecting the ancients, writ no language' (1823–4).

The balance is struck, ironically as it may seem, in the very passage where Jonson proclaims that 'truth lies open to all': these most liberating of sentiments are themselves transcribed from a book by a more recent 'authority', the *In Libros de Disciplinis Praefatio* [*Preface on Books of Learning*] by Juan Luis Vives (1492–1540). Vives was a humanist scholar, friend of Erasmus and Sir Thomas More; broadly speaking, his views were likely to be congenial to Jonson because, in ways that prefigured Bacon, he favoured empirical observations of the soul and the mind in action over traditional scholastic enquiry into the essence of things. But even here, we must not assume that Jonson simply adopts his thoughts wholesale; in the *Discoveries* he selects, paraphrases, adapts the matter to his own ends and silently interposes his own observations. The process, then, is one of accretion, of weighing and adding to what those who have gone before have already weighed and added to in their time. Vives in turn quotes his Latin from Seneca, and Jonson transposes it with minor verbal adjustments.

Given the eclectic nature of these 'borrowings', we should beware

(on the strength of them) of trying to align Jonson too closely
with particular schools of thought or consistent philosophies. A
better measure of what preoccupies him is to observe the kind of
men whose 'opinions' he consults, the kinds of minds with which
he keeps company. Aristotle was not only the most influential
thinker of classical times, but also a man close to the centres of
political power; he married the adopted daughter of Hermeias,
self-made tyrant of Atarneus and Assos who defied the encroach-
ing Persian empire; he acted for a time as tutor to Alexander the
Great, and after the latter's death suffered for his association with
the Macedonian ascendancy and his personal friendship with the
regent, Antipater. Cicero was widely regarded as the greatest
Roman orator, while his letters and essays were commonly held
to be models of the finest Latin prose; but he was also a key
figure in the politics of the last years of republican Rome, being
consul at the time of Catiline's conspiracy (which he exposed and
suppressed) and an opponent successively of Caesar and Antony
– the latter antagonism leading to his death in the proscriptions
of 43 BC. Lucius Annaeus Seneca was a Latin Stoic philosopher,
author of numerous moral letters and essays and of nine tragedies,
which were far better known and more influential in the Renaissance than the Greek tragedies which they imitated. Yet he was
also tutor to a later emperor, Nero, shared in the administration
under him when he came to power, but later lost favour and
eventually committed suicide.

In each case literary and philosophical prestige go side-by-side
with service to the state. The life of the mind and political realities
meet naturally, if not always (as it happens) fortuitously: a pattern reiterated in the case of Jonson's most forceful contemporary 'authority', Francis Bacon. Even Vives, though pre-eminently
what we should call a scholar, had known something of these
pressures as tutor to Princess (later Queen) Mary and in oppos-
ing Henry VIII's divorce from Catherine of Aragon, following which
he carefully retired to the continent under suspicion of treason.[6]
In none of these cases need we suppose that Jonson unequivocally
endorsed the man, his actions and his writings, but opinions that
had been forged or tested close to the practicalities of power are
never inconsiderable. 'I have ever observed it to have been the
office of a wise patriot, among the greatest affairs of state, to
take care of the commonwealth of learning. For schools, they are
the seminaries of state; and nothing is worthier the study of a

statesman than that part of the republic which we call the advancement of letters' (*Discoveries*, 934–9). Both of Jonson's extant tragedies explore the differences between the ethics of power and its practical application, and in *Catiline* Cicero himself becomes the pivotal figure in the drama. The equivocal nature of his triumph over the conspiracy, however, does not allow us to feel that Jonson was indulging in a fantasy projection of an ideal philosopher–statesman, an embodiment of all that is best in 'manners, arms and arts' (*For* II, 'To Penshurst', l. 98). Rather, we see an object lesson in the difference between words and action, both the strength of language and its limitations.[7] As usual, Jonson brings forward an 'authority' not simply for our endorsement, but for our scrutiny; he expects us to subject it to a process of critical judgement, to what he calls 'knowledge' (see the end of Chapter 4).

A similar distinction – between words and action, theory and practice – may well have been intended (though contemporaries scarcely conceded its existence) in the early plays where Jonson came closest to spelling out his own aspirations as a poet, a role he immediately associates with the political and cultural heart of the nation, the court. In *Cynthia's Revels* and *Poetaster* he presents idealised figures of poet-makers, Criticus in the former (Crites in the 1616 folio text), and the pairing of Horace and Virgil in the latter. Criticus is a man of learning but no money or status, who nevertheless contrives to become a member of Cynthia's royal entourage as a reward for writing a masque which, while ostensibly honouring the vain and self-indulgent courtiers who take part, actually becomes a vehicle for unmasking them. Horace and Virgil both have the ear of the emperor, Augustus. Virgil is described as 'refin'd / From all the tartarous moods of common men' (V.i.102–3) and his reading from the *Aeneid*, listened to in awed silence, is both advice to his monarch and an explanation to lesser mortals of the rightness of Augustus's actions in banishing the irresponsible poet Ovid. At a more mundane level, the long-suffering Horace has to ward off bores, poetasters and politicians maliciously inclined to further their own cause by misconstruing his writing as treason. He remains a rock of reasonableness ('knowledge') amid waves of false standards and, while he cannot pretend to the status of Virgil, he is acknowledged as a loyal defender of the state.

Detractors like Dekker, in *Satiromastix*, readily identified these figures as Jonson himself and accused him of pretentiousness: 'you must be call'd Asper, and Criticus, and Horace'.[8] But a more accurate charge would be wish-fulfilment, and not without an element of wry self-parody. Although *Cynthia's Revels* was chosen for performance at court, Jonson had as yet no ready entrée there, and the motto he adapted from Juvenal for the quarto text suggests that he was looking to shake off his dependence on the actors by attaching himself to these more exalted circles. Translated it reads: 'The actor will provide what the nobles are unwilling to give. You should not, however, scorn the poet whom the stage feeds.' But, for the time being, his bid was unsuccessful. *Cynthia's Revels* was apparently 'missliked' at court, while *Poetaster* provoked such fury that Jonson had to answer (we do not know in what context) to the Lord Chief Justice.[9] This suggests a degree of miscalculation on Jonson's part about the relationship between himself as poet and the centres of power. The monarchs he portrays on the stage are predisposed to discern the worth of his *alter egos*, to discount the misvaluations others place on them. But Jonson was relying too much on a similarly indulgent response from those in power when he projected Cynthia's court as a 'Fountain of Self-Love' and that of Augustus as peopled by dishonest lawyers, braggart soldiers and conniving politicians. Cynthia herself may be a transcendent 'Queen and huntress, chaste and fair' but her court is a sink of narcissist materialism; Augustus may be the wise ruler of the greatest empire the world has known but he is served by corrupt self-seekers.

So it is that Jonson signs his dedication of the folio *Cynthia's Revels*, addressed to the court, as 'thy servant, but not slave'. This may have been easier to articulate from the comfortable heights of 1616 than it would have been when the quarto was printed in 1601, but something of it is implicit in the original text. He is prepared to align himself with those in power, but not in an abject or uncritical way. It is hardly surprising if they saw nothing in this but that (as Dekker taunted) 'thy sputtering chaps yelp, that arrogance, and impudence, and ignoraunce, are the essential parts of a courtier' (*Satiromastix*, V.iii.188–90). When similar umbrage was taken at *Poetaster*, Jonson tried to answer the objections – in effect to clarify his own position – with an 'Apologetical Dialogue'. But that in turn 'was only once spoken upon the stage' and then not allowed into print in the 1602 quarto of the play 'since [the Author] is no less restrain'd, than thou depriv'd of it, by Authority' (*H&S*, IV, p. 317, Note to Epil. 1–12). In these plays Jonson had tacitly laid claim, as poet, to the authority of the monarchs he 'represented'. In late Elizabethan England that authority – and, indeed, the right to argue for it in public – was explicitly denied him by the actual representatives of the monarch whose patronage he sought.

BRANDING: THE 'APOLOGETICAL DIALOGUE' AND THE EPISTLE TO *VOLPONE*

The 'Apologetical Dialogue' was not finally published until the 1616 folio text of the play, when many of its key themes had been re-stated (albeit in subtly altered forms) in the Epistle to the 1607 quarto of *Volpone*. Two of these are worth examining briefly here as a prelude to considering the wider context of that Epistle, which, because of the earlier censorship, was the first sustained critical manifesto by Jonson to see print and was to prove his fullest (if not final) statement on the relationship between writing and the law, criticism and authority. The issue is not specifically formulated there in terms of the relationship between the poet and the prince (or the state), but that remains the essence of the matter. As I shall argue, the precise formulation of the Epistle owes a good deal to Jonson's traumatic experiences in the years prior to its being written – some of which still lay in the future when the 'Dialogue' was composed. But the 'Dialogue' does glance back to one of them, when Jonson's 'Author' boasts that he *could* (but will not stoop to) repay those he claims have libelled *him* over his play:

> I could stamp
> Their foreheads with those deep and public brands,
> That the whole company of Barber-Surgeons
> Should not take off, with all their art, and plasters.
> And these my prints should last, still to be read
> In their pale fronts when what they write 'gainst me
> Shall, like a figure drawn in water, fleet
>   (Appendix, p. 190)

The passage is a remarkable inversion of Jonson's own subjection to authority. Three years earlier he had killed his fellow actor

Gabriel Spencer in a duel, and only escaped hanging by claiming benefit of clergy – that is, by proving his ability to read from the Bible, an archaic exemption from due process of law which reflected the reverence of an earlier age for the literacy of holy orders. Jonson nevertheless forfeited all his possessions and had to submit to the 'deep and public brand' of a Tyburn 'T' at the base of his thumb – an ineradicable sign that his life was forfeit to the state if he transgressed again. Following classical precedent, he here turns this image of state authority into a metaphor for his own powers as a writer (however much the state may attempt to circumscribe them). We may suppose that the forfeiture and branding was even more charged for Jonson than it would otherwise have been, because it was 'then he took his religion [Roman Catholicism] by trust of a priest who visited him in prison. Thereafter he was twelve years a papist' (*Drummond*, 204–5), a dangerous change of allegiance at a time of intense Counter-Reformation pressures. The spirit of the poet resisted the authority of the state, even as the state imposed that authority upon his body.

More predictably, and less contentiously, the 'Apologetical Dialogue' also gives an early airing to one of Jonson's standard defences of himself as a satirist. His 'Author' claims that the play is 'innocent' and 'empty of offence', and when told

> they say you taxed
> The law and lawyers, captains and the players,
> By their particular names.

he asserts:

> It is not so.
> I us'd no name. My books have still been taught
> To spare the persons, and to speak the vices.
>   (ll. 81–5)

Typically, again, Jonson is following classical precedent; the last line is a direct quotation from Martial, X. xxxiii ('Parcere personis, dicere de vitiis'). His confrontation with the Lord Chief Justice over the play suggests that this pat formula was less than convincing in the real world: Jonson's own 'authority' (even backed by Martial) was insufficient to establish his 'innocence', though the later dedication of the play to Richard Martin suggests that a competent lawyer was equal to the job.[10] A writer was, however, dangerously exposed and vulnerable if this was his only defence; deprived even of the right to answer his critics in the 'Apologetical Dialogue', he was reduced to praying his readers 'to think charitably of what thou hast read, till thou mayst hear him speak what he hath written'.

But specific readers chose to think anything but charitably of his next two plays, *Sejanus* and *Eastward Ho*, both of which he wrote in collaboration, the former with an unknown 'second hand' (possibly Chapman), the latter with Chapman and Marston. As we have already observed, the Earl of Northampton had him 'called before the Council for his *Sejanus*, and accused both of popery and treason by him', while he 'was delated by Sir James Murray to the king for writing something against the Scots in a play, *Eastward Ho*' (*Drummond*, 272–3, 225–6). The precise circumstances of both accusations are far from easy to establish, and I have written about them at length elsewhere.[11] For present purposes I wish merely to observe the following points: that both occasions relate to the nervous early years of a new reign (James's accession to the English throne had been peaceful, but there were winners and losers in the race for power under him – Northampton was one such winner, at the expense notably of Sir Walter Ralegh, while the place of Scots like Murray in the English court caused much acrimony); that the accusations over *Sejanus* probably related to the 1605 printed text, which was all Jonson's own work, rather than to the play performed two years earlier, but that in either case it was almost unprecedented for the lords of the Privy Council to devote such specific attention to the author of a mere play (apparently here they distinguished between the specific authorship of such a work and the collaborative offence of staging a seditious or libellous entertainment, which is how they had viewed *The Isle of Dogs*); and that the furore over *Eastward Ho* fell under two headings – the 'something against the Scots' (which Jonson apparently regarded as so inconsiderable that he told Drummond he 'voluntarily imprisoned himself') and the fact that the play proved not to have had a proper licence for performance from the Lord Chamberlain (a very serious breach of the licensing regulations which left the authors seriously exposed – 'the report was that they should then had their ears cut and noses': *Drummond*, 228–9);[12] finally that Jonson wrote letters to a number of dignitaries while he was in prison over *Eastward Ho* and that one of these, to the king's chief minister, the Earl of Salisbury, is immediately relevant here, since passages from it were to reappear in the Epistle to *Volpone*.

One further trauma, not directly linked to his writing, probably also left its mark on that Epistle; that is the Gunpowder Plot and its aftermath. The next thing we know of Jonson, after he was released (unharmed) from imprisonment over *Eastward Ho*, is that he attended a party in the Strand, on or about 9 October 1605. This was given by Robert Catesby, leader of the Gunpowder Plot conspiracy, whose 'providential' discovery was less than a month away; several of the other conspirators were there too.[13] Immediately after that discovery (7 November) Jonson was summoned by the Privy Council to act as a go-between in their efforts to contact a certain Roman Catholic priest 'that offered to do good service to the state'; they provided him with a warrant to demonstrate both his and their own honourable intentions. Despite Jonson's earnest endeavours, conducted initially via the chaplain of the Venetian ambassador, 'the party will not be found', as he reported the next day to Salisbury personally, protesting: 'May it please your Lordship to understand that there hath been no want in me either of labour or sincerity in the discharge of this business.' He regretted his inability to resolve matters 'to the satisfaction of your Lordship and the state'.[14] As a Catholic convert Jonson may have had ready access to Catesby and the other conspirators, as well as to the Catholic priesthood. The question is whether, knowing this, Salisbury only used Jonson in the aftermath of the affair – or whether he had been using him throughout, as a double agent. His imprisonment, and threats of worse, over *Eastward Ho* would have made him all the more plausible a companion for his desperate co-religionists.

Volpone was apparently staged in February or March 1606. If Jonson's claim that 'five weeks fully penned it' (Prologue, l. 16) is true, he must have written the play immediately in the wake of the Gunpowder Plot and at a time when some of those implicated in the plot (such as the Jesuit, Father Henry Garnet) were paying the ghastly penalty.[15] Jonson's personal tension could only have increased when, in the crack-down on known Catholics after the Plot, he was 'presented' for 'correction' that January in the Consistory Court of London. He was accused of failing to take communion in the Church of England, which was required by law, and deliberate omission could be construed as treason. The charge sheet dryly noted Jonson to be 'a poet', who was reported 'by fame a seducer of youth to the Popish religion' (*H&S*, I, pp. 220–2). The charges were first heard in April, and subsequent hearings dragged on through the early summer. Jonson acknowledged his failure to take communion, over religious scruples, but pointed out that he had regularly worshipped at his local Anglican church for the past six months – in effect, since the Plot. He denied the rumour about his being a 'seducer of youth' and challenged the court to present proper evidence, which it was apparently unable to do. Jonson was required to submit his scruples to the consideration of one of a number of notable Anglican clergy, including the Dean of St Paul's and the Archbishop of Canterbury; he was to choose one of these and attend twice a week for spiritual guidance, under which terms the charges were 'stayed under seal' but not formally dismissed.

This, then, is the context in which the Epistle to *Volpone* was composed: a whole sequence of traumas and confrontations with authority, dating back to the *Isle of Dogs* affair, including conviction and branding for killing Gabriel Spencer, conversion to Roman Catholicism, problems over the ending of *Every Man Out of His Humour*, examination over *Poetaster* and the staying by authority of its 'Apologetical Dialogue', examination by the Privy Council over *Sejanus*, imprisonment and threat of mutilation over *Eastward Ho*, implication in possible government manipulation of the Gunpowder Plot, and prosecution for recusancy in the aftermath of the Plot itself. These are all addressed, implicitly or directly, in the Epistle itself or the documents upon which it demonstrably draws, the 'Apologetical Dialogue' and the letter to Salisbury. (Readers will find the next few pages easier to follow if they refer frequently to the texts of the Epistle to *Volpone* and the letter to Salisbury in the Appendix, pp. 175–9, 213–14). The Epistle first echoes the 'Dialogue' in the defence, derived from Martial, that his plays are not 'particular', and 'tax' vices not persons: 'What broad reproofs have I used? Where have I been particular? Where personal? except to a mimic, cheater, bawd, or buffoon, creatures (for their insolencies) worthy to be taxed? Yet, to which of these so pointingly, as he might not, either ingenuously have confessed, or wisely dissembled his disease?' (p. 177).

The 'Dialogue concludes with a reference back to *Poetaster* itself and what appears to be an anticipation of *Sejanus*. It promises 'something' that

must and shall be sung high and aloof,
Safe from the wolf's black jaw and the dull ass's hoof.
(p. 192)

'Ass' and 'wolf' allude to a character in the earlier play, Asinius
Lupus, an example of the 'supercilious politics' against whom
Jonson now warns in the Epistle: 'there are that profess to have a
key for the deciphering of everything; but let wise and noble
persons take heed how they be too credulous, or give leave to
these invading interpreters to be over-familiar with their fames,
who cunningly, and often, utter their own virulent malice under
other men's simplest meanings' (p. 177). Of course, *Sejanus* proved
not to be 'safe', but found its own Asinius Lupus in Northampton (a circumstance presumably alluded to in the ironic reflection
'and not my youngest infant but hath come into the world with
all his teeth', p. 177), just as *Eastward Ho* found one in Sir James
Murray.

These are matters which Jonson also addressed in his letter to
Salisbury. He composed this with the utmost care – it exists both
in an early draft and in the holograph Salisbury actually received
– partly, no doubt, because of its recipient's importance but also
because Jonson had had dealings with Sir Robert Cecil (as he then
was) as early as the *Isle of Dogs* affair. Cecil had handled the
correspondence over that business for the Privy Council as a whole.
It was probably politic of Jonson, therefore, to acknowledge it as
a genuine 'error' on his part – but one from which he had learned
his lesson, insisting on his 'innocence', his compliance with authority, ever since: 'I protest to your Honour, and call God to testimony (since my first error, which (yet) is punish'd in me more
with my shame than it was then with my bondage) I have so
attempered my style, that I have given no cause to any good man
of grief'.[16] In the Epistle, he disingenuously glosses over *any* admission of guilt by dissociating himself from all works not 'entirely mine' (p. 177), a formula which conveniently excludes both
The Isle of Dogs and *Eastward Ho*.

So carefully was the Salisbury letter phrased that significant
passages from it were to be reproduced, virtually verbatim, in
the Epistle. The first of these (like so much else) is based on Martial,
and specifically the preface to his *Epigrams*: 'My noble Lord, they
deal not charitably, who are too witty in another man's works,
and utter, sometimes, their own malicious meanings, under our

words' (p. 213). This reappears in the Epistle, in the passage on 'invading interpreters', which I have already cited.[17] The second passage is this:

> let me be examin'd, both by all my works past, and this present . . . whether I have ever (in any thing I have written, private or public) given offence to a nation, to any public order or state, or any person of honour or authority, but have equally labour'd to keep their dignity, as mine own person, safe. (p. 214)

This reappears in the Epistle as:

> howsoever I cannot escape, from some, the imputation of sharpness . . . I would ask of these supercilious politics, what nation, society, or general order, or state I have provoked? what public person? whether I have not (in all these) preserved their dignity, as mine own person, safe? (p. 177)

In both contexts, this passage leads to a very particular pay-off. In the letter to Salisbury, Jonson immediately protests: 'if others have transgress'd, let not me be entitled to their follies'. This was not in the early draft of the letter, and is clearly a careful afterthought. Jonson is hinting at something made much more explicit in a letter by Chapman to the king over his and Jonson's joint predicament: 'our chief offences are but two clauses, and both of them not our own' (*ed. cit.*, p. 218). Two particular passages in *Eastward Ho* had apparently caused offence, rather than the play as a whole. The usual construction of Jonson's and Chapman's letters is that they were both implicitly blaming Marston (who may have contrived to avoid imprisonment) for these 'clauses', though it is equally possible that they meant they were interpolations by the actors. But, where Chapman effectively admits that an offence has been committed (though he and Jonson are not guilty of it), Jonson himself turns the issue towards his own rectitude. He does not enter into the question of other persons' guilt, but is concerned to establish his own *consistent* innocence; he has not 'transgressed' but respected 'authority'.

This, in more general terms, is the issue he also takes up at the parallel point in the Epistle to *Volpone*: 'My works are read, allowed (I speak of those that are entirely mine); look into them'.

His own works submit themselves to the licensing required by authority, both for performance and for publication: he thus dissociates himself in this from *Eastward Ho*, which was neither 'entirely mine' nor, apparently, 'allowed'. The observation that his 'works are read, allowed' adds a crucial new dimension to the whole argument. Tongue-tied by authority in the publication of *Poetaster*, he could only beseech his reader to 'think charitably of what thou hast read'. Here in the Epistle he recognises that 'nothing can be so innocently writ, or carried, but may be made obnoxious to construction', though he continues to protest his 'innocence' (p. 177). But this acknowledgement of the process of 'allowance' whereby the Master of the Revels licensed a play for performance and the officers of the Church High Commission gave it another for print, points to a degree of control over what *other* readers could legitimately find in his writing.[18] They had deemed it acceptable to the state, and who was to challenge their reading? By acquiescing to a form of policing which he had previously found irksome, Jonson paradoxically acquired a power to determine (delimit) the meaning of what he wrote (and so his integrity as an author) which he had never enjoyed before.

Once that is perceived, we are better placed to appreciate the strategy of the Epistle as a whole. The dedication of the play to those 'most learned Arbitresses', the universities (Epistle, p. 178), can be seen – like the invocation to classical authorities (notably, here, Strabo, Martial and Horace) – as an appeal to timeless, a-political values, placing art in a transcendent framework of disinterested scholarship, abstracted from the social and political conditions of its own composition. But this is belied by the manner and location of the Epistle itself. In the quarto text, the portentous capitals of the dedication stand over the laconic invitation: 'There follows an *Epistle*, if you dare venture on the length' and the document itself is subscribed 'From my house in the Blackfriars, this 11 of February 1607', locating it very specifically in a world of writers and readers, time and place (p. 179). The universities themselves, invoked as judges, were no more outside the structure of authority than those other courts – civil, criminal and ecclesiastical – which Jonson so regularly confronted, even if he more readily concurred with their judgement on this particular play. Indeed, their leading luminaries were key names in Jonson's history: the Chancellor of Cambridge was Salisbury; its High Steward was Lord Chamberlain Suffolk (whose missing licence was such a key element in the *Eastward Ho* affair though he also seems to have been the person responsible for effecting the release of Jonson and Chapman[19]). The Chancellor of Oxford was Thomas Sackville, Earl of Dorset, the Lord Treasurer, who in his youth had part-authored that intensely topical play *Gorboduc*. He would be a very plausible candidate for the unnamed lord of the third in the sequence of Jonson's letters from prison over *Eastward Ho*, the more so when we recall that Jonson is supposed to have declared: 'I laid the plot of my *Volpone*, and wrote most of it, after a present of ten dozen of palm sack from my very good Lord Treasurer' (*H&S*, I, p. 188). As we have seen, the composition of *Volpone* certainly followed hard on his release from prison, and such a gift would have befitted the occasion.

Whatever we make of specific occasions and personalities, however, it remains inescapable that a dedication to the universities was inevitably also a dedication to the power-brokers in the Privy Council. To invoke the 'equal sisters' as 'arbitresses' in literary matters should perhaps be put alongside the performance of the Court of Avocatori within *Volpone* itself as judges in civil and criminal ones. The burden of the Epistle is very much that of the 'Apological Dialogue', to justify Jonson's claim that he properly fulfils 'the offices, and function of a Poet' in contradistinction to 'the too-much licence of poetasters in this time' (p. 176). But Jonson lifts the argument into a different frame of reference by linking his definition of 'a poet' with Strabo's 'universal' dictum about 'the impossibility of any man's being the good poet, without first being a good man' (p. 176).[20] At a time when Jonson was still formally under investigation for failing to conform to the state religion, and when the virtuous intentions of his last three plays had all been impugned in one context or another, the question of his 'goodness' is a challenging one: by whom, and in what court, is this to be determined? Jonson immediately follows this with a broad encomium of 'a poet', beginning: 'He that is said to be able to inform young men to all good disciplines' and latterly including among his accomplishments, 'a teacher of things divine, no less than human'. This might almost be taken to parody the charge he had faced in the Consistory Court: 'a poet, and by fame a seducer of youth to the Popish religion'. But if anyone had challenged Jonson for mocking authority here he could (as with the annotations in the quarto of *Sejanus*) have cited the chapter and verse of the innocent derivation of the whole passage: Minturno's *De Poeta* (1559), p. 8.

From such equivocal foundations, Jonson launches out against 'this bold adventure for hell', which is how he characterises much current 'dramatic, or, as they term it, stage poetry' and from which he is determined to distinguish his own writing. Denying that he has ever engaged in 'prophaneness' (an issue of particular topicality, since in 1606 Parliament had passed an Act of Abuses to prevent blasphemy and profanity on public stages, which the Master of the Revels was charged with enforcing) or 'bawdry' (p. 176), it is here that he addresses 'the imputation of sharpness', drawing on the classical precedents of Horace and Martial, as re-worked in the 'Apologetical Dialogue' and the letter to Salisbury, to deny that he has ever been 'particular' or provoked any 'nation' or 'public person'. He asserts that his works – confining the term to 'those that are entirely mine' – are 'read, allowed', conforming to the requirements of authority. He insists that 'it is not rumour can make men guilty, much less entitle me to other men's crimes' – picking up the theme of unwarranted 'fame' or 'rumour' that runs from the 'Apologetical Dialogue', through the letters from prison, to the trial for recusancy, hammering home his point in attacking 'these invading interpreters' (who, he warns 'wise and noble persons', may also be 'over-familiar with *their* fames': my emphasis) and a breed of satiric writers who 'care not whose living faces they entrench, with their petulant styles' (p. 177) to gain notice and popularity: he declines 'so preposterous a fame'. Jonson's implicit claim to be himself a good man and a true poet is thus advanced on two fronts: dissociation from three forms of contamination – from the company of 'poetasters', from misreadings (malicious and otherwise) and from guilt-by-association with what other writers have done to gain a reputation – and a protestation of 'mine own innocence', the authority for which he cannot generate himself but must derive from being 'allowed'. His private intentions are guaranteed by a very public subjectivity.

Jonson then turns the terms of the argument away from intention and interpretation, towards dramatic form, sympathising with 'those severe, and wiser patriots' (p. 177) who would prefer a return to older, unsophisticated styles of drama (with fools and devils) rather than be subjected to the lampoons and state satires of the current stage. He ascribes to a 'lust in liberty' the vogue for 'misc'line interludes [variety entertainments] . . . where nothing but the filth of the time is utter'd, and that with such impropriety of phrase, such plenty of solecisms, such dearth of sense, so bold prolepses, so racked metaphors' (pp. 177–8). It is to rebut such examples, and to restore poetry to its former dignity 'that were wont to be the care of kings, and happiest monarchs' (as depicted in *Poetaster*), that Jonson claims he has laboured in *Volpone* 'to reduce [bring back], not only the ancient forms, but manners of the scene: the easiness, the propriety, the innocence, and last the doctrine, which is the principal end of poesy, to inform men in the best reason of living'.

All of this he reiterates in the Prologue to the play, where he promises 'rhyme, not empty of reason' (4), and 'no eggs are broken; / Nor quaking custards with fierce teeth affrighted' (20–1) in an example of 'quick comedy, refined, / As best critics have designed' (29–30); he invokes Horace in the ambition 'To mix profit with your pleasure' (8) and Aristotle in his claim 'The laws of time, place, persons he observeth' (31) as he distances himself from the tasteless lawlessness of the 'misc'line interludes' elsewhere on the contemporary stage.[21] He acknowledges in the Epistle that his 'catastrophe' may be criticised for being over-severe (with Mosca consigned to the galleys and Volpone to a lingering mortification in the hospital for incurables) but points out that it was deliberate policy not slip-shod work, that it was done to give the lie to those 'that cry out, we never punish vice in our interludes', and that he could find classical precedent for it anyway: 'fitly, it being the office of a comic poet to imitate justice, and instruct to life, as well as purity of language, or stir up gentle affections' (p. 178). This might readily be construed as an ironic reading of the 'catastrophe' of *Volpone*, where the 'justice' meted out is hard to distinguish from the revenge of a self-seeking, hood-winked court.

But the ironies could be compounded several times over if we recall that, only weeks before the play was written, the author of this Epistle himself had written to the king's chief minister (in a letter from which he was now borrowing passages), complaining of being 'un-examined, or unheard, committed to a vile prison' (to Salisbury, p. 213) and contemplating worse penalties yet. Furthermore, around the time he wrote the play itself, he was subject to another court's investigation into his religious and political orthodoxy. To 'imitate justice' and to 'instruct to life' may not be co-terminous exercises for 'a poet'. Jonson does not, however, enforce any of these contextual ironies as he consigns his copy to the printer from his house in the Blackfriars in February 1607, merely promising (in the quarto text): 'To which, upon my next opportunity toward the examining and digesting of my notes, I shall speak more wealthily, and pay the world a debt' (p. 178). This is presumably the long-promised 'observations upon Horace', whose failure to find print I have already commented upon. If it actually had more to say about the proper functions of the poet, the relationship between his intentions and his reception, or the proper balance between his own liberty and the authority of the state, its loss is of even greater consequence than I have suggested so far. It may, however, provide a further explanation for why he never saw fit to publish it.

Jonson rounds the Epistle off with a final obeisance to the universities, a promise to 'raise the despised head of poetry again', and a fierce final denunciation of those who 'keep her in contempt', for the terms of which he returns to the theme of branding first explored in the 'Apologetical Dialogue'. Here it is translated into a venomous threat to the detractors of poetry: 'she shall out of just rage incite her servants . . . to spout ink in their faces, that shall eat, farther than their marrow, into their fames; and not Cinnamus the barber, with his art, shall be able to take out the brands, but they shall live, and be read, till the wretches die, as things worst deserving of themselves in chief, and then of all mankind' (p. 179). Cinnamus is celebrated in Martial (VI.lxiv.24–6) for his skill in removing brands. This contrasts with the beguiling geniality of the prologue to *Volpone*, where he promises to remove the acid from his ink, leaving only salt, to replace branding with laughter:

> All gall and copperas, from his ink he draineth,
>   Only a little salt remaineth,
> Wherewith he'll rub your cheeks, till red with laughter
>   They shall look fresh, a week after.

(p. 180)

In the 'Apologetical Dialogue' Jonson had reserved the threat of branding for those who had libelled his own writing. In the Epistle he claims more generally for poetry (a term he has consistently and exclusively identified with his own works) the right to inflict public mutilation upon its detractors – a right which the state had so recently ('the report was that they should then had their ears cut & noses') threatened to exercise a second time upon his own person. In the prologue (where, as he wryly remarks, 'From no needful rule he swerveth', line 32) Jonson promises to forgo that right, exercising the prerogative of mercy which – in the end – had been extended to Chapman and himself. The key issue, here as throughout, is that of authority: the authority of the state and of the poet, and of the relationship between them. This public flourishing of his own branding – for the first time, as far as the reading public was concerned – emphasises the paradox of Jonson's position, the subject turned authority.

James D. Redwine Jr has observed that: 'The importance of the *Volpone* criticism . . . can scarcely be stressed too often – it marks a turning point in the development of Jonson's critical theory. Up to the time he wrote *Volpone*, his attitude toward the so-called laws would seem to be one of respectful independence.' He cites a dialogue between Cordatus and Mitis in the Induction to *Every Man Out of His Humour* (see Appendix, pp. 169–70) as evidence of Jonson's earlier view of the 'licence' or 'liberty' that may properly be exercised by modern poets. But

from *Volpone* onward . . . 'licence, or free power, to illustrate and heighten our invention' is more likely to be attacked as a dangerous tendency of an illiterate age than to be defended on the grounds of classical precedent. . . . Throughout [the Epistle to *Volpone*] it is the 'liberty' or 'licence' of contemporary poetry that he attacks most bitterly. And in the *Volpone* prologue, three of Mitis' 'too nice observations' are brought forth as necessary elements ('needful rules') of 'quick comedy'.[22]

I am less inclined to see the *Volpone* material in this way, as a watershed in Jonson's critical thinking, though I agree that it most forcefully represents one end of the spectrum of his thinking about the 'licence' or 'liberty' of poetry. For one thing, Redwine underplays the extent to which some of Jonson's most libertarian observations on the freedom of poets (such as the 'guides, not commanders' passage in *Discoveries*, about the authority of the ancients) were written much later in his career. More importantly, he completely ignores the very specific historical context within which this was written, and the enormous pressures this placed on Jonson, to which he responds by very provocatively running together the 'rules' of poetry and the 'laws' of the state. Once that is appreciated, we can see that his entire vocabulary – of law and arbitration, innocence and branding, allowance and mulcting, liberty and licence – is, if not positively ironic, at least double-edged. His own subjective 'innocence' (for which we might substitute 'honesty') is not defined by the laws of the state, any more than it is by the authority of the ancients, but these are useful markers when the alternative is to be misread, misconstrued, misreported in a world where reception is governed by the lowest common denominators of ignorance, spite and the suspiciousness of those with power.

This seems to me a good example of what Martin Elsky means when he says (as quoted above): 'Jonson points to the monarch as the guarantor of his word, though he does not go to the extreme of seeing his entire poetic as being constituted by the authority of the king.' The final reservation tacitly marks a difference between Elsky's position (and my own) and that of Jonathan Goldberg in *James I and the Politics of Literature*, who argues with Foucauldian pessimism that Jonson's entire identity as an author is subsumed in the ideological authority of the King: intention is beside the point in a world where language writes us (rather than *vice-versa*) and meaning is entirely defined by the power which sanctions that language.[23] This is an elegant post-structuralist double-bind, but it is one which needs to be confronted with the equal and opposite deconstructionist proposition, deriving from the supposedly arbitrary processes of signification, and rendered with deliberate crudity by Stanley Fish as 'there are no determinate meanings and . . . the stability of the text is an illusion'.[24] It is not monarchs, writers or texts which generate or sanction meaning: but readers, in all their perplexing variety. In the Epistle to *Volpone* Jonson was, in effect, mediating between the Scylla of Goldberg and the Charybdis of Fish, the tyranny of state-determined 'allowance' and the terror of endless misreading. If he settles, in this instance, for the former over the latter, he does so in a context where the very fact of mediation preserves a separate authority for the writer, a distinct identity for the author, though (as we shall see) this can easily be overlooked.

These are matters of some moment, because what Redwine views simply as a change in Jonson's critical priorities can be construed as symptomatic of a much more fundamental re-orientation of his career. Put at its crudest, it could be said that he was turning his back on the rebellious 'liberty' which had been such a hallmark of his early life and writing, and becoming a creature of the state. My own reading of the Epistle to *Volpone*, in the context of all the confrontations with authority from which it derives and to which it refers, has stressed the ironic transpositions involved, Jonson appropriating to himself the language of law and authority which had so repeatedly and until so recently been applied to his own person and writings: words that had helped gain his release after 'transgressing' in his previous work (*Eastward Ho*) here celebrate the 'authoritative' reception of his new one. Seen in this light, it is potentially a very subversive document indeed, mocking those who would seek to restrain his art (as they had repeatedly restrained his body) just as much as he reviles those who denigrate or misconstrue it.

Yet there is no doubt that Jonson's career actually took a more establishment turn from this point. His brushes with authority diminished in number and severity, and by the time he received a royal pension in 1616 he was in all but name Poet Laureate, regularly polishing the court's self-image with his masques. What was this if not selling out? Jonson had concluded his letter to Salisbury with the hope that he 'will be the most honour'd cause of our liberty, where freeing us from one prison you shall remove us to another, which is eternally to bind us and our Muses to the thankful honouring of you and yours to posterity; as your own virtues have by many descents of ancestors ennobled you to time. Your Lordship's most devoted in heart as words. / Ben. Jonson' (p. 214). Is this Jonson's offer, in the most literal of terms, to become Salisbury's poet, as perhaps he also had to agree to be his spy? If so, it truly freed Jonson from one prison to remove him to another, and may explain the bitterness with which – when Salisbury was dead, and he was free to do so – Jonson berated his muse for betraying him 'to a worthless lord', in a context which makes it perfectly plain that it was Salisbury he had in mind; it would also explain the decision to omit that poem to Salisbury (interestingly, the one which makes most of his 'ancestry') from the *Epigrams*.[25] We do not know if Jonson felt it necessary to consult Salisbury before reproducing in public parts of the letter he had written him, but at the very least he could hardly have re-used that material without being conscious of his dependence on a whole structure of institutionalised power, with Salisbury at the centre of it.

Moreover, in appropriating the language of authority, Jonson may be said to have made himself indistinguishable from it. In boasting that his works are 'allowed' and that he subscribes to the 'law' (that of the ancient critics as much as of Jacobean England), Jonson has indeed become 'Salisbury's poet', not necessarily in a personal sense, but in the sense that *poetic* and *critical* authority are recognised as cognate with that of the state and not divisible from it. Where the Augustus of *Poetaster* defers to Virgil, Jonson's poet/critic acknowledges that his first allegiance is not to some transcendent reality (the truth, justice, antiquity, the laws, the universities) but to the state – though in acknowledging as much he is empowered to employ all those resonant abstract verities in his own service, which is also that of the state. In this rather limited sense, the Epistle to *Volpone* remains an intensely ironic text, because it fully acknowledges the permissive prison within which the author recognised himself as trapped (and so remains *potentially* subversive in allowing for its possible deconstruction, or the author's possible escape).

But it is, so to speak, only the 'establishment' side of the equation – the law-abiding author/citizen – which later generations (like Dryden, Rymer and even Redwine) recognised or at least acknowledged, as the modern concepts both of responsible authorship and of literary criticism emerged alongside it. Jonson himself doubtless furthered the process in the text's subsequent manifestations: the self-deprecatory reference to the Epistle's length, and its dating and placement from the Blackfriars in 1607, disappeared from the 1616 folio version, immediately casting it as a more 'authoritative', out-of-time document. And, because of the respect the *Works* enjoyed, this is the version best known to posterity (taking precedence, for example, in Herford and Simpson). The promise, referring to 'the office of a comic poet' that 'upon my next opportunity toward the examining and digesting of my notes, I shall speak more wealthily, and pay the world a debt' is toned down to a bland 'To which, I shall take the occasion elsewhere to speak'. As we have repeatedly observed, Jonson never did so speak in public. The 'observations on Horace his *Art of Poesy*' apparently burned in the fire, and with them the last chance that Jonson might have spoken more conclusively or radically about his own authority as a writer; in this respect, it is a loss as tantalising as that of Aristotle's treatise on comedy, which absorbed Umberto Eco so entertainingly in *The Name of the Rose*. In its absence, Jonson has branded himself to posterity as a keeper of the laws, an 'allowed' poet, more thoroughly than the authorities could ever have done: 'and not Cinnamus the barber, with his art, shall be able to take out the brands' (though the present writer is subjecting them to a more sympathetic scrutiny than they have received hitherto). Dryden, Rymer, and Jonson's other immediate successors did not trouble to scrutinise them, because it entirely suited their purposes to take them at face value.[26] Jonson s hardwon compromise in the Epistle to *Volpone* in fact laid the groundwork for a *modus vivendi* for writers for the next century or more, as they defined their literature in terms of formalistic and moralistic neoclassical laws and the authority of the ancients, and so largely avoided confrontation with the laws and authority of the state which licensed their self-expression.

LICENCE: THE INDUCTION TO *BARTHOLOMEW FAIR*

There remains, however, one dimension to the 'licence'/'liberty' debate which is obscured if we try to tie the *Volpone* criticism too narrowly to one side of the equation or the other. That is Jonson's frank acknowledgement that, whatever 'laws' a writer obeys, his meaning will not be circumscribed by them: 'nothing can be so innocently writ, or carried, but may be made obnoxious to construction'. Submission to the authority of the state's censors may absolve the author of responsibility for the consequences of signification being a random process, but it does not remove *the fact*: there remains an area of free-play between what is written and how it is received. And it is something that an enterprising author (however law-abiding) can turn to his advantage, as Jonson demonstrates with consummate self-assurance in the Induction to *Bartholomew Fair* (see Appendix, pp. 196–200). The central issue there – teased out with all the ingenuity of a conceit by Donne – is the relationship between the 'real' fair and the literary one that Jonson has invented. The Stage-Keeper condemns it as 'like to be a very conceited scurvy [play], in plain English' – scurvy *in that* it is conceited (witty, ingenious), at the expense of entertaining real-life 'Bartholomew-birds' like the bully, little Davy, the itinerant tooth-drawer, Kindheart, and the juggler 'with a well-educated ape' (pp. 196–7). It is also scurvy, in his view, because not only does it not have such elements of the *real* fair, but those it does have are not a patch on the stage-clowns of the last generation,

Dick Tarlton and John Adams (both explicitly named) and Will Kempe (evoked in a scene from *Much Ado About Nothing*, where he is known to have played Dogberry, p. 197). Pursuing his usual tactic of disabling contrary voices before advancing his own, Jonson thus uses the Stage-Keeper as a comic stalking-horse to undermine the cases for both artless verisimilitude and an earlier, less sophisticated stage-craft: Tarlton and his successors were the comic counterparts of the tragedies '*Jeronimo*, or *Andronicus*' (that is, Kyd's *The Spanish Tragedy* and Shakespeare's *Titus Andronicus*), whose devotees the Scrivener will sarcastically commend for their 'virtuous and stayed ignorance' (p. 199).[27]

The Book-Holder and the Scrivener between them introduce a totally new set of principles into the equation. The 'Articles of Agreement' they bring with them are a joke precisely because they attempt to set limits to that which is beyond control: the reception of a work by an audience, which is always unpredictable, but never more so than in the unstable marketplace of the theatre. They nevertheless articulate some ground-rules: the play the audience is about to see is a commercial product, bought and sold on mutually agreeable terms; these must include the recognition that it *is* a play, not reality, and so to be judged in terms of its appropriateness as a play and not otherwise; moreover, in as much as individual members of the audience have paid strictly finite sums to be there, they are not entitled to make unreasonable demands of the author in respect of what he delivers in return (such demands would include not only artless verisimilitude but also the artistic standards of an earlier era); moreover, the fact that they have paid and entered this quasi-contractual situation sets the audience in a different relationship to this play from that they might have understood in earlier times – they are not part of a communal, festive experience, but judging spectators of a work of art; by the same token, the event they are to experience does not have the 'Land of Cockaigne' indeterminacy or 'out-of-time' quality of the carnivalesque – it is located in a very particular place and time: 'the Hope on the Bankside, in the County of Surrey . . . the one and thirtieth day of October 1614, and in the twelfth year of the reign of our Sovereign Lord, James' (p. 198); furthermore the play itself, for all its Brueghel-like apparent shapelessness, will closely observe the 'laws' of time and place as part of its definition as a work of art. The fact that the play *depicts* a very traditional festive occasion, the annual St Bartholomew's Day fair, held at Smithfield every 25 August, and that Jonson goes out of his way to emphasise its carnival quality by making the eating of Bartholomew-pig the symbolic nub of the action, only ironises and intensifies each of these last three points. As Jonathan Haynes observes: 'The play is of course built directly on the representation of the festive marketplace, and nowhere does Renaissance literature bring us closer to the sights and sounds and smells of a popular celebration.'[28] But the whole point of the Induction, and other manifestations of critical 'law', is to distance us from the sensual/festive/popular even as we are exposed so overwhelmingly to it.

In such ways Jonson draws a line between himself and the drama of the immediate past, very much as he was to do in the prologue to the folio *Every Man In His Humour*. But he also creates an intriguing speculative space between his play and that which it represents, a space that is occupied by his 'judging spectators'. It is succinctly outlined by the Scrivener as he draws to a close: 'though the Fair be not kept in the same region that some here, perhaps, would have it, yet think that therein the author hath observed a special decorum, the place being as dirty as Smithfield, and as stinking every whit' (p. 200). *Like* the Fair (and still more like it in as much as the Hope, which doubled as a bear-baiting pit, was even less salubrious than other public theatres) but *not* the Fair. And he can list specific differences: for the Stage-Keeper's little Davy 'a strutting horse-courser', for Kindheart the pig-woman, for the juggler a 'wise Justice of Peace meditant'. But beyond such specifics, who can police the line of Jonson's imagination? When he tries to make it the final article of his agreement with 'the foresaid hearers and spectators, that they neither in themselves conceal, nor suffer by them to be concealed, any state-decipherer, or politic picklock of the scene, so solemnly ridiculous as to search out who was meant by the gingerbread-woman, who by the hobby-horseman, who by the costermonger, nay, who by their wares' (p. 199), he is attempting to confine the unconfinable – and he knows it.

The role of Justice Overdo, in particular, cries out for statedecipherers 'to search out who was meant'. That the embodiment of law in the play should deliver a diatribe against tobacco (II.vi) can hardly be accidental in a work whose epilogue addresses the very King James who was author of *A Counterblast to Tobacco*; moreover, Overdo himself commends 'a worthy worshipful man, sometime a capital member of this city, for his high wisdom, in

this point, who would take you, now the habit of a porter; now
of a carman; now of a dog-killer . . .' (II.i.13–16), referring to an
actual Lord Mayor of London known to use disguises as he himself was doing.[29] In such ways the text taunts us with the possibility of making 'applications', eliding the distinction between fact
and fiction; but, at the same time, it denies us any comfortable
closure on such matters. Overdo *may* to a degree represent King
James, and/or an actual Lord Mayor, but he is also just another
manifestation of a long line of theatrical law-givers who use disguise to pursue their goal, a line that stretches from Pentheus in
Euripides' *The Bacchae* to the dukes in Shakespeare's *Measure for
Measure* and Marston's *The Malcontent*.[30]

The more, therefore, that Jonson advertises the formalist integrity of his drama, its subjection to the best precedents and rules
of art, the freer he paradoxically becomes to point up the ways
his art may actually mirror life – or, more precisely, the freer his
consumers are to construe it as so doing. The 'allowance' of the
Master of the Revels and other censors is thus a vital agency in
the circulation of meaning, and Jonson's public subjection to it (a
subjection of his works *as fictions* rather than as commentaries on
the times, though so easily represented to post-Romantic minds
as a forfeiture of his integrity) was in many ways a sensible expedient, one by which he could justifiably describe himself as the
'servant, but not slave' of the state. This extends, in different ways,
to areas of his writing other than for the public stage. In respect
of non-dramatic verse written in honour of aristocrats (so insincere in its flattery to modern stomachs), his first line of defence
must have been the number and range of people so addressed –
something which the publication of these works made a matter
of public record. Although the selections contained in the 1616
folio show a demonstrable bias towards the Pembroke faction
ascendant at the time, they do not do so without a proper deference towards the king himself, Aubigny and his wife, Salisbury,
Suffolk, and others of lesser stature, sufficient to show Jonson as
a *central* figure, honouring the state in general through its luminaries.[31] In acknowledging the patronage of so many, he is tacitly
proclaiming a degree of independence from them all.

More specifically, in arraying the poems in these selections, he
invites readers (as the poems so often do internally) to compare
and contrast, to discriminate between different forms of praise
and grounds for praising.[32] In so doing, in ways analogous to his

emphasis on the formal qualities of his plays, he draws attention to the poems as literary constructs and emphasises the degree of poetic convention present in the 'representation' of those they honour. To that extent he acknowledges a distance (which may, or may not, be construed as a difference) between what he evokes in words and the reality of his subject. In this he is being consistent with a commonplace of Renaissance critical theory, which clearly underlies both his panegyric poetry and his court masques and entertainments, though Jonson himself rarely refers to it directly. This is the notion of *laudando praecipere* (to teach by praising), an intensification of Horace's central proposition that all poetry should 'mix profit with . . . pleasure' (Prologue to *Volpone*, l. 8).[33] The contention here is that poems which praise individuals, or masques which glorify them, are conceived not as literal images of their subjects but as idealised projections of how such persons should fulfil the role in life to which they are born; the emotional force of such works is thus not dishonestly wasted on flattering their subjects but attempts to inspire them to live up to their potential, a very specific version of 'the principal end of poesy, to inform men in the best reason of living' (Epistle to *Volpone*, p. 178). This is to make such poetry identical in spirit, if antithetic in method, to satire, and is specifically what Jonson has in mind in the dedication of the *Epigrams* to Pembroke: 'if I have praised, unfortunately, anyone that doth not deserve, or if all answer not in all numbers the pictures I have made of them, I hope it will be forgiven me, that they are no ill pieces, though they be not like the persons' (Appendix, p. 193). Verisimilitude in poetry is not the same as truth.

It is, of course, a slippery doctrine, since there is every danger that a patron will simply not recognise a distinction between the ideal and the real. On the other hand, patrons are not the only readers of works addressed to them: the works are likely to circulate in manuscript and may indeed emerge in print. Then it literally falls to other readers to match the poem with its subject. Jonson repeatedly invokes the concept of the *reader par excellence*, embodied in Aubigny for *Sejanus*, Pembroke for *Epigrams* and *Catiline*, the king himself for *Bartholomew Fair*, but essentially an abstract principle, the potential 'understander', discrimination itself: 'if I prove the pleasure but of one, / So he judicious be; he shall b' alone / A theatre unto me' ('Apologetical Dialogue', p. 191). And if the reality markedly falls short of what the poem evokes, as Jonson bluntly puts it in 'To My Muse' (*Ep* LXV):

Whoe'er is raised
For worth he has not, he is taxed, not praised.

As I have observed, in the context of the *Epigrams*, this seems
pointedly aimed at Salisbury. But the general principle stands as
an admonishment over all Jonson's panegyric works.

The issue arises, *extremely* tactfully and obliquely, in a letter
dedicating the quarto of *The Masque of Queens* to Henry, Prince of
Wales:

> When it hath been my happiness . . . but to see your face . . . I
> have, with as much joy, as I am now far from flattery in pro-
> fessing it, called to mind that doctrine of some great inquisi-
> tors in nature, who hold every royal and heroic form to partake,
> and draw much to it of the heavenly virtue. For, whether it be
> that a divine soul, being to come into a body, first chooseth a
> palace fit for itself; or, being come, doth make it so or that
> nature be ambitious to have her works equal; I know not: but,
> what is lawful for me to understand, and speak, that I dare;
> which is, that both your virtue, and your form did deserve your
> fortune. The one claimed, that you should be born a prince;
> the other makes that you do become it.   (*H&S*, VII, p. 280)

Jonson does not exactly concur with the neo-Platonic theory that
'royal and heroic' persons are always endowed with forms befit-
ting their rank (the physical supposedly reflecting the spiritual
grace, a notion perhaps most familiar today from characters like
Perdita and Miranda in Shakespeare's late plays); nor will he
commit himself to how it might happen, if it were true. But, in
the case of Prince Henry, he enthusiastically agrees that the outward form suits the inner man: he is every inch a prince (though
'I am now far from flattery in professing it'). It is characteristically
tortuous of Jonson both to pay the expected compliment and simultaneously to distance himself from the premises on which it would
conventionally be based. He *knows* (but tactfully does not say)
that there is no *necessary* concurrence between aristocracy and either
virtue or beauty; indeed, it could be said that one premise of the
theory of *laudando praecipere* (here as true in the visual arts as the
verbal) was that it sought to make good the unfortunate deficiencies of nature, to further a process which in a perfect world
would have been completed at birth.

These ironies are particularly resonant in the court masques, those self-indulgent 'spectacles of state' which some would always prefer for Inigo Jones's 'design' over Jonson's 'invention'.[34] The first function of such works was always 'to glorify the court' and with it 'the most royal princes, and greatest persons (who are commonly the personators of these actions)'.[35] That being so, there were any number of occasions when the reality conspicuously failed to live up to the ideal which it was being exhorted to emulate. The fact of this was all the more unavoidable once the printed texts of these pieces had given them an immortality to rival that which their participants *ought*, as understanders, to have derived from the experience ('Else the glory of all these solemnities had perished like a blaze and gone out in the beholders' eyes': *Hymenaei*; Appendix, p. 174). A notable example proved to be *Hymenaei* itself, written to celebrate the wedding of the young Earl of Essex and Lady Frances Howard (a match designed to reconcile the Devereux with the Howards, and so with the Cecils, under the royally fruitful union of James and Anne, and paralleling the political union of England and Scotland into Great Britain).[36] The marriage actually ended in a scandalous divorce six years later on the dubious grounds of non-consummation (intensely ironic in the light of the masque's heavy emphasis on union, fertility and fruitfulness), though it was widely assumed that the king brow-beat the clergy involved into a verdict which would make possible a marriage between Lady Frances and her new lover, his favourite, the Earl of Somerset. Jonson not only did not balk at writing a celebratory piece for the new wedding (*A Challenge at Tilt*, the sexual innuendo of which is quite unabashed), but also republished *Hymenaei* in the 1616 folio.[37] The main change he made to the text was to remove the names of all participants (artists as well as aristocrats), so that he had to inform Drummond 'That epithalamium that wants a name in his printed works was made at the Earl of Essex's marriage' (345–6).

Doubtless there were other readers, not least of the quarto text, who did not need to be told that. By 1616, Somerset and Lady Frances had been convicted of complicity in the murder of Sir Thomas Overbury, so that the folio text of *Hymenaei* stood not only as testimony to the failed ideals of one marriage but also as a mute indictment of the values of a second, and more generally as an accusatory finger at a court in which such behaviour could flourish. A rather different example of such ironies is provided, as Dale B. J. Randall has demonstrated, by *The Gypsies Metamor-phosed*, a daringly double-edged work which contrives simul-taneously both to praise and amuse the king and to remind him of the *parvenu*, 'gypsy' provenance of the man who commissioned the piece, his favourite, Buckingham.[38] In these, as in virtually everything he wrote (and particularly in everything he published), Jonson was exploiting a conscious gap between the formal integrity of what he wrote and the possible ways in which it might be interpreted. That is, he was turning to his own advantage a point made succinctly by Sir Philip Sidney, about the poet defined as a maker of fictions: 'Now for the poet, he nothing affirms, and there-fore never lieth ... though he recount things not true, yet be-cause he telleth them not for true, he lieth not.'[39] In Jonson's case, as a writer in and around the court, but without its inherent auth-ority, this was an *enabling* distinction, one that made it possible to submit to censorship without losing integrity, to write in pub-lic praise of those about whom he might have private reserva-tions, and to believe of himself what he boasted to Drummond, that 'he would not flatter, though he saw death' (278). It is in the prefatory material to *Volpone* and the Induction to *Bartholomew Fair* that he most fully articulates the complex conditions and understandings which make that possible.

4

The 'Laws' of Poetry

I am not of that opinion to conclude a poet's liberty within the narrow limits of laws which either the grammarians or philosophers prescribe. For before they found out those laws there were many excellent poets that fulfilled them. Amongst whom none more perfect than Sophocles, who lived a little before Aristotle.

Discoveries, 2579–84

As we have observed in various contexts, but specifically in relation to the Epistle to *Volpone* and the Induction to *Bartholomew Fair*, there is a demonstrable connection between Jonson's sense of his place as an author within the state (the law of the land) and his respect for the formal 'laws' of literature, often (though not always) derived from classical precedent. We have also observed that this respect, although the emphasis might vary from context to context, was that owing to 'guides, not commanders'. Thirdly (a point which shadows the other two, and which I want here to develop), we have seen how Jonson's appeal to the 'laws' is always a function of his attempts to define himself as an author by differentiating his own writing from that of various precursors, notably that of the 'playwrights' who wrote simply to entertain the audiences of the London theatres, and of the 'amateur' coterie poets of the court and its hangers on. In respect of both of these categories, though for different reasons in either case, the appeal to the 'laws' is (for at least the first half of his career) concomitant with a defence of print culture, though there are cases – Spenser is an example – where Jonson will also invoke aspects of the 'laws' to draw lines between himself and others who have gone before him into print. In all cases perhaps the prime consideration for Jonson is that the relationship between himself and his reader be contractually unambiguous, though even that lack of ambiguity (as in the Induction to *Bartholomew Fair*) may in itself be provocatively suggestive.

'THE UNITIES'

Take, for example, the declaration in the Prologue to *Volpone* that 'The laws of time, place, persons, he observeth, / From no needful rule he swerveth' (31–2). He is invoking Aristotle, though an Aristotle simplified and distorted by subsequent commentators. In the so-called 'unities' of time and place it was argued that the time spanned by the dramatic action should be confined to what was mimetically credible (often put at twenty-four hours), that the events should all take place within a comprehensible geographical locale (though not necessarily literally in the same spot), and that characters should be consistent in themselves, while comic and serious characters should not mingle in the same plot. These are not strictly ascribable to Aristotle, who said nothing at all about place in the *Poetics*, and only discussed time in the spirit of what he saw as best practice rather than as a strict rule. Jonson's third 'law', of persons, similarly seems to derive from Aristotle's observation (rather than rule) that comedy is an imitation of characters of a lower type (socially and morally), tragedy an imitation of characters of a higher type. It was Aristotle's interpreters in the sixteenth century, and notably Castelvetro in his 1570 edition of the *Poetics*, who hardened these observations into so-called laws. Jonson says nothing here (though he does, as we shall see, in the *Discoveries*) about what Castelvetro and others dubbed the third 'unity', which is that of 'action', the requirement that all the elements of a literary work should relate organically and proportionately to its central conception. The fact that he does not mention it here perhaps suggests that he did not feel hidebound by the accumulated wisdom of the past. But most of his own published plays do very largely subscribe to the 'needful rules'. That he was self-conscious about them while writing is clear from his disqualification of *Sejanus* as 'no true poem, in the strict laws of time', as well as numerous other choric interventions.

There are many facets to these 'laws', and several grounds on which they may be justified. Jonson comes closest to mounting a systematic argument in relation to them in the closing sections of the *Discoveries* (2648–838), a discussion of 'the parts of a comedy and tragedy' which he very largely bases on passages from two works by the Dutch classical scholar Daniel Heinsius, his *Dissertation: On the Judgement of Horace concerning Plautus and Terence* (1618) and *Concerning the Constitution of Tragedy* (1611). His dependence on Heinsius is such that he follows him in a serious misreading (2654ff) of what Aristotle said about the relationship of laughter to comedy. It is important to observe (a point to which I shall return) that the general context of this is a slightly garbled discussion of the faults and virtues of various early comic writers, and more particularly of the superiority of the Latin New Comedy of Plautus and Terence, which focused on the ludicrous behaviour of certain generalised character-types, over the Greek Old Comedy, pre-eminently represented by Aristophanes, which scurrilously mocked known individuals.

In the course of this he focuses on the question of 'the magnitude and compass of any fable' (2701), the fable being the 'plot' or unifying thread that gives cohesion to any 'poem':

The fable is called the imitation of one entire and perfect action, whose parts are so joined and knit together as nothing in the structure can be changed or taken away without impairing or troubling the whole, of which there is a proportionable magnitude in the members. . . . Whole we call that, and perfect, which hath a beginning, a midst, and an end. So the place of any building may be whole and entire for that work, though too little for a palace. As to a tragedy or a comedy, the action may be convenient and perfect that would not fit an epic poem in magnitude . . . as in every body, so in every action which is the subject of a just work, there is required a certain proportionable greatness, neither too vast nor too minute. For that which happens to the eyes when we behold a body, the same happens to the memory when we contemplate an action. I look upon a monstrous giant, as Tityus, whose body covered nine acres of land, and mine eye sticks upon every part; the whole that consists of those parts will never be taken in at one entire view. So in a fable, if the action be too great, we can never comprehend the whole together in our imagination. Again, if it be too little, there ariseth no pleasure out of the object; it affords the view no stay; it is beheld and vanisheth at once. . . . The same happens in action, which is the object of memory, as the body is of sight. Too vast oppresseth the eyes, and exceeds the memory; too little scarce admits either. . . . And every bound, for the nature of the subject, is esteemed the best that is largest, till it can increase no more; so it behoves the action in tragedy or comedy to be let grow till the necessity ask a conclusion; wherein two things are to be considered: first that it exceed not the compass of one day; next, that there be place left for digression and art. For the episodes and digressions in a fable are the same that household stuff and other furniture are in a house. (2703–71, with omissions)

As so often, there is nothing here that is actually new, but Jonson disposes his precedents with a very particular emphasis: the work of art must not only be organically whole and proportionable in its parts, but *comprehensibly* so; it must be such that an observer can consider the *entirety*, if not at a single glance then in memory. This is not, however, an argument for functional minimalism; comedies and tragedies should 'be let grow till the necessity ask a conclusion', while place should be 'left for digression and art', the proper embellishments of the bare frame. The latter would include, for example, the 'fullness and frequency of sentence' [*sententiae* or pithy aphorisms], which he claims it to be among the 'offices of a tragic writer' to deploy, and which he considers to be a feature of his *Sejanus* (Appendix, p. 173). Perspective is, in a sense, all: the observer must be able to comprehend the whole and be able to relate the parts to that whole. And the 'rules' are functionally subordinate to that requirement. Jonson regards it as axiomatic that 'the action in tragedy or comedy' should 'exceed not the compass of one day', but that is not adduced as an end in itself; it (and, we may infer, the 'law of place') is part of a wider sense of how the dramatic text should relate to its audience, and be appreciated by them. The compression furthers both the organic unity and the comprehensibility of the whole, narrowing the sight-lines and the imaginative distance. All of these emphases are of a piece with a preference for the closed, classical text, as opposed to the open-endedness of festive performance.

The 'law' of 'persons' is related to the generic differences between tragedy and comedy, and the need to police those differences. But Jonson readily concedes that the 'parts of a comedy are the same with a tragedy, and the end is partly the same. For they both delight and teach' (2648–50). The differences between them, such as the concentration in tragedy on 'dignity of persons' ('To the Readers', *Sejanus*), while comedy 'sport[s] with human follies, not with crimes' (Prologue to *Every Man In His Humour*), is thus functional rather than essential. Confining attention to limited areas of the metaphysical, social and ethical spectra contributes to the unity of a particular text, and so to the opportunity the audience has to comprehend the fable in its entirety. In all these formalist discussions of generic definition and dramatic proprieties, that is, we find Jonson implicitly looking for his ideal consumer, the individual understander, marked off by 'knowledge' from the indiscriminate (and undiscriminated) audience associated with popular theatre ('the great herd, the multitude', or again 'the beast, the multitude', *Discoveries*, 1464, 2682–3).

OLD AND NEW COMEDY

This in part suggests a reason why such a discussion should arise from Jonson's observations on the difference between Old and New Comedy. The former (pre-eminently represented by Aristophanes) he judged at fault because it aimed at the lowest common denominators of human sensibility, the very antithesis of man's ability to discriminate:

> what either in the words or sense of an author, or in the language or actions of men, is awry or depraved doth strangely stir mean affections, and provoke for the most part to laughter. And therefore it was clear that all insolent or obscene speeches, jest[s] upon the best men, injuries to particular persons, perverse and sinister sayings – and the rather unexpected – in the Old Comedy did move to laughter, especially where it did imitate any dishonesty, and scurrility came forth in the place of wit; which who understands the nature and genius of laughter cannot but perfectly know. (2666–76)

He cites as an example the guying of Socrates in Aristophanes' *The Clouds*, concluding: 'This is truly leaping from the stage to the tumbrel again; reducing all wit to the original dung-cart' (2699–700).

Such a disavowal of the freakish (an issue, for example, in both *The Alchemist* and *Bartholomew Fair*) strongly implies the existence of a commonly-understood inverse measure of what is normal or natural, something that runs through much of Jonson's thinking. 'To Penshurst' (*For* II), for example, is constructed around an affirmation of an indissolubly 'natural' hierarchy of physical, social and supernatural worlds, in which everyone and everything has a knowable place; and such a comprehensible order of things has implications for the language in which it should be represented.[1] But this quickly shades here into other matters: 'jest[s] upon the best men, injuries to particular persons, perverse and sinister sayings' – the array of worries at the heart of the Epistle to *Volpone*. The Old Comedy was actually guilty of what Jonson's plays prior to that had been *accused of*: particularity, libel of identifiable individuals, sedition. The New Comedy, by contrast, concentrated on the manners and *mores* of the times but avoided personal insults and questionable commentary on affairs of state. A key feature of Jonson's own comedies after *Volpone* (a notable touchstone here being the revised *Every Man In His Humour*) is that they are, with increasing specificity, about contemporary London. As he slyly puts it in the Prologue to *The Alchemist*:

> Our scene is London, 'cause we would make known
> No country's mirth is better than our own.
>
> (ll. 5–6)

At the same time, however, Jonson consistently argues that no particular applications are intended, or should be inferred. Yet, within that play, the whole business of Dapper being subjected to the attentions of 'the Queen of Faery' curiously parallels the swindling of one Thomas Rodgers, then the subject of a notorious case in Chancery.[2] Jonson would no doubt claim that this was a vindication of the general thesis of his play – proof that he had caught the pulse of the times or 'clime' (Prologue, 7) – rather than evidence that he was being 'particular': 'For here, he doth not fear, who can apply' (l. 19).

The nub to such a claim lies in the status of *The Alchemist* itself *as art*, as a piece of New Comedy (it echoes Plautus's *Mostellaria* in places), which triumphantly abides by all the Aristotelian 'laws': it all takes place within a certain day (1 November 1610 to be precise), all the action is in or about Lovewit's house in the Blackfriars, and the characters are a plausible cross-section of the middling and lower orders of Jacobean society. In its observance of the mechanical 'rules' of *mimesis* it lays claim to existing in a separate, essentially aesthetic realm, observing its own 'laws' rather than falling into the lawlessness of 'particularity', libel or sedition. 'Judging spectators' (l. 3) will recognise the distance between the formal regulation of the work of art and contingent reality, as Horace had 'vindicated [Plautus] against many that are offended, and say it is a hard censure upon the parent of all conceit and sharpness' (*Discoveries*, 2626–8). Jonson then spells out Horace's eminent qualifications to make such a judgement, 'especially being a man so conversant and inwardly familiar with the censures of great men that did discourse of these things daily amongst themselves' (2634–6). But if Horace defended Plautus, he reserved his highest praise for Terence: 'Horace did so highly esteem Terence's comedies as he ascribes the art in comedy to him alone among the Latins, and joins him with Menander [the Greek dramatist, often credited as the first major writer of New Comedy]' (2642–4). In fact Horace did *not* so join Terence with Menander: Jonson's scholarship may be weighty, but it is far from flawless. The essential point remains, however, that he is determined to weave here a tradition of informed critical commentary (to which Horace is central) in which adherence to the generic constraints of New Comedy is simultaneously a measure of formal artistic excellence and a guarantee of authorial 'innocence' (here that of Plautus).

If we take the *Discoveries* to date from the second half of Jonson's career, we might well read this as a retrospective repudiation of his self-alignment with Old Comedy in the three plays that he specifically dubbed 'comical satires' (as distinct from 'comedies'), *Every Man Out of His Humour*, *Cynthia's Revels* and *Poetaster*. As I have argued, however, it is not particularly fruitful to characterise Jonson's different emphases, in disparate contexts or at discrete stages of his career, as recantations or reconsiderations, stages en route to a definitive conclusion. As the career unfolded, different pressures required different responses. *Discoveries*, written without the pressure of defending specific works of his own, has more than a little of 'father' Ben about it, the patriarch law-giver. At the outset of the much earlier first 'comical satire' he has a character, Cordatus, describe it as 'strange, and of a particular kind by itself, somewhat like *Vetus Comoedia* [O2ld Comedy]: a work that hath bounteously pleased me, how it will answer the general expectation, I know not' (Appendix, p. 169), and in the 'Apologetical Dialogue' appended to the last, he defends himself against the charge of railing (implicitly in all of them):

> If all the salt in the old comedy
> Should be so censur'd, or the sharper wit
> Of the bold satire, termed scolding rage,
> What age could then compare with those, for buffoons?
> What should be said of Aristophanes?
> Persius? or Juvenal? whose names we now
> So glorify in schools, at least pretend it.
>   (Appendix, p. 190)

In this he follows J. C. Scaliger and other Renaissance critics in linking Aristophanic Old Comedy with the kind of virulent, abusive Latin satire most commonly associated with Juvenal.[3] Hence Asper, the central satiric voice in *Every Man Out of His Humour*, presents himself as a latter-day Juvenal, brushing off the alarm of his more cautious companions, Cordatus and Mitis:

> I'll strip the ragged follies of the time,
> Naked, as at their birth . . .
>   . . . and with a whip of steel,
> Print wounding lashes in their iron ribs.
>   (Grex, After the Second Sounding,
>   Appendix, p. 164)

Or again:

>   Well, I will scourge those apes;
> And to these courteous eyes [the audience] oppose a mirror,
> As large as is the stage, whereon we act:
> Where they shall see the time's deformity
> Anatomiz'd in every nerve, and sinew,
> With constant courage, and contempt of fear.
>   (p. 166)

Images of the beadle's whip and the surgeon's knife (and elsewhere the doctor's purgative) cohere around that of the stage as corrective mirror: the tone is harsher than that he adopts later (and it is far from clear that we should suffer this '*furor poeticus*' uncritically) but the model of the poet as one whose essential function is that of reminding people what they can and ought to be is constant throughout.

DRAMATIC STRUCTURE: THE PARTS OF A PLAY

In the comical satires, however, the stridency of the Juvenalian tone *seems* to be off-set by a more relaxed attitude to the laws of dramatic structure:

MITIS   Does he observe all the laws of comedy in it?
CORDATUS   What laws mean you?
MITIS   Why, the equal division of it into acts, and scenes, according to the Terentian manner, his true number of actors;
the furnishing of the scene with grex, or chorus, and that the
whole argument fall within compass of a day's business.
CORDATUS   O no, these are too nice observations.   (p. 169)

This, and similar disclaimers, are in fact more ironic than they may seem. Cordatus goes on to cite the practitioners of New Comedy as precedents for dispensing with a chorus, and so more generally for the pragmatic flexibility of the 'laws' as actually applied in classical times. Yet Cordatus and Mitis are themselves a grex or chorus of sorts, supplying that which Asper (as the supposed 'author' of the play) has omitted. Jonson's *own* practice as author, that is, undercuts the theoretical freedoms being claimed by his characters on stage, and it must always be questionable to what extent *any* of his on-stage choric characters 'represents' Jonson himself. Even when they seem most sympathetic to his cause (perhaps especially then) their function is to place a critical framework between the action and the audience, not to constitute an absolute authority.

Later on, Cordatus, for example, seems to give the lie to his own casual dismissal of the need for 'the equal division of [the play] into acts and scenes'. He quietens Mitis as the action is about to recommence: 'Here comes Macilente, and signior Brisk, freshly suited, lose not your self, for now the *epitasis*, or busy part of our subject is in act' (Grex after III.viii, lines 100–2). This invokes the tri-partite division of dramatic works, expounded by the fourth-century grammarian Donatus, into *protasis* (beginning of the action/argument and presentation of characters), *epitasis* (complication and entanglement of the argument, leading to a *summa epitasis*, or ultimate confounding, in which lie the seeds of a solution), and finally the *catastrophe*, the sudden resolution of affairs in a happy (or tragic) conclusion. Jonson's fullest exposition of the formula emerges in *The Magnetic Lady* where the author's Boy chides the foolish Damplay for expecting to see something concluded in the *protasis*: 'Do you look Master Damplay, for conclusions in a *protasis*? I thought the law of comedy had reserv'd 'em to the *catastrophe* and that the *epitasis*, as we are taught, and the *catastasis*, had been intervening parts to have been expected' (Chorus after Act I; Appendix, p. 208). *Catastasis* here, a term borrowed from Scaliger, seems to be the equiv2alent of the more conventional *summa epitasis*, that final piling on of complication which seems almost to defy resolution and is such a feature of Jonson's own most enduring comedies, *Volpone* and *The Alchemist*. As the Boy puts it to Damplay: 'Stay, and see his last act, his *catastrophe*, how he will perplex that, or spring some fresh cheat, to entertain the spectators, with a convenient delight, till some unexpected, and new encounter break out to rectify all, and make good the conclusion' (Chorus after Act IV; Appendix, p. 212).[4]

The terminology here, in which 'last act' and 'catastrophe' are virtual synonyms, points to Jonson's conventional Renaissance conflation of the tri-partite divisions of dramatic structure proposed by Donatus with Horace's recommendation in the *Ars Poetica* of a five-act structure, as best exemplified by the plays of Terence. So in a prefatory outline of *The New Inn* he could observe: 'Here begins, at the third Act, the *epitasis*, or business of the play' and 'The fifth, and last Act is the *catastrophe*, or knitting up of all' ('The Argument', H&S, VI. pp. 348–401, ll. 64–5, 104–5).[5] It is one of the features of Jonson's presentation of his plays on the printed page that he invariably follows the five-act model, hitherto reserved for the Latin works of Terence, Plautus and Seneca (though he also usually follows the conventional *playhouse* practice of indicating a change of *scene* whenever there is a significant change of personnel on stage, and not just when there is a change of locale or lapse in time, as the modern practice would be).[6]

This is very much part of Jonson's early alignment with print culture, as well as (paradoxical as it may seem) with classical tradition: *Every Man Out of His Humour* was the first of his plays to see print, and however much Cordatus may argue that 'I see not then, but we should enjoy the same licence, or free power, to illustrate and heighten our invention as [the early comic dramatists] did' (Grex, After the Second Sounding; Appendix, p. 170), the play actually presents itself *to the reader* as very much subject to the best received laws of dramatic construction, which are denoted by methods of transcription associated pre-eminently with the key New Comedy dramatist, Terence. With the *folio* texts of *Cynthia's Revels* and *Poetaster* this remains the case, even though they are partially re-written in ways that make them less 'actorly' and more 'readerly', a point acknowledged in the prologue to the former (not in the early quarto text), where Jonson asserts that his 'poesy . . . affords / Words above action: matter, above words' (*H&S*, IV, p. 43). Language has priority over stage action, but the *substance* of the text (as distinct from its style or formal structure) has priority over both of these. This may betray a belated unease with what were very much experimental plays, inspired primarily by the *non-dramatic* models of Roman satire (Horace largely supplanting Juvenal by the time of *Poetaster*), but throughout the comical satires he teasingly reminds the audience that he is well aware of the classical 'rules', even when he may seem to be breaking them: a far remove from contemporary playwrights who are either ignorant or wilfully disregard them.

HUMOURS

These playful paradoxes revolve to a large degree around Jonson's distrust of the 'communal' verdict of the playhouse and his determination to enforce on his audience/reader the contractual responsibility to deliver an individual verdict.[7] This is perfectly mirrored within the plays by (a much maligned and misunderstood topic) his 'humour' theory of characterisation. The key passage is in the Grex, After the Second Sounding, of *Every Man Out of His Humour*, where Asper explains what *he* means by 'humour':

Why, humour (as 'tis *ens* [in essence]) we thus define it
To be a quality of air or water,
And in itself holds these two properties,
Moisture, and fluxure . . .
          . . . and hence we do conclude,
That whatsoe'er hath fluxure, and humidity,
As wanting power to contain itself,
Is humour. So in every human body
The choler, melancholy, phlegm, and blood,
By reason that they flow continually
In some one part, and are not continent,

Receive the name of humours. Now thus far
It may, by metaphor, apply itself
Unto the general disposition:
As when some one peculiar quality
Doth so possess a man, that it doth draw
All his affects [passions], his spirits, and his powers,
In their confluctions, all to run one way,
This may be truly said to be a humour.
But that a rook, in wearing a pied feather,
The cable hat-band, or the three-piled ruff,
A yard of shoetie, or the Switzer's knot
On his French garters, should affect a humour!
O, 'tis more than most ridiculous.
                                        (Appendix, pp. 165–6)

It was for years the practice to gloss this passage with long
disquisitions on Galenic theories of psycho-pathology and of the
relationship between key bodily fluids and temperamental disposition – theories which have left terms like sanguine, choleric
and bilious as part of our vocabulary of human character. Such
terms are implicitly *normative* in as much as they suggest that the
proper function of medicine is to keep such fluids (and character
traits) in a healthy balance. At the same time it was necessary to
explain the last few lines in relation to a late sixteenth-century
vogue for actually affecting 'humorous' excess (particularly sat-
urnine 'melancholy': think of Jaques in *As You Like It*) on the
grounds that it betokened, not disease, but a touch of distinction,
or even genius. In reality, this might amount to nothing more
than wearing exotic fashions or adopting eccentric behaviour merely
to be distinctive, things that naturally attracted ridicule in both
of Jonson's *Humour* plays, as they had done earlier in Chapman's
An Humorous Day's Mirth (performed 1597): Jonson neither coined
the term in dramatic circles nor was alone in making such material part of his comic mode.

But such affectation was not the nub of Jonson's interest in
humour-psychology, nor indeed was Galenic medicine. As the
passage makes clear, he only uses the medical terminology *as a
metaphor*, while Asper ridicules the claims of foppish posing to
be considered the true mark of a 'humour'. A character may truly
be described as 'humorous' only 'when some one peculiar quality
/ Doth so possess a man, that it doth draw / All his affects, his

spirits, and his powers, / In their confluctions, all to run one way' – an obsessive single-mindedness which, while it may be described in pathological terms, is actually a moral or social condition since it marks a resistance to the consideration of others, an assertion of self over the interests of the wider community, which runs contrary to the most fundamental humanist principles.[8] A classic example of this is Morose in *Epicoene*, whose hypersensitivity to all noise (except the sound of his own voice) is not seen as a medical affliction but represents an egotism that alienates him from the community of which he should be a leading member. The relentless logic of Jonsonian comedy is to expose, anatomise and finally 'explode' such a misdirection or hoarding of social energy, with a singular lack of compassion. Dauphine's dismissal of his uncle, Morose – 'Now you may go in and rest, be as private as you will, sir. I'll not trouble you till you trouble me with your funeral, which I care not how soon it come' (V.iv.214–17) – is typical of the heartless symbolic deaths to which such characters are subjected.[9]

Jonson does not discuss this aspect of his characterisation, except obliquely in the Epistle to *Volpone*, in which he seeks to justify the 'rigour' of his 'catastrophe' where (following many ancient precedents) 'the bawds, the servants, the rivals, yea, and the masters are mulcted' (Appendix, p. 178). But in many ways it is only a logical corollary of the theory as propounded by Asper: character itself, in these terms, is an aberration and it is the duty of comedy to treat it as such. This has led to a long-standing complaint that Jonsonian comedy is heartless and two-dimensional (especially by contrast with that of Shakespeare), charges often compounded with supposed psychological defects in Jonson himself. As A. C. Swinburne complained: 'it is difficult to believe that Ben Jonson can have believed, even with some half-sympathetic and half-sardonic belief, in all the leading figures of his invention'.[10] This was a heart-felt cry from a man who admired Jonson yet who felt the compelling force of the character-realism of the late Victorian novel. But the whole point of Jonson's formalist approach to literary matters was precisely to acknowledge that he did not 'believe' (in this naive and sentimental way) in the dramatic worlds he created: the important thing was that, however much they might *resemble* the real world, they were actually separate from it, and the elements that comprised them (in this instance, the characters) lived by different laws of being. The world and the stage were separate theatres, for all that they might mirror one another.

This point of *difference* was precisely what the audience/reader existed to observe, appreciate and police – quite the opposite of the melting suspension of disbelief for which Swinburne yearned. In this we can see that the 'humorous' character is a curious mirror-image of the individuated 'judging spectator' or 'reader extraordinary' to whom all of Jonson's works (and critical pronouncements) are directed.[11] That is, these characters are graphically defined *as individuals*, sites of consciousness at odds with the community around them. Yet where, in the case of the spectator/reader, this is a desirable way of establishing identity, in the case of the 'humorous' characters the opposite is true: the identity to which they so stridently cling, and by which they seek to distinguish themselves from their rivals (since in this context all human intercourse is a matter of competition, even – or especially – that between the sexes), is essentially *false*, a concatenation of empty words, language reduced to the level of noise. This makes the example of Morose particularly apt, though the varieties of cant which are such a hallmark of Jonsonian comedy all point to a similar vacuity: the game of 'vapours' in *Bartholomew Fair* ('which is nonsense: every man to oppose the last man that spoke, whether it concerned him or no', sidenote at IV.iv.30) carries this to its logical conclusion.

Since the emphasis in this whole approach to character is very much on the unsatisfactory individual, Mitis has a fair point when he suggests that 'the author' of *Every Man Out of His Humour* 'might have altered the shape of his argument, and explicated [the humours] better in single scenes'. But Cordatus counters: 'That had been single indeed: why? be they not the same persons in this, as they would have been in those? and is it not an object of more state, to behold the scene full, and relieved with variety of speakers to the end, than to see a vast empty stage, and the actors come in (one by one) as if they were dropped down with a feather, into the eye of the spectators' (Grex after II.iii, lines 292–301). That is, he argues for variety on the grounds that it affords 'relief'. By this he does not mean 'alleviation' or even (I suspect) simply 'an agreeable change of object': he is surely closer to a technical sense in the visual arts, in which objects achieve definition in separate planes by virtue of their relationship to each other.[12] The full effect of such character-drama, that is, depends upon how it is perceived by the audience, who are in a position to compare and contrast the various figures placed before them: their role is not simply one of passive reception, as it might be if the characters were presented 'one by one' (like eye-drops from a quill is the analogy he uses, suggesting a lack of controlling difference and distance), but of active discrimination, prompted by a sense of perspective.

It is commonly observed, of course, that Jonson's best plays are not the 'comical satires', with this Old Comedy-style concentration on individual 'humours' (however 'varied' in their presentation), but the comedies from *Volpone* to *Bartholomew Fair*, where complex action and intrigue sets the agenda, prompted by a New Comedy emphasis on plot construction and the more generalised ridicule of character-types. Yet Jonson never formally renounced his theory of 'humours' as a basis for 'character' in his plays. As I have already suggested, Morose, in what is generally regarded as one of his finest comedies, is a classic exemplum of the notion (despite Dryden's slightly embarrassed claim that it was a portrait of a real person: 'I am assur'd from divers persons, that Ben. Johnson was actually acquainted with such a man'). And late on Jonson himself claimed to see a career-long continuity in his character writing, as we have seen in the Induction to *The Magnetic Lady, or Humours Reconciled*.[13] The fact is that the move to more intricate New Comedy plotting ('quick comedy, refined, / As best critics have designed', as he puts it in the Prologue to *Volpone*) is for him only an intensification and elaboration of the principle of 'variety' that he had espoused from the outset, and does not undercut humour-characterisation as such.

In the comedies therefore (as distinct from the 'comical satires'), the audience is confronted with an orchestration of humours, where (say) the mechanistic plots of *Volpone* and *The Alchemist* throw one vacuous identity into relief against another in a parodic model of the organic community whose values they corporately reject. The same mechanistic plots ensure that the 'utmost bound' of the 'fable' is reached around the end of Act 4 or the beginning of Act 5, in moments of *catastasis*, which perfectly demonstrate that 'the nature of the subject, is esteem'd the best that is largest, till it can increase no more; so it behoves the action in . . . comedy to be let grow, till the necessity ask a conclusion' (*Discoveries*, 2763–7). These are the moments when the 'humorous' characters begin successively to be 'exploded', forced to confront their own vacuity, disempowered, rendered voiceless (or, like Sir Epicure Mammon, ironically left just enough voice to 'go mount a turnip-cart, and preach / The end o'the world, within these two months': *The Alchemist*, V.v.81–2). Conversely, these are exactly the moments that the 'judging spectators' are required to be most clearly aware of themselves as individuals, able to appreciate the particular justice of each 'explosion' as well as the artistry of the orchestration as a whole. So, as a false identity disintegrates on stage (or on the page), a true one is expected to crystallise in registering that fact. This is what the wry paradoxes of the Induction to *Bartholomew Fair* attempt to prepare 'the understanding gentlemen o'the ground' for, while Zeal-of-the-Land Busy's misconceived denunciation of Littlewit's puppet-show in that play is a parody of what is expected. In so confidently exercising his private judgement he reveals the emptiness of his own identity and manhood, and is appropriately silenced by the revelation that the 'actor' he accuses of transgressive cross-dressing is a sexless marionette, an artefact, a function of the 'author's' authority, not the subject of his own.

It has been recognised since at least the time of L. C. Knights's *Drama and Society in the Age of Jonson* (1937) that a link of sorts is likely between the intensely individualist, acquisitive and materialist aspirations of Jonson's 'humorous' characters and the proto-capitalist developments in the society of the day (enclosures, colonial ventures, legally sanctioned monopolies, and so on), especially as they impinged on the court as the centre of law and government and on London as the rapidly expanding centre of trade. The precise nature of that link, and of Jonson's own position within it, remains a moot point. Knights himself emphasised Jonson's espousal of traditional anti-acquisitive attitudes, in defence of quasi-feudal communal values; more recent critics, notably Raymond Williams, Don E. Wayne and Walter Cohen, have argued from different perspectives that Jonson, as the dependant of a court with deeply suspect value-systems and as a self-assertive 'author', was himself either compromised by, or at least a symptom of, the changing attitudes he ostensibly resists.[14]

The very nature of humour-characterisation, and the particular contractual demands it places on audiences, clearly relates to this debate. The Galenic metaphor purports to be timeless, to express something inalienable to the human condition, as we see in the masque *Hymenaei*, where he allegorises the relationship between the Humours and Reason:

Here out of a Microcosm, or Globe, (figuring Man) with a kind
of contentious music, issued forth the first Masque of eight men.
These represented the four Humours, and four Affections
[Passions], all gloriously attired . . .

HYMEN　The four untempered Humours are broke out.
And, with their wild affections, go about
To ravish all religion. If there be
A power, like reason, left in that huge body,
Or little world of man, from whence these came,
Look forth, and with thy bright and numerous flame
Instruct their darkness, make them know, and see,
In wronging these [i.e. those celebrating the marriage],
　　they have rebelled 'gainst thee.

(ll. 109–28)

Yet, as even this allegory suggests, humours are only an issue
at all because their effects are inherently anti-social, because those
driven by them transgress implicit codes of behaviour. And definitions of the anti-social or codes of behaviour are not fixed, but
change as the culture changes. In this respect it cannot be accidental that, as Jonson adopts the tighter New Comedy structures
for the plays that follow the 'comical satires', he focuses with
increasing sharpness on the urban scene. *Volpone*, set in Venice,
is the first of the comedies with a clearly articulated urban land-
scape; *Epicoene* is the first play to build the social geography of
London into its satiric structure, a feature of virtually all his subsequent comedies. It is the pressures and rhythms of urban life
that inform the 'variety' of the 'humorous' characters in these
plays, even when (as pre-eminently in *Bartholomew Fair*) the plays
evoke earlier patterns of existence, marked by Lenten and
carnivalesque alternations. Anne Barton has argued influentially,
in *Ben Jonson, Dramatist*, that Jonson's later plays, in particular,
hark back to the festive forms of Elizabethan romantic comedy
which he had earlier scorned.[15] But it seems to me that this is
still marked by scepticism, a recognition that the new traffic of
the metropolis has obliterated the slower and seemingly eternal
rhythms of the past, however much he and we may regret the
fact. Jonson's humour-characterisation is a corollary of his recur-
rent self-definitions as an author; both are attempts to find new
expressions of identity at a time when all forms of social expression,
exchange and placement were in flux.

Susan Wells has described the city of Jonson's comedies, in terms derived from Bakhtin, as a marketplace in transition from being 'of the people', a gathering place 'governed by an ideology of communal exchange', to a place authorised by bureaucracy and 'official order', though its activity is actually 'governed by no law or custom other than the need to accumulate', a site of pure exchange and profit.[16] We may see, in the history of the period, the survival of older, 'festive' structures in the early modern world (as John Stow did in his *Survey of London*, 1598 and 1603), or point to the breakdown of traditional social ties, as proto-capitalist forms of trade and industry set a more competitive, more nakedly acquisitive style (an issue raised in Parliament in the monopoly and enclosure debates): both social modes existed side-by-side. Jonson's 'humorous' characterisation is a response to this duality, to the fact of change itself, to a lack of confidence in existing explanations of the individual and his/her place in society (and to a dissatisfaction with earlier representations of such individuals in dramatic texts).[17] That Jonson chose to explain what he was doing here in conservative and traditional metaphors should not blind us to the fact that what he was responding to was a new and disorientating way of life. As Don E. Wayne observes, humour-characterisation 'amounts to a rudimentary social psychology, a technical apparatus for diagnosing the changes that affected English society in the Renaissance; and as such it involves an anticipatory awareness of the phenomenon of alienation in both the Marxian and existentialist senses of the term'.[18] In adopting the New Comedy of Plautus and Terence, he was following the best model the classical world (indeed, European history) had to offer, ancient Rome being the closest precedent then known to the increasingly urbanised London. The more fiercely he 'anatomises' and 'explodes' his 'humours' the more eloquently he acknowledges that (for better or worse) this is – a properly artful representation of – the reality of life in a London expanding as rapidly and inexorably as his own paunch.

As I have already suggested, these tensions, which manifest themselves in his plays in the contradiction between the painstaking accumulation of detail in the creation of his characters and the sudden savagery with which he obliterates it, are (he hopes) inversely reflected in the experience of the audience/reader, whose 'knowledge' should crystallise, judgement be delivered, and individuated manhood be confirmed as Jonson's artistic strategy

declares itself complete.[19] There is a savage parody of this reading process in the tragedy *Sejanus*, which maintains a form of
'humorous' characterisation in the depiction of political processes
and exchange of power, analogous to the depiction of social and
economic intercourse in the comedies. Tiberius's 'character' of
Sejanus is read, tantalisingly and circuitously, to the Senate. But
in place of the considered judgement for which the absent Tiberius
craftily calls, the 'character' is condemned to a peremptory be-
heading, which instantly turns into total dismemberment at the
hands of 'the rude multitude'. The frenzied violence is described
in graphic detail, to the point where 'Sejanus' is atomised and
loses all identity: 'Each little dust covers a little part / So lies he
nowhere, and yet often buried' (V.vii.834–5).[20] Jonson himself
analogised the fate of Sejanus at the hands of the mob to the
treatment the play received at its first performance: 'It is a poem
that . . . suffered no less violence from our people here, than the
subject of it did from the rage of the people of Rome' (Dedication to Aubigny, Appendix, p. 192). He looked to Aubigny for a
self-possessed, 'knowledgeable' reading both of the 'characters'
in the plays and of the play itself, in contradistinction to the un-
disciplined 'rage of the people' in whatever context. The non-
dramatic verse, for which an individual readership is assured
(though, with print, it is an individuality replicated anonymously
many times), adopts a different strategy, but aimed at exactly the
same type of hypothetical reader, as we see in the dedication of
both *Catiline* and the *Epigrams* to the same man, the Earl of
Pembroke.

PURE AND NEAT LANGUAGE: NON-DRAMATIC VERSE

Jonson has less to say about the *formal elements* (and so 'laws') of
non-dramatic verse than he does about plays, though here too
his practice repeatedly demonstrates an awareness of classical
precedent and a willingness to adapt them to contemporary needs.
Among the most obvious examples are his use of Martial as a
primary model for the *Epigrams* and of Catullus as the basis for
the 'Celia' poems in *The Forest*, and (as late as 1629) the composition of the first true Pindaric Ode in English (the Cary/Morison
Ode, *Und* LXX).[21] But most of his comments on such matters are
collected together in *Discoveries*, where they present themselves

as considered judgements in the humanist tradition rather than (as with so many comments about plays and masques) as self-promotions in the marketplace. As I have argued, however, such appearances are deceptive. The parts of *Discoveries* which offer a commentary on poetry (and, indeed, those parts of the *Conversations with Drummond* which comment on poets and versification) are most intelligible as reflections on Jonson's own career as a writer of such verse rather than as Olympian conclusions. They spell out an agenda for that career at the same time as they attempt to cultivate a sympathetic readership. Yet in tracing the parallels between the criticism and the practice – in noting, for example, the rationale of a preference for plain style, or his predilection for the heroic couplet – we must beware of a complacent circularity, in which the example of the verse confirms the theory of the commentary, which in turn locates Jonson in a clearly-defined tradition, which finally claims both the verse and the author for its own, shielding it from other discourses.

Jonson and his writing can readily be located in a tradition of humanist thought; but, as we have observed, this is never entirely a comfortable location for him. His humanism is always one under pressure: not at ease with the political or economic structures it confronts, or indeed with his own anomalous status as a professional writer within those structures. We must suspect that Jonson tacitly admitted this to himself when he excised Lorenzo Jr's paean of praise for the 'true poet' ('than which reverend name / Nothing can more adorn humanity') from the revised text of *Every Man In His Humour* (see Appendix, p. 171). The speech is admittedly something of a distraction at that point in the text, and deserved to be cut on those grounds; but its naive humanistic enthusiasm, its bland indifference to the embattled realities of a literary life (so apparent in the texture of Jonson's most mature work), may well have seemed positively embarrassing to Jonson by the time he came to revise the text, and he omitted it along with several other idealistic references to poets and poetry.[22] This embattlement manifests itself elsewhere in those features of awkwardness, discontinuity and evasion highlighted both by Don Wayne in his study of the semiotics of Penshurst and by Stanley Fish in his reader-response analysis of the non-dramatic verse.[23] Similar signs of tension have been identified, in particular, in Jonson's panegyric verse and the questions it raises about his ambivalent relationship with the aristocracy, by, among others, Robert C. Evans and William E. Cain.[24] His verse is never a comfortable retreat from reality, however much at times it may labour to give the impression of being so: the Penshurst idyll is always to an extent *known* to be an illusion (a literary construct), and never a secure one. In the critical theory that parallels it, Jonson implicitly admits as much even as he strives to deny it.

A central preoccupation in Jonson's discussion of poetry is the attempt to clarify the poet's ideal relationship with his reader (and so, in a sense, his own authorial identity), focusing on the nature of language itself as a medium of communication: 'Language most shows a man: speak, that I may see thee. It springs out of the most retired and inmost parts of us, and is the image of the parent of it, the mind' (*Discoveries*, 2049–51). This is both proverbial and, here, suggested by Vives, but it is a conventional wisdom that Jonson repeatedly deploys in his assertions about poetic language. As the 'humours' of his dramatic characters are registered in the affectations and abuses of the words they use, and equally in their capacity for misconstruing or misvaluing the words of others, Jonson looks in his own poetry, and in that of his contemporaries, for the opposite: a clear, honest use of language, based on mutual respect between writer and reader.

This neither means, however, that he feels assured of finding such mutual respect, nor that he sees language as a transparent or uncomplicated medium, with an unproblematic relationship between words and what they convey or represent. There is a very telling double-think on this in Drummond, under the section headed 'His opinion of verses': 'That verses stood by sense without either colours or accent; which yet other times he denied' (333–4) – as if at times Jonson wanted to believe that the 'sense' of a poem could be divorced from the linguistic structure in which it was embedded, but at other times he saw the impossibility of this. On the whole, he recognises that words are artefacts just like the poems into which they may be constructed, and as such, every bit as liable to frivolous or spiteful misuse by authors and misunderstanding or misconstruction by readers. Indeed (the central point around which he constantly revolves, though he never confronts it openly) language itself may be inherently unreliable and unpredictable: there is only the custom of the tribe, its consensual usage, to prevent its being so. And how far can you trust those? That being so, all his preferences are for forms of poetic language that minimise such slippage. He claims 'authority' for

many of these from Quintilian, whom he particularly pressed on
Drummond: 'He recommended to my reading Quintilian (who,
he said, would tell me all the faults of my verses as if he had
lived with me)' and 'that Quintilian's 6, 7, 8 books were not only
to be read, but altogether digested' (9–10, 104–6). It is from the
last of these that Jonson himself borrows in this passage in *Discoveries*: 'But talking and eloquence are not the same: to speak,
and to speak well, are two things. A fool may talk, but a wise
man speaks, and out of the observation, knowledge, and use of
things. Many writers perplex their readers and hearers with mere
nonsense. Their writings need sunshine. Pure and neat language
I love, yet plain and customary' (1882–8).

A subsequent passage which observes that 'Metaphors far-fet
hinder to be understood; and affected, lose their grace' (1923–4)
derives in fact from Vives, but he in turn was working over
Quintilian. 'Metaphor' (Greek) is a form of 'translation' (Latin):
both are forms of 'carrying over'. Jonson is concerned first that
the reader should be able to perceive *how* something is 'carried
over' and applied to something else: if the link is too far-fetched
it will hinder communication, not help it. Hence the judgement
that 'Donne himself, for not being understood, would perish'
(*Drummond*, 158). By the same token, the 'carrying over' must
serve a purpose, be functional and not merely 'affected', or it will
lose its expressive power, however inventive. Drummond found
this the most impressive feature of Jonson's own writing: 'His
inventions are smooth and easy; but above all he excelleth in a
translation' (615–16). So Jonson's instincts (like Bacon's) are for
matter over words, sense over eloquence and, other things being
equal, brevity over expansiveness: 'Of the two (if either were to
be wished) I would rather have a plain downright wisdom than
a foolish and affected eloquence. For what is so furious and Bedlam-
like as a vain sound of chosen and excellent words, without any
subject of sentence or science mixed?' (*Discoveries*, 347–51).[25] Or
again: 'For too much talking is ever the indice of a fool' (371–2).
In as much as prolixity derives from an attempt to impress by
being new for its own sake, that too is misguided. Novelty or
surprise, as ends in themselves, are not to be encouraged in any
area of writing, since they generate the wrong kind of interest,
idle curiosity rather than understanding: 'Nothing doth more invite a greedy reader than an unlooked-for subject' (300–1).

In all such judgements, however, Jonson implicitly acknowledges the brinkmanship of his own poetic practice, the danger of loss of control, and so of authority itself. We may wonder, in this context, whether Jonson's ultimate failure to write poems on the scale of *The Faerie Queene* or *Paradise Lost* was linked to these concerns over brevity and the avoidance of prolixity. The *Conversations with Drummond* open with 'That he had an intention to perfect an epic poem, entitled *Heroologia*, of the worthies of his country roused by fame, and was to dedicate it to his country' (*Drummond*, 1–3). But this is the first and last we ever hear of it; it is not mentioned in 'An Execration upon Vulcan' as being lost in the 1623 fire, and Digby apparently found nothing of it after Jonson's death. However we explain this absence, we should bear it in mind in relation to what he had to say about Spenser (which I shall address later), whose *Faerie Queene* in particular made him an intimidating precedent for Jonson.[26]

Similar considerations of the dangers of linguistic slippage and prolixity govern his views on verse-form, metre and style. His personal preference for rhyming iambic pentameter couplets (but only sparingly end-stopped) would be self-evident from a casual reading of his verse, even if he had not told Drummond: 'It [his intended epic *Heroologia*] is all in couplets, for he detesteth all other rhymes' (3). But he also: 'Said he had written a discourse of poesy both against Campion and Daniel, especially this last, where he proves couplets to be the bravest sort of verses, especially when they are broken like hexameters; and that cross-rhymes and stanzas – because the purpose would lead him beyond eight lines to conclude – were all forced' (3–8). This non-extant 'discourse' may have been part of the lost preface to his translation of Horace's *Art of Poetry*, and was presumably a reply to both Campion's *Observations in the Art of English Poesy* (1602), which attacked the 'childish titillation' of rhyme and Daniel's *A Defence of Rhyme* (1603), which approved of rhyme in principle, but found 'those continual cadences of couplets used in long and continued poems . . . very tiresome and unpleasing'. Jonson's point to Drummond about couplets being 'the bravest sort of verses, especially when they are broken like hexameters' (that is, the stop not coinciding with the end of the line and hence the rhyme) is presumably a truncated version of his argument for a varied and flexible iambic pentameter couplet, where the complex counterpointing of rhythm, rhyme and grammatic structure might belie the charge of being 'tiresome and unpleasing' (at least to an attentive reader).

On the other hand, Jonson himself found Drayton's use of *hex-ameter* couplets in the *Poly-Olbion*) unacceptable: 'His long verses pleased him not' (*Drummond*, 19–20). We are not told exactly why, but we may infer that it was precisely because they lacked the flexibility and variety that he himself brought to pentameter by breaking it 'like hexameters'. By the same token, his rejection of 'cross-rhymes' (i.e. rhymes not linked in couplets) and 'stanzas' (poems divided into groupings of lines greater than couplets) specifically explains his reservations about the unique verse form Spenser devised for *The Faerie Queene*, having nine lines intricately cross-rhymed: 'Spenser's stanzas pleased him not' (*Drummond*, 15). In both of these instances the underlying issue seems to be (as we saw earlier in relation to larger literary structures) Jonson's concern for the reader's concentration or attention-span: he wanted the reader to be actively engaged but not to be overwhelmed with intricate details; he wanted him to be able to grasp the whole of the structure in a single moment of concentration, so as to be able to appreciate the relationship of the parts to the whole. In the case of *Poly-Olbion* the inference seems to be that the hexameters were too slack to engage real attention, while the 300–500-line 'Songs' into which the poem is sub-divided may have seemed over-expansive, barely comprehensible as a single unit. In all of this, while we may respect a professional's command of language as the tool of his trade, the anxiety that underlies his position is all too apparent. Can it ever be profitable for an author to at-tempt to second-guess or police his readers' response in this way? It is rather like trying to contain water in a sieve. In the Epistle to *Volpone* and the Induction to *Bartholomew Fair* an acknowledge-ment of the formal properties of plays as artefacts (representational artefacts, perhaps, but clearly differentiable from the surround-ing 'reality') is sufficient to allow Jonson to draw lines, beyond which he can 'trust' his audience (or, at least, cease to worry about them). There is no such sticking-point in his criticism of the non-dramatic verse, possibly because its fictions are so much more intimate, so much closer to the real sites of identity and subjec-tivity. As Michael McCanles observes, 'Jonson's poetry is the most clearly autobiographical of his productions, because in it Jonson literally wrote his own life, in the sense of constructing a life's career out of verbal dialogue with himself [and] with those around him.'[27]

In the case of *The Faerie Queene* Jonson seems to have judged that the over-elaboration of the versification simply hindered understanding; his comments to Drummond rapidly expand to include the whole scope of the poem and its allegorical complexities, as if to suggest that he was antipathetic to the whole mode of what Spenser himself called a 'dark conceit', of which the versification may have seemed merely the first symptom: 'Spenser's stanzas pleased him not, nor his matter, the meaning of which allegory he had delivered in papers to Sir Walter Raleigh' (*Drummond*, 15–16), glossing later that 'by the Blating Beast the Puritans were understood; by the false Duessa, the Queen of Scots' (143–4). Part of this seems to contradict what he says in *Discoveries*, where he suggests that 'Spenser, in affecting the ancients, writ no language; *yet I would have him read for his matter*' (1823–5, my emphasis).[28] And the latter would seem to square with his contention that 'for a heroic poem . . . there was no such ground as King Arthur's fiction' (*Drummond*, 114–15), which does indeed provide the framework for *The Faerie Queene*. Unless he changed his mind, the apparent discrepancy must hang on the looseness of the term 'matter', especially in relation to an allegory as complex as *The Faerie Queene*. What seems to be beyond doubt is that, irrespective of the poem's 'matter', he objected to its 'manner', to the versification, use of archaic language and over-involved allegory, all of which in their different ways 'hinder to be understood'. Nevertheless, it is clear, even from Riddell and Stewart's preliminary report of the marginalia in Jonson's copy of Spenser, that he was extremely *attentive* to Spenser as a predecessor (see above, p. 64). It may well be that the vagaries of what happened to get into the public domain – his talking with Drummond was not meant for print, while *Discoveries* is patchy and incomplete – has done less than justice to his most considered views, which may moreover have changed as his own career developed.

What he has to say about Spenser's heroic poetry does, however, coincide substantially with what he has to say about those of his contemporaries whom later generations would loosely dub as 'metaphysicals'. To Jonson, they seem to lose sight of the *point* of writing, in contorting their words to demonstrate their wit. He always seems to have respected Spenser's high seriousness even when he did not approve of the poetry it produced; that cannot be said of the 'metaphysicals', even Donne. 'But now nothing is good that is natural; right and natural language seems to have least of the wit in it; that which is writhed and tortured is counted

the more exquisite. . . . Nothing is fashionable till it be deformed;
and this is to write like a gentleman' (*Discoveries*, 585–7, 591–2).
The sarcastic comment at the end of this passage goes to the heart
of the matter. This was a poetry of the coterie, for circulation in
manuscript among (mainly) young men probably on the fringes
of court, probably products of the universities and the Inns of
Court, for whom writing was at one level a way of establishing
their élite social status and demonstrating their 'natural' superiority to the lower orders. They eschewed print as demeaningly
public and contaminated by associations with labour, preferring
a private rivalry in which they could display their learning and
verbal skills like peacocks, without having to consider the common reader. This led to some dubious practices: 'Donne said to
him he wrote that epitaph on Prince Henry, "Look to me, faith",
to match Sir Ed[ward] Herbert in obscureness' (*Drummond*, 93–4)
and 'Donne's *Anniversary* was profane and full of blasphemies.
That he told Mr Donne, if it had been written of the Virgin Mary
it had been something; to which he answered that he described
the idea of a woman, and not as she was' (325). In both instances
(in Jonson's view) the concentration on ingenuity and verbal pyro-
technics had led to a lack of perspective and proportion, the all-
important 'matter' getting lost in wilful obscurity or (even worse)
blasphemously over-blown imagery.

These vices are paralleled by the example of those who perversely affect irregular styles: 'Others, that in composition are
nothing but what is rough and broken. . . . And if it would come
gently, they trouble it of purpose. They would not have it run
without rubs [rough patches on a bowling green], as if that style
were more strong and manly that struck the ear with a kind of
uneven[n]ess. These men err not by chance, but knowingly and
willingly' (*Discoveries*, 707–13). Here again, Donne would seem
to be one of the culprits he had in mind: 'Donne, for not keeping
of accent, deserved hanging' (*Drummond*, 36). Jonson was, however, almost right that 'Donne, for not being understood, would
perish', precisely because his own programme for poetic language
and practice (what Foucault called 'the neoclassical paradigm')
prevailed from the middle of the seventeenth century to the end
of the eighteenth, creating a climate of critical opinion in which
Donne's verse looked increasingly perverse and unnatural. Dr
Johnson's 'Life of Cowley', with its scathing denunciation of 'the
metaphysical school of poetry', is the ultimate vindication of his
namesake's reservations.

The comicall Satyre of

EVERY MAN

OVT OF HIS
HVMOR.

As it was firſt compoſed by the Author B. I.

Containing more then hath been publikely
ſpoken or acted.

With the ſeuerall Character of euery perſon.

Non aliena meo preſſi pede | ⸭ ſi propiùs ſtes
Te capient magis | ⸭ & decies repetita placebunt.

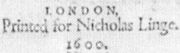

LONDON,
Printed for Nicholas Linge.
1600.

1. *Every Man Out of His Humour,* title-page of the 1600 Quarto

SEIANVS.

San.I,and get more. Lat.More Office, and more Titles.   Dio, *ibid.*
Pom.I will not loose the part,I hope to ſhare
In theſe his Fortunes, for my *Patrimony*.
Lat.See how *Arruntius* ſits,and *Lepidus*.
Tri.Let 'hem alone, they will be markt anone.
Sen.Be doe,with others . Sen.So will I. Sen.And I.
Men grow not in the State,but as they are planted
Warme in his fauors. Cot.Noble *Seianus*.
Hat.Honor'd *Seianus*. Lat.Worthy and great *Seianus*.
Arr.Gods !how the Spunges open,and take in !
And ſhut againe ! Looke,looke 'Is not he bleſt
That gets a ſeate in eye-reach of him ? more,
That comes in eare, or tongue-reach ? O but moſt,
Can claw his ſubtle elbow,'or with a buzze
Flieblow his eares. Pratt,Proclaime the *Senates* peace;
And giue laſt ſummons by the Edict.Prae.Silence.
In name of Caesar,and the Senate.Silence.

[a]MEMMIVS REGVLVS. and. FVLCINIVS.   [a] *Vid.Briſ.*
TRIO. consvl's. these. present. kalendes. of. ivne. vvith.   ſonum : *de*
the . first . light . shall . hold . a. senate . in . the . temple.   *formul.*
of. [b]APOLLO palatine . all . that . are . fathers . and.   [b] Lipſium
are . registred . fathers . that . have . right . of . entring.   Sat.Menp.
the . senate . vve. vvarne. or. commavnd.yov. be. frequent-   [b] Palatinus,
ly. present. take. knovvledge. the. bvsinesse. is . the . com-   *à monte*
mon. vvealthes. vvhosoever.is. absent. his. fine. or. mvlct.   Palatino,
vvill. be.taken .his. excvse. vvill. not. be.taken.   *dillus.*

Tri.Note,who are abſent,and record their names.   [c] *Solemnis*
Reg.[c]Fathers Conscript. may vvhat i am to vtter,   *praefatio*
Tvrne good and happy for the common vvealth.   *Conſilium*
And thou Apollo,in whoſe holy Houſe   *in relatio-*
We here are met,Inſpire vs all,with truth,   *nibus.*
And liberty of Cenſure to our thought.   Dio. *pag.*
The Maieſtie of great *Tiberius Cæſar*   *718.*
Propounds to this graue *Senate*,the beſtowing
Vpon the man he loues,honour'd *Seianus*,
The [d] *tribuniciall* dignity.and powers   [d] *Vid.* Suet.
Here are his Letters,ſigned with his ſignet: Tib.*cap.*65
                    M   What

---

2. *Sejanus*, 1605: Quarto Sig M1 recto.
    Jonson uses the resources of typography and enforces the authority
    of his own sources alongside Tiberius's edict

3. *The Masque of Queens*: dedication of the holograph copy to Queen Anne

TO THE MOST NOBLE

AND MOST ÆQVALL
SISTERS

THE TWO FAMOVS VNIVERSITIES,

FOR THEIR LOVE
AND
ACCEPTANCE

SHEW'N TO HIS POEME
IN THE PRESENTATION:

BEN: IONSON

THE GRATEFVLL ACKNOWLEDGER
DEDICATES
BOTH IT, AND HIMSELFE,

There followes an *Epistle*, if
you dare venture on
the length.

¶

4. *Volpone,* 1607: Quarto: The Dedication

These are more, however, than vagaries of changing taste. At the heart of Jonson's objections to Donne and his confederates is a resistance to the idea of the playfulness of language, to the idea of language as an entertaining puzzle (he told Drummond 'He scorned anagrams', 375), where the reader engages to be baffled, outraged, amused, amazed and intrigued by the poet's wit, a collaborator in the bizarre and the outlandish. Such notions are, for Jonson, as disturbing as they are dangerous. He did not, however, expect merely a passive role of his own 'understanding' readers, charging them to 'judge only out of knowledge. That is the trying faculty' ('To the Reader in Ordinary', *Catiline*, Appendix, p. 184). We have already seen what he has to say about many categories of *mis*-reading, and his promotion of D'Aubigny, Pembroke, Lady Bedford and the King as embodiments of the ideal reader.[29] An observation on the art of epigrams, a form which preoccupied much of his early verse writing, gives us a more specific sense of what he was looking for: 'A great many epigrams were ill because they expressed in the end what should have been understood by what was said: as that of Sir John Davies' (*Drummond*, 323–4).[30] That is, the reader was not simply to be a passive receptor, admiring or drinking in what the poet 'expressed'; he or she was expected to *complete* the process of meaning, to make sense of what was less than explicit, to respond to nuances, to discriminate between possibilities, and so to 'understand'. To that extent the active participation of the reader is an essential element of communication, however dangerously indeterminate (remember the Epistle to *Volpone*) that makes the whole process.[31]

Which is why so much of his theory is aimed at circumscribing that indeterminacy. Though often disappointed, he never entirely despairs of finding the 'rare friends' that 'rare poems ask' ('To Lucy, Countess of Bedford, With Mr Donne's Satires', *Ep* XCIV). This poem ever so obliquely invites Lucy Harington to compare the experience of reading itself, with that of reading Donne's *Satires*, for which she has asked: the two will be different, perhaps qualitatively different, though he leaves to be 'understood' what he does not 'express'. What he looks for is a much more constrained and directed role than the one Donne requires, much less imaginative and speculative, the terms of it much more predetermined by the author's own linguistic and epistemological co-ordinates: in a word, less creative, if arguably more discriminating.[32] Here again, Jonson's prime consideration is his own authority over the text he writes. He translates his own determination to retain such authority into a series of strictures on both Donne's abuse of his own authority and his frivolous surrendering of it.

This seems to contradict his very public respect for Donne, expressed for example in Epigrams XXIII and XCVI. However, Jonson is nothing if not measured in his criticism, and even where he finds something to admire, that will not prevent him voicing less complimentary views of other parts of the subject. So it is with Donne: 'He esteemeth John Donne the first poet in the world in some things. His verses of the lost chain he hath by heart, and that passage of 'The Calm', that dust and feathers do not stir, all was so quiet' (*Drummond*, 86–8). At the same time, however, he affirmed 'Donne to have written all his best pieces ere he was twenty-five years old' (99), which would certainly have excluded the *Anniversaries* and the poem on Prince Henry. Donne is a very fine poet in some things, especially his early work:

> Whose every work of thy most early wit
>   Came forth example and remains so yet
>   (*Ep* XXIII)

but he is not a role-model Jonson can recommend unequivocally, because – at his most mannered – his intellectual ingenuity, and verbal and metrical waywardness, are simply too exclusive, too much the product of a clique writing for itself and its own admiration, to engage the reader in a process of mutual discriminations (the basis of 'knowledge' and 'understanding') as Jonson himself would seek to do. At its worst Donne's playfulness is blind to the moral implications of what it can degenerate into – 'profanity' and 'blasphemies' – which for Jonson is a logical corollary of abandoning what is 'natural'. Manner and matter are so closely associated in Jonson's mind that faults of style, anything that wanders too far from 'pure and neat language . . . plain and customary', is *prima facie* evidence of serious flaws in the poet's integrity as a whole. One senses a quiet satisfaction in Jonson telling Drummond of Donne's own belated recognition of this in connection with what promises to have been one of his most outrageously witty compositions:

The conceit of Donne's 'Transformation' or μετεμψυχοσιζ was that he sought the soul of that apple which Eva pulled, and thereafter made it the soul of a bitch, then of a she-wolf, and

so of a woman. His general purpose was to have brought in all
the bodies of the heretics from the soul of Cain, and at last left
it in the body of Calvin. Of this he never wrote but one sheet,
and now, since he was made doctor [of Divinity] repenteth highly,
and seeketh to destroy all his poems. (97–103)

Nevertheless, Jonson had some respect for the capacity of such
poets at least to think for themselves and not be bound by conventions, whereas 'He cursed Petrarch for redacting verses to
sonnets, which he said were like that tyrant's bed, where some
who were too short were racked, others too long cut short' (60–3).[33]
Petrarch, in fact, never *prescribed* the sonnet-form as a model for
later poets, but it had been adopted as almost the hallmark poetic
form of the humanist courtier and his imitators. For Jonson it
was as much an infringement of the poet's freedom as a 'maker'
to be constrained by an over-rigid verse form as it was to be
bound by other artificial 'laws': a subject must find its proper
length, and the poet demonstrate his judgement in recognising
it. By the same token, for all the other deficiencies of the 'metaphysicals', as Dr Johnson observed, 'To write on their plan, it
was at least necessary to read and think.'[34] It was also necessary
for *their readers* to think in order to elicit any sense from what
they wrote, albeit not to think in the manner, and within the
parameters, that Jonson himself would prescribe. Both of these
conditions were missing in another category of poetry with which
he found fault:

> Others there are that have no composition at all, but a kind of
> tuning and rhyming fall in what they write. It runs and slides
> and only makes a sound. Women's poets they are called, as
> you have women's tailors.
>
> > They write a verse as smooth, as soft, as cream,
> > In which there is not torrent, nor scarce stream.
>
> You may sound these wits, and find the depth of them, with
> your middle finger. They are cream-bowl- or but puddle-deep.
> (*Discoveries*, 722–30)

It is less immediately obvious whom Jonson has in mind here,
though Samuel Daniel ('a good honest man, had no children: but
no poet', *Drummond*, 17) is a possibility. The chief indictments,

though, are clearly aimlessness and intellectual shallowness, producing a verse of musical charm but no substance.

DECORUM: WRITERS AND READERS

The emphasis in so much of this is negative (what Jonson does not like, cannot approve) that it is only right to balance it with some of his spontaneous enthusiasms, though he is less explicit than we might have liked about precisely what it is he finds so attractive: 'Sir Edward Wotton's verses of a happy life he hath by heart, and a piece of Chapman's translation of the thirteen of the *Iliads*, which he thinketh well done' (123–5); 'He hath by heart some verses of Spenser's *Calendar*, about wine, between Colin and Percy' [from the October Eclogue of *The Shepheardes Calendar*, 104–8, which praises wine as an inspirer of poetry] (128–9); 'Southwell was hanged; yet so he had written that piece of his "The burning babe", he would have been content to destroy many of his' (180–2). It is also clear, however, that none of his criticism is wilfully or capriciously negative: where Jonson finds fault with his contemporaries he does so with a consistent view of the qualities that poetry *ought* to have, and most particularly of the relationship that ought to pertain between poet and reader. What he says about letter-writing, although in many ways a truism, is also a key to this: 'respect to discern what fits yourself, him to whom you write, and that which you handle, which is a quality fit to conclude the rest, because it doth include all' (*Discoveries*, 2305–8). That is, find a proper relationship between yourself as writer and those you expect to read you, and find an equally proper relationship between your subject-matter and the words with which you will express it (including all the grammatical, rhetorical, rhythmic and musical skills with which you will employ those words). This is the essence of poetic *decorum*: that which is fitting. No more than any other critical 'law' does this amount to an immutable list of prescribed rules: everything is determined by context. We noted earlier (see p. 8) Jonson's insistent reiteration to Drummond of his view that Sidney, Lucan and Guarini had all been at fault in making shepherds, and others of the lower orders, speak as well as themselves.

Absolute verisimilitude may not be called for – Jonson never argues in favour of realism simply for its own sake – but it cannot be true to the given situation that aristocrats and shepherds should speak alike (a flaw in the decorum of manner/matter relations), while if everyone speaks as well as the best people speak, readers will not be able to discriminate between them socially or intellectually (a flaw in the decorum of writer/reader relations, in as much as the writer is duty bound to offer, and the reader to expect, a text within which the principle of discrimination is respected, since that is the basis of the communication between them). Jonson is convinced that the poet is more likely to get this right by patient application than by casual inspiration: 'he wrote all his first in prose, for so his master Camden had learned him' (*Drummond*, 321–2); 'things wrote with labour deserve so to be read, and will last their age' (*Discoveries*, 2488–9). And what he says of composing sentences has a wider application to writing as a whole, not least because in the simile he uses he lays himself open to the taunts which dogged him all his life about the manual labour (bricklaying) to which he had been apprenticed in his early life: 'The congruent and harmonious fitting of parts in a sentence hath almost the fastening and force of knitting and connection; as in stones well-squared, which will rise strong a great way without mortar' (1995–8). Writing poetry *is* a craft, bringing the parts *decorously* together a matter of skilled labour, though never in the demeaning sense of hack-work.

When all this is said, however, we are left with a vacuum of sorts at the heart of this vigorous and coherent critical energy. His constant insistence that there *is* such a thing as 'right and natural language', that it is *inherently* 'manly', that there *are* self-evident laws of decorum, and that there *is* a readily discernible relationship between an author, his subject-matter, his style and his (understanding) reader: in the end, insistence is all it can be, a species of wish-fulfilment, which he defends (as do the legacy-hunters in *Volpone* and the seekers of alchemical power in *The Alchemist*) in the face of all evidence to the contrary, in the face of reason itself. Curiously, therefore, it is when Jonson is at his most Olympian (or, with Drummond, unbuttoned) that his criticism is most vulnerable to the charge of fantasising conditions of reading and writing that were pre-Babel, even pre-lapsarian. That is, they censor out the tensions inherent in all social discourse, and especially those in Jacobean England, where social and economic conditions were in such flux, and the status of spoken, written and printed words was in such a process of transition.

The protestations of objective, verifiable and *natural* criteria by which acceptable poetry may be distinguished from non-acceptable boil down, in the end (like the prefatory matter of the masques and plays), to a re-statement of the agenda for his own verse, and a determination to fashion a readership for it. Its refusal, however, to accept so limited a role for itself, to insist upon its universal application, is a mark, not of assurance, but of embattled – and, at times, thin-skinned – insecurity: qualities never too far below the surface of the poetry itself.

Jonson tends to be at his least insecure, because least dogmatic, in relation to these issues when he addresses them within fictional frameworks, usually within dramatic structures, where the nature of dialogue, or the dynamics of plot and action, ironise or disperse the authorial voice. So, for example, the question of poetry as a laboured craft is one that he addresses in the unperformed 1624 masque *Neptune's Triumph for the Return of Albion*, which opens with a witty dialogue between the 'Poet' and a 'Master-Cook'. The latter attempts to prove that 'a good poet differs nothing at all from a Master-Cook. Either's art is a wisdom of the mind' (Appendix, p. 202). The nub of his argument is that the cook has to be a skilled artificer:

> He designs, he draws,
> He paints, he carves, he builds, he fortifies,
> Makes citadels of curious fowl and fish;
> Some he dry-ditches, some moats round with broths;
> Mounts marrow-bones; cuts fifty-angled custards
> (p. 203)

who knows the 'influence of the stars, upon his meats' (99), and – crucially – knows what his patrons want and expect, and is prepared to provide it. 'But, what if they expect more than they understand?' asks the idealistic Poet. 'That's all one, Mr Poet' replies his 'brother', 'You are bound to satisfy them' (p. 202). Don K. Hedrick suggests that the Cook 'argues successfully' and that: 'With self-irony Jonson has accepted his role as cook to the cannibals [the meat-devouring audience] rather than as the sort of critic–reformer we saw earlier' [i.e., earlier in his career: the argument is that the later Jonson settles for the role of entertainer of his patrons, rather than would-be reformer].[35] This surely makes the mistake of identifying Jonson with his 'Poet' and entirely underplays the degree of 'self-irony'. The best the Cook-as-poet can manage to produce is a non-speaking 'olla podrida' (stew) of an anti-masque which is only a minor (if enjoyable) element in the achievement of the masque as a whole. In the figure of the Cook (his own creation) Jonson acknowledges the element of hired manual labour in his work, and the extent to which he is constrained to satisfy the expectations of his patrons.

But in placing the Cook within the wider 'mysteries' of the masque (which he neither appreciates nor understands) Jonson also distances himself from him, reserving to his own authoritative role as poet an imaginative independence which also implies a lack of final subservience to his audiences. (That, at least, is *my* understanding of this passage: the fact that Mr Hedrick disagrees is a measure of how right Jonson was to worry about leaving too much to a reader's discretion.) These distinctions surfaced again in his bitter quarrel with Inigo Jones, his collaborator on the masques, whom he accuses of believing that 'painting and carpentry are the soul of the masque' in this 'money-get, mechanic age' ('An Expostulation with Inigo Jones', Appendix, p. 216). It is not simply that Jones, as the scenic designer, is a manual craftsman of sorts; that, in itself, is not demeaning. It is the suggestion that these plastic arts are the 'soul' of the masque that incenses him, implying that it is right to surrender uncritically to the audience's taste and expectation for visual finery and trickery. Jonson reserves to himself as poet the authorial 'invention', which must of course attend to his patrons' requirements, but is not constrained within them and may even interrogate them.

KNOWLEDGE

The aim of the Horatian poet's 'invention' is 'To mix profit with [the reader's] pleasure' (Prologue to *Volpone*). More precisely, for Jonson the nature of 'profit' is the promotion of 'knowledge', while the 'pleasure' of the poetry (of whatever sort) inheres in its verbal and narrative felicities, those features of the text with which the attentive reader may enjoyably engage. 'Knowledge' in this context is not an accumulation of information; it is the faculty of discrimination itself, 'the trying faculty' as he calls it in 'To the Reader in Ordinary' prefacing *Catiline*, where it distinguishes men from lesser beings. As he observes in the *Discoveries*, drawing on

Seneca, 'Knowledge is the action of the soul, and is perfect without the senses, as having the seeds of all science and virtue in itself; but not without the service of the senses; by those organs the soul works: she is a perpetual agent, prompt and subtle, but often flexible and erring, entangling herself like a silkwork; but her reason is a weapon with two edges, and cuts through' (*Discoveries*, 823–9). Knowledge, informed by reason, is the bedrock of Jonsonian discrimination; those who fail to apply it are less than human. The pleasure of poetry works upon the senses in order to service knowledge. 'I know no disease of the soul but ignorance [the antithesis of knowledge]: not of the arts and sciences, but of itself' (814–15): and that is a disease to which poetry may minister, if it properly engages the reader. The 'laws' of poetry are only valid in as much as, and to the extent that, they help promote this delicate, reciprocal relationship with its patient, the reader.

Put this way, with all the high seriousness of humanist theory, this must sound both portentous and arcane. But we can find parallels to the mechanics of the relationship between poet and reader here proposed in modern reception and reader-response theories. Rather than pursue this, however, we may allow Jonson to make what he is saying more intelligible in his own words, if we observe that the song 'Come, my Celia, let us prove' (*Volpone*, III.vii.165–82, reprinted with amendments as *For* V, 'Song. To Celia') comically *enacts* the essential principles which he propounds. It is, in the first place, an avowed seduction poem, language deployed as richly and complexly as possible to dull the mind and morals of the lady to whom it is addressed while simultaneously arousing her senses. In Jonson's terms, *all* poems are a seductive mix of ideas and emotive language (to which a narrative superstructure may or may not be added) and our function as readers is not simply to succumb to this mix but to resist it critically. As Volpone performs the song in the play he is, of course, deaf and blind to any resistance Celia may actually be mounting, but the principle is ironically enforced by the presence of the concealed Bonario, a very different 'reader', totally impervious to the charms of the song.

These dramatic ironies in turn implicate a further 'reader', the audience itself (who, of course, substitute for both Celia and Bonario when they confront the song on the printed page). To reformulate what Jonson said in relation to 'ill' epigrams, how much have we 'understood' of what the song 'expressed in the end'? If the song were merely the pagan hymn to sensuality that Volpone presents it as, there would be little more to do than surrender to its verbal felicity. But in fact the author is Jonson (with no little help from Catullus), not Volpone, and there is a good deal going on beneath the lyric charm, of which the most pointed example is the line 'Suns that set may rise again', which on one level enforces Volpone's *carpe diem* theme ('seize the day') but on another, punningly opens up a whole perspective of Christian resurrection which flies in the face of the pagan amorality 'expressed' so forcefully throughout the lyric.[36] How we should resolve these contradictions, and whether we believe Celia should (or indeed, left to her own devices, could) have resisted the force of the song, are not matters on which Jonson directs us. He has, rather, charmingly invited us into a situation which requires those alert enough to recognise the fact to apply judgement and discrimination, to engage the 'trying faculty' of 'knowledge', and so 'understand'.

He expects no less in any other poem or play we read, and judges other writers in terms of their capacity similarly to *engage* their readers in serious matters (even if comically expressed) rather than simply entertain, flatter or baffle them. If he spells this out in terms of the 'laws' of poetry he does so because this is the only vocabulary he has for describing (and reducing to order of a kind) what post-structuralists among us would recognise as the slippery and dangerous games we play in trying to communicate, in trying to resolve meaning. Volpone's seduction of Celia is left unresolved by Bonario's (in)opportune cutting short of the proceedings; in the pages of *The Forest*, too, we have no way of knowing if she succumbed. Such indeterminacies are, in the end, what generate the moral and aesthetic tensions of Jonson's own best writing. It is a measure of the tensions within his chosen role as 'the poet' that so much of his critical theory was bent on exploring the dangers such effects, so diligently policing their hypothetical borders.

5

Jonson and Shakespeare

I loved the man, and do honour his memory, on this side idolatry, as much as any.

Discoveries, 665–6

We actually know nothing of the personal and professional relationship between Ben Jonson and William Shakespeare beyond the fact that the latter's company (the Lord Chamberlain's/King's Men) staged six of Jonson's plays (*Every Man In His Humour, Every Man Out of His Humour, Sejanus, Volpone, The Alchemist* and *Catiline*) while Shakespeare was alive, and Jonson records that Shakespeare himself acted in the first and third of these. But what we like to think we know beyond this (the mythology) is deeply embedded in the literary culture of Britain, and reveals a good deal of what later ages made of what was – only belatedly and for a very mixed bag of reasons – hailed as a golden age of English letters. In assessing Jonson's criticism of Shakespeare, we need carefully to steer round the very potent constructions that those later ages have placed upon their relationship.

No one has chronicled the process of those constructions more scrupulously than Sam Schoenbaum, though he has usually fought shy of cultural explanations as to *why* they should have occurred.[1] I start, therefore, with his brief account of some symptomatic anecdotes:

> In the seventeenth century, hearsay anecdotes found a place in the notations of Sir Nicholas L'Estrange, Nicholas Burgh, and Thomas Plume. These anecdotes (with one exception) show agile Will overcoming ponderous Ben. In a merry tavern meeting Jonson begins his own epitaph ('Here lies Ben Johnson that once was one'), then passes the pen to Shakespeare, who completes it:

Who while he lived was a slow things [*sic*],
And now being dead is nothing.

Shakespeare, standing godfather to one of Jonson's children, and faced with the necessity of thinking of an appropriate christening gift, comes out of 'a deep study' inspired. 'I'll e'en give him a dozen good latten spoons', he tells Ben, 'and thou shalt translate them.' For modern readers this feeble jest requires a gloss: *latten* was a brass or brass-like alloy. In Plume's version of the latten spoon anecdote, the roles are reversed; so Shakespeare does not invariably have the last word.[2]

We cannot entirely rule out the possibility that these are indeed 'hearsay', passed down by word of mouth from people who actually witnessed such events. But it is, to say the least, highly suspicious that both the jokes appear to derive from information put into print and the public domain by Jonson himself. In the Prologue to *Volpone* he admits that he has been accused of being slow ('when his plays come forth, think they can flout them / With saying, he was a year about them'), while in *Discoveries* he levels the opposite charge against Shakespeare: 'he flowed with that facility that sometime it was necessary he should be stopped' (669–79). It would not take a very fertile wit to marry the two pieces of information and come up with the lame joke about the epitaph. By the same token, the latten spoons joke may well be a fanciful elaboration on Jonson's famous observation that Shakespeare had 'small Latin, and less Greek' (Appendix, p. 195). In short, I suspect we have the ironic situation that the mythology derives from Jonson's own words, but twisted in such a way as to show *him* in the poorer light, which of course was never his own intention.[3]

Why that twisting should take place is a larger question than we can fully address here, but part of the answer may be inferred from one of the most famous of the seventeenth-century Jonson/Shakespeare anecdotes, that in Thomas Fuller's *History of the Worthies of England* (1662):

Many were the wit-combats betwixt him and Ben Johnson, which two I behold like a Spanish great galleon, and an English man-of-war; Master Johnson (like the former) was built far higher in learning; solid, but slow in his performances; Shakespeare

with the English man-of-war, lesser in bulk, but lighter in sail-
ing, could turn with all tides, tack about and take advantage of
all winds, by the quickness of his wit and invention.[4]

As Schoenbaum observes, the 'I behold' betrays this as imagination rather than factual reminiscence.[5] To the matters of intellectual speed Fuller has grafted questions of physical bulk, which
again may well be derived from Jonson's own words. He would
not, of course, have access to the *Conversations with Drummond*,
which were not made public for another fifty years, but it was
one of Jonson's strategies for engaging with readers and audiences in later years to make an open issue of his great size: see,
for example, 'My Picture Left in Scotland' (*Und* IX), 'Epistle to
Mr Arthur Squib' (*Und* LIV) and the Induction to *The Staple of
News*, where Mirth describes the author within 'rolling himself
up and down, like a tun' (*H&S*, VI, pp. 279–81, ll. 61–3).

But Fuller has also added an entirely extraneous dimension to
this imagined scene: the gratuitous nationalism which projects the
intellectual rivalry between the two dramatists against the on-
going maritime conflict between England and Spain in the last
half of Elizabeth's reign. This conflates Jonson's 'learning' with
foreign, indeed inimical forces, while Shakespeare's 'wit and invention' are natively English. There is, perhaps inevitably, a strain
of naive jingoism in a *History of the Worthies of England*, but this
needs to be set alongside Dryden's *Essay of Dramatic Poesy* (1668),
the dialogue of which unfolds against the sound of gun-fire at
sea, which proves to be the Battle of Lowestoft fought between
the British and the Dutch navies. The *Essay* in turn proves to be
quite nationalist in tenor, favourably comparing modern (i.e. Restoration) English drama not only with that of Elizabethan times
but also with the plays of classical Greece and Rome and those
of recent neoclassical France, notably the works of Corneille and
Molière. Literary history in the 1660s, that is, was inextricably
tied up with a newly emerging sense of national identity which
was partly a response to naval and commercial rivalry with continental Europe. Fuller's 'beholding' of Jonson conveniently casts
him as an un-English rival to Shakespeare, the quintessential
Englishman, a step in the slow promotion of the latter's adoption
as the national poet, a role that was not finally secured for another century. (Ironically again, Jonson can lay first claim to *that*
myth, though his detractors have rarely noticed this: see 'To the

memory of . . . William Shakespeare', Appendix, pp. 194–6, 'Triumph my Britain, thou hast one to show / To whom all scenes of Europe homage owe').

Nicholas Rowe takes all this one step further in his 'Some Account of the Life, &c. of Mr William Shakespear' attached to his edition of the latter's plays (1709), in which he introduces a note of sourness, even envy (on Jonson's part), into the supposed rivalry:

> His acquaintance with Ben Johnson began with a remarkable piece of humanity and good nature; Mr Johnson, who was at that time altogether unknown to the world, had offer'd one of his plays to the players, in order to have it acted; and the persons into whose hands it was put, after having turn'd it carelessly and superciliously over, were just upon returning it to him with an ill-natur'd answer, that it was of no service to their company, when Shakespear luckily cast his eye upon it, and found something so well in it as to engage him first to read through it, and afterwards to recommend Mr Johnson and his writings to the public. After this they were profess'd friends; though I don't know whether the other ever made him an equal return of gentleness and sincerity.[6]

Again, while we cannot entirely rule out the possibility that Rowe had access to hearsay information, much of this is palpably fantasy – and, ironically yet again, it seems to have derived from Jonson himself. It was the 1616 folio of his *Works* which would have given Rowe the idea that *Every Man In His Humour* was his first play, and also strongly associated Shakespeare with it, since his name is given there at the top of an appended list of the original actors. Rowe knew nothing of Jonson's work for Henslowe, of *The Case is Altered*, or of *The Isle of Dogs*, all of which (but especially the latter) make a nonsense of the claim that he 'was at that time altogether unknown to the world'. The snide doubting 'whether the other ever made him an equal return of gentleness and sincerity', conjuring up images of an envious and ungrateful younger man, should be regarded in the same way as a pure piece of fiction.

I have pursued the question of the Jonson/Shakespeare relationship at some length because it is so deeply engrained in our cultural mythology that people can hardly read what Jonson said about Shakespeare without doing so in its light. Yet, as I hope I have sufficiently demonstrated, the mythology itself derives from multiple misreadings – generated by any number of pressures within late seventeenth-century English culture – of Jonson's own words. To approach Jonson's criticism of Shakespeare as the words of an envious, pedantic newcomer and lesser spirit is grotesquely to damn it with distorted echoes of itself. We must try to rid our minds of those echoes and to see the criticism as their contemporaries might have seen it.

The earliest public comment that Jonson *may* have aimed at Shakespeare must be treated cautiously, because its application to him is far from certain. It is, nevertheless, instructive in its own right. As we have already observed, *Poetaster* contains a number of observations on the dubious status of the patented acting companies in the London region.[7] One of these (albeit by the totally untrustworthy character, Tucca) contrasts the status in law of unregulated actors as 'rogues and sturdy vagabonds' with the pretensions of some of their more established fellows, who aspire to coats of arms to assert their respectability: 'They forget they are i'the statute, the rascals; they are blazoned there, there they are tricked, they and their pedigrees: they need no other heralds, iwis' (I.ii.52–5).[8] The shareholder–players in the Lord Chamberlain's and Lord Admiral's Men, who performed regularly at court and would be taken into direct royal patronage when James I came to the throne, were already well on the way to the social standing on which John Cocke would sarcastically reflect in 1615: 'players may not be called rogues: *For they be chief ornaments of his Majesty's revels'.*[9]

Of these, one of the few who had actually acquired a coat of arms by 1601 (albeit in his father's name, and on the strength of his former standing as bailiff of Stratford) was William Shakespeare, whose family's right to bear arms was established in 1596. This was sufficiently contentious that when in 1602 the York Herald quarrelled with Garter, King of Arms, one of the cases he cited of the latter's permitting unfit persons to bear arms was the grant to 'Shakespear the Player, by Garter'. The comment in *Poetaster* is too generalised for us to conclude that Jonson had Shakespeare particularly in mind. But in the earlier *Every Man Out of His Humour* he has Sogliardo, the rustic clown, lay out £30 for a coat of arms, to which is added the 'word' or motto, *Not Without Mustard* (III.iv.86). It *seems* that the Shakespeare motto was *Non Sanz Droict* (*Not Without Right*), in which case this would be a much more telling 'application', adding a charge of country-boy *arrivisme* to the later generalised smear about the actors' pretensions.[10] It *is* clear that Jonson had Shakespeare's *works* in mind while he was writing this play, since he quotes two lines from *Julius Caesar*, then only weeks old, and mentions some characters, notably Falstaff. But, apart from Mitis's objection that the play lacks 'cross-wooing, with a clown to their serving-man' (Grex after III.vi.199), which might be construed as a hit at Shakespeare's romantic comedies, it would be difficult to argue that this was any more than topical banter.[11] In judging the force of any of this we have to bear in mind that the Lord Chamberlain's Men actually performed the play, though Shakespeare himself was not in the cast (as he had been in *Every Man In His Humour* and was again to be in *Sejanus*). This suggests a degree of in-joking rather than of vindictive satire. On the other hand, we need also to remember that this is the first play Jonson himself published, 'as it was first composed by the author, B. J., containing more than hath been publicly spoken or acted'. Could any of the possible references to Shakespeare be part only of the written text, and not of what was performed? If so, they would carry a different force, and might be seen (though only by someone who knew both versions of the text) as part of the printed play's repudiation of its performance origins.

The evidence is so inconclusive in any of this that it would be a mistake to make very much of it at all. Nevertheless, *Poetaster* in particular underlines Jonson's life-long ambivalent relationship with the acting profession – of which, only quite recently, he had been a member. The published text is a deliberate renunciation of that past, drawing a careful line between 'the author' (who had begun to emerge in print with *Every Man Out of His Humour*) and the actors. One of the points of the satire in Dekker's *Satiromastix* is to ridicule this as a fiction, recalling how Horace/Jonson had ambled '(in a leather pilch) by a play-wagon, in the high way' and played 'mad Hieronimoes part' in Kyd's *The Spanish Tragedy* 'to get service among the mimics' (IV.i.130–2). Jonson's own scorn, of course, is aimed at the patented acting companies and their pretensions, rather than at the lowly travelling companies, like Pembroke's Men, to which he had been attached, so he is not strictly being hypocritical.[12] But he *is* at pains to establish for himself the role of the free-spirited author, rather than of anyone formally attached to the socially dubious institution which is the professional theatre. And if there *is* a specific glance at the Shakespeare motto, the striking thing is that Jonson is only concerned with him as a representative type of the upwardly-mobile *actor*. He makes no reference at all to him as a writer of plays. The 'ordinary poet' of the Lord Chamberlain's Men was primarily a creature of the theatre in the scale of values within which Jonson was attempting to define his own very different status as an 'author'.

This remains in essence true of a range of comments, including some of the most famous, that Jonson made about Shakespeare between 1614 (when he alluded extensively to Shakespeare in the Induction to *Bartholomew Fair*, and indeed the text itself) and 1619 when he spoke to William Drummond. Between those dates he published the 1616 folio of his *Works*, with its revised *Every Man In His Humour* and new Prologue. It may be significant that Jonson said nothing publicly about Shakespeare while the latter was still active in the theatre. *Henry VIII* (by 29 June 1613) and *The Two Noble Kinsmen* (possibly later that year) are the two latest plays with which we can connect him, and the latter was a principal target for Jonson's criticism in *Bartholomew Fair*. But Jonson kept his peace (at least in public) about the older man until he had retired to Stratford, and then in effect put himself forward to fill the gap which that retirement had created. John Fletcher, who probably worked with Shakespeare on both his last two plays, *literally* filled that gap by becoming 'ordinary poet' to the King's Men. Jonson's bid, however, was not for a specific post, but for the authoritative space he had vacated.

As we have already seen, the Induction to *Bartholomew Fair* is largely devoted to establishing a contractual relationship (or a working understanding) between 'the author' and his audience.[13] Part of Jonson's strategy for achieving this is, characteristically, comparative analysis, calling into question the nature of the relationships they have enjoyed with other writers. And Shakespeare, overwhelmingly the most successful dramatist of the past two decades, is inevitably the central figure. This need not be construed as envy or sour grapes; it is a simple fact of professional life. If Jonson wishes to establish himself as an authoritative and independent voice, he has to distance himself from the most dominant theatrical voice of recent times. Shakespeare is never actually mentioned by name, but the range of his plays alluded to is telling. The first of these is *Much Ado About Nothing*, a scene from which the Stage-Keeper is enthusiastically commending just when the Book-Holder and Scrivener enter to cut him short: 'And then a substantial watch to ha' stolen in upon 'em, and taken 'em away with mistaking words, as the fashion is in the stage-practice' (p. 197). So the Watch, primed by Dogberry and his 'mistaking words' (with more of their own), take away Conrad and Borachio in *Much Ado*, III.iii. The context here is revealing. The Stage-Keeper evokes this in the course of remembering comedians of yester-year, starting with Richard Tarlton and going on to a fellow member of the old Queen's Men, John Adams; Tarlton himself was dead by 1588 and his troupe was a spent force by the plague of 1593/4, so this is well in the past by 1614. Comedians of that ilk had been something of a law unto themselves, personalities in their own right, whose integration into the plays they performed in was often only notional: they were there to do their 'business', to entertain the audiences with familiar routines. This, in essence, was 'the fashion' of the *then* 'stage-practice', where all other con-siderations were secondary to entertaining the audience.

Much Ado About Nothing really belongs to a later era than this, and Shakespeare had actually stamped a much greater authorial presence on his plays than anyone had imposed in the playing conditions which the Stage-Keeper waxes lyrical about. But the principal comedian working with the Lord Chamberlain's Men at that time, Will Kempe (who we know played Dogberry) was clearly in the tradition of Tarlton and kept alive some of his clown-ing practices.[14] In this way Jonson tacitly accuses Shakespeare of retaining links with an older, outmoded and (as he sees it) an-archic 'stage-practice' which is alien to his own authority as a writer. In *Discoveries* he is quite categorical: 'Nor is the moving of laughter always the end of comedy; that is rather a fowling for the people's delight, or their fooling. . . . In short, as vinegar is not accounted good until the wine is corrupted, so jests that are true and natural seldom raise laughter with the beast, the multitude. They love nothing that is right and proper' (2652–4, 2680–3): there is a pun on 'fowling' = hunting fowl, fouling, and fooling. The comedian who departs from the truth and natural-ness of a written script (key qualities, as Jonson saw it, of his own comic mode) merely for the sake of cheap laughs compro-mises the author's integrity; an author who connives with this calls into question his own principles.[15]

The next Shakespearian text invoked raises slightly different issues, since it has more obvious pretensions to 'learning' of a kind than *Much Ado*: 'He that will swear *Jeronimo* or *Andronicus* are the best plays yet, shall pass unexcepted at here, as a man whose judgement shows it is constant, and hath stood still these five and twenty, or thirty years. Though it be an ignorance, it is a virtuous and staid ignorance; and next to truth, a confirmed error does well' (p. 199). *Titus Andronicus* was an old play, possibly Shakespeare's first exercise in tragedy, in the gory Senecan style popularised by Thomas Kyd's *The Spanish Tragedy* (*Jeronimo*). Perversely, as Jonson sees it, both of them have retained their popularity, and are used by some as a yardstick of excellence with which to castigate more recent works. There may well be an element of *self*-castigation in this, since we know that Jonson himself was paid by Henslowe in 1601/2 for 'additions' to *The Spanish Tragedy*, which must have helped to perpetuate the popularity of the old pot-boiler even if what he actually wrote may be said to display the superiority of his own 'words' to Kyd's 'action'.[16] The key issue *now* is to revive people's critical faculties, to get them to see that something is not necessarily good because it is old and popular, to prepare them mentally for something new and different. The irony here, of course, is that what Jonson actually offers as new is informed by critical principles millennia old, be it his own tragedies *Sejanus* and *Catiline* (both disastrous popular failures) or his post-*Volpone* comedies with their New Comedy spirit of decorum. In rejecting *Titus Andronicus* Jonson is rejecting one kind of accommodation with the classical past in favour of another, which, he insists, has more integrity; it is also thereby, in a calculated double-think, more *modern*.

This sets Jonson up for his most sustained attack on Shakespeare, on his most recent plays, which are very much the current fashion, an attack which will be carried over into the play itself. In spelling out the 'author's' Articles of Agreement, the Book-Holder disdainfully observes: 'If there be never a servant-monster i' the Fair; who can help it? he says; nor a nest of antics? He is loth to make Nature afraid in his plays, like those that beget *Tales, Tempests*, and such like drolleries, to mix his head with other men's heels, let the concupiscence of jigs and dances reign as strong as it will amongst you' (p. 199). The missing 'servant-monster' must be Caliban, who is so nominated three times in the first eight lines of III.ii. of *The Tempest*, and does 'mix his head with [Stephano and Trinculo's] heels' in II.ii; similarly, the 'nest of antics' (grotesques) is almost certainly the dance of twelve satyrs in *The Winter's Tale* (after IV.iv.340). '*Tales, Tempests*' only reinforce these identifications, while 'drolleries' may glance at the dumb-show of 'several strange shapes' in *The Tempest*, which is there called 'a livery drollery' (III.iii.21). As Ian Donaldson has observed, the primary function of this attack is to stake a claim for Jonson's own 'realistic' drama in the face of the 'romance conventions' popularised by Shakespeare.[17] *Bartholomew Fair* itself systematically parodies the romance conventions of lost-and-found, the vindication of innate nobility, and the wondrous workings of divine providence, especially in the contest between Quarlous and Winwife (a latter-day Palemon and Arcite) for the hand of Grace Wellborn. This is so thoroughgoing as to suggest that Jonson rejects romance conventions altogether, rather than merely some recent examples of the genre. But closer examination indicates that this is not so, and that this objection is specifically to Shakespeare's examples in this form.

One indication of this is the final sneer at 'the concupiscence of jigs and dances'. Jonson is implying that things have come full circle (or, indeed, may never have changed): jigs and dances were the hall-marks of clowns like Tarlton and Kempe. These 'romances' may masquerade as new and modish, but they are basically contaminated by the same old 'stage-practice'. Another lies in the reference to a very different 'stage-practice', that associated with the 'nest of antics'. It is generally agreed that the dance of 'satyrs' or 'saltiers' in *The Winter's Tale* is imported from the masque of *Oberon* (given at court on 1 January 1611), and that this is glanced at within the text when we are told 'One three of them, by their own report, sir, hath danced before the King' (IV.iv.335–6).[18] The King's Men had played the comic and speaking roles within that masque, would still have access to the costumes, and so would have no difficulty incorporating this element of it into Shakespeare's play. But this means that Jonson was objecting, in essence, to something of his own devising, since *Oberon* and the satyrs within it were very much his own 'invention', though he would not personally have been responsible for the choreography. He does not, however, appear to be objecting to the 'plagiarism' as such – rather, to the questionable taste of Shakespeare's use of this item in his play. By implication, the objection is to the artlessness of the borrowing, perhaps to the incongruity of using material devised for the unique conditions of the court masques on the public stage. In the Prologue to *Volpone* he is scathing about those who bring in 'a gull, old ends reciting, / To stop gaps in his loose writing' and emphasises that he himself 'makes jests to fit his fable' rather than stealing them from elsewhere. If there are to be borrowings from elsewhere, whatever their inherent quality, they must be fully integrated in the new work.

To pursue further the question of Jonson's precise attitude to 'romances', and to those of Shakespeare in particular, we need to go well beyond the Induction to *Bartholomew Fair* and into most of his other comments on Shakespeare. We also need to consider questions of generic definition that remain vexed to this day. Heminge and Condell, the editors of the Shakespeare first folio, placed *The Winter's Tale* and *The Tempest* among the comedies. Of the other works which the twentieth century has dubbed 'late plays', they included *Henry VIII* among the histories, and *Cymbeline* among the tragedies (omitting *Pericles* and *The Two Noble Kinsmen* altogether, presumably on the grounds that they were not solely or primarily by Shakespeare). So the 'late plays' they included were distributed among the only three genres they recognised – comedies, histories and tragedies. And the two on which Jonson's ridicule particularly falls were deemed 'comedies', which chimes with his 'jigs and dances' suggestion that they are in some respects like his clown-ridden earlier comedies.

Yet Jonson's insistence that there is something *particularly* ridiculous about these two plays (they 'make Nature afraid'), which is echoed in the zeal with which *Bartholomew Fair* itself then parodies *The Two Noble Kinsmen*, gives some credence to the supposition that he saw all three as essentially *different* in some respects, an intuition which the twentieth century has largely endorsed.[19] I have myself followed J. F. Danby, Northrop Frye and others in recognising that difference with the label 'romances', though this is problematic in that the Renaissance did not itself use the term to describe theatrical works. It understood it well enough, however, in relation to courtly tales of princely disguising and knight-errantry, of which the most notable English examples were Sidney's *Arcadia* and Spenser's *The Faerie Queene*. The modern use of the label 'romance' for Shakespeare's last plays largely derives from the conviction that he was translating into dramatic terms what they had rendered as prose and verse narratives.[20] It is not a usage we could expect Jonson to have endorsed, though he would doubtless have understood it.

In as much as the Jacobeans had a separate critical category for plays that dealt with such material, it was 'tragicomedy', though the term itself related primarily to formalistic questions of the balance between tragic and comic elements in the same play rather than to the subject-matter. Here again, the term is commonly used today of Shakespeare's late plays, though there is no evidence that Jonson or any other contemporary so described them.[21] Indeed, the terms 'romance' and 'tragicomedy' are used interchangeably and indiscriminately, in ways that W. H. Herendeen is sure Jonson would not have countenanced:

> The modern tendency has been to blur the boundaries between romance and tragicomedy; this is largely the influence of the Shakespearean model and is not otherwise established on a historical basis. Jonson distinguishes between them – as a rigorous classicist he found his unShakespearean model in Plautus and as a theorist he found in the Italian neoclassicists descriptions of the genre that distinguish it from romance.[22]

He certainly found in Plautus's *Cistellaria* a justification for bringing a near-suicide into his own *Every Man Out of His Humour*, so endangering its comic decorum (see Grex after III.ix. 86–93). But he does not actually describe that play as a 'tragicomedy'. He also knew Giambattista Guarini's *Il Pastor Fido* (the most renowned Italian neoclassicist tragicomedy, the legitimate status of which its author had very carefully theorised), since he told Drummond that 'Guarini in his *Pastor Fido* kept not decorum in making shepherds speak as well as himself could' (47–8), which is not exactly high praise but does not imply real antipathy. He did, moreover, also remark that 'Fletcher and Beaumont ten years since hath written *The Faithful Shepherdess*, a tragicomedy well done' (184–5); what is more, he had written a commendatory poem for the published text, consoling Fletcher for the response of the audience who 'before / They saw it half, damned thy whole play' – a fate which befell more than one of his own experimental plays.[23] Perhaps most tellingly, he chose to place the figure of Tragicomedy in the most dominant position on the frontispiece to his *Works*, even though that volume contained no such work by himself. So we may reasonably infer that Jonson was not opposed to tragicomedy *in principle*, even if he identified some stylistic faults in Guarini's own work. In the Epistle to *Volpone*, where he defends his own transgressions against 'the strict rigour of comic law', he shows himself not unsympathetic to flexibility in the drawing of generic boundaries, which was the objection most often raised *against* tragicomedy.

Yet he finds fault with those of Shakespeare's plays which come closest to that form. Either he did not identify these plays as tragi-comedies or, if he did, he felt them to be poor examples of the genre. There is, finally, insufficient evidence to determine which was the case, though the *Conversations with Drummond* offer possible hints that it was the latter. Jonson had less to say about Shakespeare to Drummond (himself a poet, and not a dramatist) than he had, for instance, about Donne, but the two comments the Scot recorded have figured highly in the mythology of Jonson as the envious and narrow-minded classicist: 'That Shakespeare wanted art' (37) and 'Shakespeare in a play brought in a number of men saying they had suffered shipwreck in Bohemia, where there is no sea near by some 100 miles' (168–70). The two are not necessarily connected, but if we do take them together they constitute the bare bones of a critique of those plays which 'make Nature afraid'.

The offending piece of geography occurs in *The Winter's Tale*, can be traced to Shakespeare's source (Robert Greene's *Pandosto*), and for many readers is simply of a piece with the calculated defiance of realistic expectations evident throughout the play. But Jonson thought it worthy of comment, even though Drummond probably did not know the play, which was not printed until 1623. It showed a lack of attention on Shakespeare's part, a lack of the care which for Jonson was always a hallmark of 'art'. And such derelictions were for Jonson the principal signs of Shakespeare's allegiance to a pre-print culture, partly to that of the common stage (the heritage of Tarlton, Kempe etc.) but partly also, given the status that the actors had latterly acquired at court, to that of the gentleman 'amateur' poet, with his *sprezzatura*-style affectation of a nonchalant ease about his writing, the very anti-thesis of Jonson's own acknowledged 'labour', and this he found a particularly pronounced feature of the late plays. The two notions fuse in his most detailed and considered statement about Shake-speare, that in *Discoveries*:

I remember the players have often mentioned it as an honour to Shakespeare, that in his writing, whatsoever he penned, he never blotted out line. My answer hath been, 'Would he had blotted a thousand'; which they thought a malevolent speech. I had not told posterity this but for their ignorance, who choose that circumstance to commend their friend by wherein he most faulted, and to justify my own candour: for I loved the man, and do honour his memory, on this side idolatry, as much as any. He was, indeed, honest, and of an open and free nature; had an excellent fantasy, brave notions, and gentle expressions; wherein he flowed with that facility that sometime it was necessary he should be stopped. '*Sufflaminandus erat* [he needed to be braked]', as Augustus said of Haterius. His wit was in his own power; would the rule of it had been so too. Many times he fell into those things, could not escape laughter: as when he said in the person of Caesar, one speaking to him, 'Caesar, thou dost me wrong'; he replied, 'Caesar never did wrong, but with just cause': and such like: which were ridiculous. But he redeemed his vices with his virtues. There was ever more in him to be praised than to be pardoned.   (ll. 658–79)

This was apparently a response to the comments of Heminge and Condell 'To the Great Variety of Readers' in the Shakespeare first folio, where they observe that 'as he was a happy imitator of nature, [he] was a most gentle expresser of it. His mind and hand went together, and what he thought, he uttered with that easiness that we have scarce received from him a blot in his papers'.[24] In this his old colleagues in the King's Men may have had half an eye on the dedicatees of the volume, the Herbert brother Earls of Pembroke and Montgomery, and the other half on the standing of their own troupe: their most famous poet was 'gentle' most especially in a social sense, a Groom of the Chamber fit to rub shoulders with other gentleman versifiers at court. To that extent, although the Shakespeare first folio in some respects follows the example set by Jonson's *Works*, its editors seek positively to associate it with a different tradition of authorship. Shakespeare is *not* presented as an author of 'works' in the classical sense, but of 'Comedies, Histories and Tragedies', products of the Elizabethan theatre, belatedly gentrified. It is about this that Jonson here attempts to set the record straight.

The line from *Julius Caesar* is perplexing in several ways. For one thing it does not appear as Jonson quotes it in the 1623 folio, its earliest printing, where it is given as 'Know, Caesar doth not wrong, nor without cause / Will he be satisfied' (III.i.47–8). Did Jonson misquote, or did Shakespeare or his editors amend it in response to Jonson's criticism? The former seems unlikely, since

Jonson was sufficiently convinced that the line was ludicrous that he made fun of it again in the Induction to *The Staple of News*:

EXPECTATION   I can do that too, if I have cause.
PROLOGUE   Cry you mercy, you never did wrong but with just cause.

(ll. 35–7)

Just as perplexing is *why* he should have thought it was ludicrous. As *he* quotes the lines, they are 'elliptical rather than nonsensical'.[25] They encapsulate a view of autocracy bordering on tyranny, making only moral – not psychological, political or verbal – nonsense. But that may have been enough for Jonson, given his views on the relationship between language and morality. At all events, this obviously registered with him, alongside the seacoast of Bohemia, as signs of Shakespeare's want of 'art', a lack of serious application which prevented his 'excellent fantasy, brave notions, and gentle expressions' from achieving the finished perfection of which they might have been capable.

From this perspective we may look back to various unresolved questions about Jonson's mockery of the late plays in the Induction to *Bartholomew Fair*. We may surmise that he was not being hypocritical in deriding the 'nest of antics' which was of his own devising: more likely he was calling attention to a lack of 'art' in Shakespeare's not making it more convincingly a part of his own 'invention'. And, whether or not he thought of those plays as tragicomedies, it is clear that he felt they lacked the formal integrity necessary to make their improbabilities acceptable, as he apparently conceded that Guarini and Fletcher had on occasions succeeded in doing. Jonson's own masques, after all, sport grotesques as fantastic as the 'servant-monster', Caliban (or, indeed, that 'nest of antics'), and scenarios as 'wondrous' or 'admirable' as anything Prospero contrives. But they did so within an artful context of 'understanding' which Jonson himself had been at pains to define and insist upon, drawing on the most compelling authorities at his disposal. In his adherence to 'stage-practice', in his apparently willing subjection to the tyranny of the audience, Shakespeare had broken or ignored the 'necessary rules' by which an author shapes his works. For Jonson those rules are essential, primarily because they help an author protect his own integrity by defining a proper relationship between the writer, the text, and his audience/readers. 'To mix his head with other men's heels' is not only a specific piece of stage-nonsense: it is also a metaphor for everything that Jonson finds questionable about Shakespeare's art as a dramatist, a measure of the extent to which he was content to remain a 'playwright', rather than a 'poet'.

This is essentially the case that Jonson spells out in the Prologue to the folio *Every Man In His Humour*, which extends the argument much wider than the late plays and is such a carefully-structured document that it needs to be followed closely (see Appendix, p. 184). The final emphasis on styles of comedy is clearly tailored to the play it introduces, but its horizons are so much broader that it is reasonable to suppose Jonson intended it to serve as a more general preliminary statement about the whole of the folio which followed it, and – as we have repeatedly observed – the carefully edited version of his career to date which it contained.

With one eye squarely on contemporary tastes and practices, his vision expands to introduce a range of classical precedent and commentary which place them in perspective. Aristotle and 'the laws of time, place' (Prologue to *Volpone*) stand behind the strictures on plays with plots which widely transgress the 'compass of a day's business' (*Every Man Out of His Humour*, Grex, After the Second Sounding, line 241) and casually waft audiences 'o'er the seas'. 'Foot-and-half-foot words' is Jonson's own rendition of Horace's *'sesquipedalia verba'* (*Ars Poetica*, 79), identifying the Elizabethan taste for bombast (originally the cotton stuffing of padded clothes, metaphorically verbose and exaggerated language) as one of a very long line of abuses of language, English and otherwise. Shakespeare is never named in the catalogue of contemporary 'abuses', some of which it would hardly be fair to lay at his door: squibs were a particular feature of the old 'devil' plays such as *Dr Faustus* and its predecessors, which Shakespeare did not essay (though Jonson himself was ironically to revive the form in *The Devil is an Ass* that same year), while no character actually passes from the cradle to the grave in his plays (though the translation of Perdita from birth to a lady of sixteen years, 'grown in grace', is close in spirit to what Jonson finds objectionable). But there are enough unequivocal pointers to suggest that, as Shakespeare was the most popular and successful dramatist of the last twenty years, Jonson inevitably had him strongly in mind in castigating the tastes and practices of the period.

Shakespeare may not have invented the English chronicle history play (the anonymous *Famous Victories of Henry V*, for example, probably antedates his first tetralogy of histories), but no one was more identified with plays on the Wars of the Roses, on which much of his early reputation rested. *Pericles* (which Jonson elsewhere dismissed as a 'mouldy tale'[26]) is not the only play in which a deity comes down in a 'creaking throne', but it does rely on a range of such would-be exotic effects and has, in ancient Gower, a chorus who repeatedly 'wafts [us] o'er the seas', as (perhaps more famously) does the otherwise more realistic *Henry V*. (Jonson was not against choruses in their place, and was self-conscious that *Sejanus* lacked one;[27] but its function was primarily to analyse and moralise the action for the audience, not to facilitate extravagant shifts in locale.) *Cymbeline* rings the changes on the 'throne' in having Jupiter descend on an eagle, but he does that to the accompaniment of thunder – produced, no doubt, by the 'rolled bullet' (cannonball rolled over the wooden floorboards), an effect also essential in *King Lear*, as was the 'tempestuous drum' heralding the storm. Caliban was not the only stage-creation Jonson might have dubbed a 'monster', but the fact that he had unequivocally identified him as such in the Induction to *Bartholomew Fair* leaves the strong suspicion that he is reiterating the same complaint here, if perhaps only to epitomise a whole 'monstrous' breed of plays. And so on. Shakespeare was not alone in employing any of these themes, styles or devices, but hardly anyone else could supply such a comprehensive catalogue of examples.

In all of this the stated concerns are twofold: first, that the business of keeping the lowest common denominator in the audience entertained ('the boys to please') has taken precedence over all other considerations, including artistic and moral ones; secondly, that the price of 'purchas[ing their] delight at such a rate' must be self-disgust, integrity squandered in the marketplace. But there remains a less fully articulated concern, at least as pressing as the other two. Jonson starts the Prologue to *Every Man In His Humour* by proclaiming that he 'hath not so loved the stage' as to subject himself to its tyranny, even for financial necessity (perhaps, in this, conveniently forgetting his work for Henslowe, which will *not* be commemorated in the following pages). But he stops just short of acknowledging his more fundamental reservations about the theatre as marketplace under *any* conditions, given the volatility of the crowd and the pressures of instant judgement.

So much of what he objects to here – characters ageing a lifetime in the course of a performance, locales casually wafted hither and yon, cheap stage devices to mimic the great forces of nature, 'monsters' totally alien to 'deeds, and language, such as men do use' – amounts to a rejection of imaginative freedom, to a demand for its curtailment.

This is a demand not just for limits to be placed on the 'excellent fantasy, brave notions' that he recognises in a Shakespeare, but also for controls to be placed on the free-for-all of a marketplace which is the theatre, where the imagination of the audience knows no bounds and constantly threatens anarchy. It is an outright rejection of what Clifford Geertz calls the 'collective text'.[28] True communication requires mutually-agreed terms of exchange (such as the Induction to *Bartholomew Fair* ironically attempted to define) and, in Jonson's terms, is impossible where they do not exist. He told Drummond: 'He had an intention to have made a play like Plaut[u]s' *Amphitrio*, but left it off for that he could never find two so alike others that he could persuade the spectators they were one' (360–2). Such considerations seem not to have inhibited Shakespeare, who made the identical appearance of twins key hinges to the plots of *The Comedy of Errors* and *Twelfth Night* (in the latter case even the identical appearance of twins of different sexes). It is a totally different attitude to that 'willing suspension of disbelief' of which Coleridge judged audiences to be capable: Shakespeare approached it as a theatrical resource to be exploited, Jonson as a problem to be overcome in the pursuit of 'understanding' and the cultivation of 'knowledge'. He recommends the severe limits, and clear terms of exchange, of a low-key realism ('deeds and language such as men do use') within a modest brand of New Comedy (which 'sport[s] with human follies, not with crimes') as the aesthetic of his ideal marketplace. These are the conditions which the 'laws' of his criticism constantly sought to cultivate, and which for so long Shakespeare's 'authority' inhibited.

Nor should we simply ascribe this to an envious *lack* of imagination on Jonson's part. He told Drummond of a mystic experience in relation to the death of his first son: 'he saw in a vision his eldest son, then a child and at London, appear unto him w[i]t[h] the mark of a bloody cross on his forehead, as if he had been cutted w[i]t[h] a sword; at which, amazed, he prayed unto God; and in the morning he came to Mr Camden's chamber to tell him, who persuaded him it was but an apprehension of his fantasy, at which he should not be disjected. In the meantime comes th[e]r[e] letters from his wife of the death of th[a]t boy in the plague. He appeared to him, he said, of a manly shape, and of that growth that he thinks he shall be at the resurrection', and again: 'He hath consumed a whole night in lying looking at his great toe, about which he hath seen Tartars and Turks, Romans and Carthaginians, fight in his imagination' (216–24, 268–70). These are hardly symptomatic of a man starved of imagination. On the contrary, Drummond's impression was that he was 'Oppressed with fantasy, which hath ever mastered his reason, a general disease in many poets' (614–15), a more extreme case, it would seem, than the 'excellent fantasy, brave notions' that Jonson identified in Shakespeare. He committed himself to an aesthetic which severely straitjacketed his own natural inclinations, rather than one that compensated for any inherent deficiencies in his qualifications as a 'maker'.

In recognising that Shakespeare and Jonson were both creatures of 'fantasy' we may concur to an extent with Russ McDonald's recent attempt to emphasise the *similarities* between them as artists rather than the differences:

> Obviously Shakespeare and Jonson were fascinated by some of the same topics: imagination, language, self-delusion, obsession, evil, theatricality, power. They were capable of taking similar attitudes toward such topics. Occasionally, they even developed their concerns by means of some of the same dramatic strategies. Both were capable of imagining an ideal, both of scourging its opposite. Their very greatest works proceed from similar antiromantic impulses. The manifest differences should not obscure the areas of genuine mutual interest. . . . With both Shakespeare and Jonson, there is something of the other in each.[29]

This is true to a point, and within the critical horizons which McDonald chooses to recognise. By the same token, we should acknowledge the point most forcefully made by Alexander Leggatt, that (even allowing for the adventitious circumstances in which Jonson's criticism was formulated) it is possible to identify a number of contradictions between his theory and his practice as an artist, contradictions which at times highlight how like Shakespeare he could be, even as he protests the opposite.[30]

But, as a critic, Jonson's own attention was always on the differences between the two of them, differences (as I have tried to argue) not just over style and taste, but over their whole perception of themselves as writers, over their definitions of the authority they wielded as text-makers. It was Jonson himself who started drawing lines between the two of them; his criticism was the first attempt to place their works in different conceptual boxes. It may be that he was as consistent and strident about this as he was precisely because he recognised the potential similarity between them, or (to put it another way) appreciated the weight of debt he owed to the older man, whose example was as inhibiting as it was inescapable. On the other hand, one has to say that the differences which Jonson insisted upon were neither trivial nor artificial: in his allegiance (at least up to 1616) to print culture and in his resistance to what he saw as the imaginative and communicative chaos of the public theatres, Jonson was a portent of the future, while much of Shakespeare was in serious danger of being consigned to an unrecorded and largely unremembered past.

That this did not happen we have to thank the 1623 folio of his *Comedies, Histories and Tragedies*. As we have already observed, this would probably have been an unthinkable publication if Jonson's own 1616 *Works* had not paved the way. Yet in many ways it is a very different sort of book. It does not, for example, contain any non-dramatic works, as Jonson's did: *Venus and Adonis*, *The Rape of Lucrece* and the *Sonnets* were all already in print, and it may simply be that Heminge and Condell were unable to obtain the copyrights. But the effect is to make that volume a celebration of Shakespeare's life in the theatre, and especially of his long and fruitful relationship with the Lord Chamberlain's/King's Men, while at the same time giving the whole profession a genteel gloss which would have looked totally unrealistic at the time that Shakespeare started out as an actor and jobbing playwright, without the assurance of royal and aristocratic patronage. His own long, successful and intensely respectable career, as much as anything else, had dictated the terms of its own retrospective perception, a solipsism which the longest-surviving members of the King's Men are happy to overlook. Shakespeare had graced a profession which he had thereby helped to change. So in commemorating Shakespeare, they reinforce their own status by perpetuating the memory of the 'ordinary poet' who helped to create it. As we have seen, Jonson protested against elements of this in what he had to say about Shakespeare in *Discoveries*. But, before that, these considerations weighed with him in the composition of his own contribution to the Shakespeare first folio, the memorial poem, very carefully titled 'To the memory of my beloved, The AUTHOR Master William Shakespeare: And what he hath left us' (Appendix, p. 194).

To generations brought up on the notion of an envious or grudging Jonson, this has seemed at best an insincere exercise in Jacobean panegyric, at worst a piece of sheer hypocrisy. In this, as in so much else, Dryden led the way, castigating it as 'an insolent, sparing, and invidious panegyric'.[31] In this view, the 'small Latin and less Greek' is the condescension of a man over-fond of his own learning, the 'not of an age, but for all time' empty words; the more he protests 'To draw no envy . . . on thy name', the more be betrays his own envy. I hope I have done something to recast these terms of reference. The keys to the poem are its very prominent address to an 'AUTHOR' and to 'what he hath left us', that is the book itself. Seven years after Shakespeare's death and the publication of his own *Works* (both 1616), Jonson is now able to see him, not as a rival from whom he must distinguish himself, but as a more-than-worthy forerunner whose example justifies Jonson's own vocation as a poet. As in *The Golden Age Restored*, where he celebrates modern Britain in a parade of its poetic worthies, so when he creates a modern pantheon of dramatists by

>   tell[ing] how far thou didst our Lyly outshine,
> Or sporting Kyd, or Marlowe's mighty line

he cannot but draw attention to the continuation of that line into the present, even as he seeks to extend it back to its supposed origins in 'insolent Greece or haughty Rome'. Shakespeare is no longer the antithesis of what Jonson seeks to achieve, but proof that he has been right all along. And nowhere more so than in the fact of folio publication itself, where belatedly, posthumously and despite himself, Shakespeare has become the 'author' he conspicuously had not been in his lifetime. In the confines of those pages, which (rather than the man himself) are the true 'monument without a tomb', he can be seen as the man who brought 'art' to his natural talents ('For a good poet's made as well as born'), even if he did not do so as a result of careful study of the 'laws' and the ancients. Like Sophocles, whose successor he here appears as, he is one of the 'many excellent poets that fulfilled' the laws before the grammarians or philosophers found them out (*Discoveries*, 2582–3). His works themselves are proof of his sweated labour, 'strik[ing] the second heat / Upon the muses' anvil' to produce 'his well-turnèd and true-filèd lines'.

There is no wonder, then, that Jonson was displeased to find Heminge and Condell, *in the same volume*, recording in awed tones that 'what he thought, he uttered with that easiness that we have scarce received from him a blot in his papers' and that he felt it necessary (as he would see it) to set the record straight in *Discoveries*. He was not being somehow 'truer' or more honest in the relative privacy of his commonplace book, merely making a different point. In the *Bartholomew Fair* criticism and his own 1616 *Works* Jonson had 'excluded' Shakespeare, in a conscious act of Oedipal aggression. In the 1623 folio he had hoped, via the commendatory poem, to reclaim that in Shakespeare which seemed to him worth preserving – only to find that the actors had muddied the water, both in the very theatrical provenance of what it contained and in their prefactory address. I have argued eleswhere that part of what both Heminge and Condell, and Jonson, were responding to was a Shakespeare who allowed his plays (as he surely allowed his 'sugared sonnets') to circulate in manuscript, as we know that the plays of the Beaumont and Fletcher canon were later to circulate.[32] The evidence for this is complex and circumstantial, and I will not repeat it here: it is not critical to the current argument. But I mention it to emphasise the complex range of possible 'publication' for an early modern dramatist, each with its own social ethos: performance in the public theatre, performance at a private venue, manuscript circulation, cheap quarto print (authorised or unauthorised), expensive folio print (self-induced, or posthumous).

The objective truth behind the two very different 'Shakespeares' claimed by Heminge and Condell on the one hand, and Jonson on the other – the gentleman of the newly gentrified theatre, and the 'made poet' taking his place in the literary canon – is now beyond recall: they are metaphors for different kinds of writers, different notions of literary authority, and we must be content to recognise them both as the constructions they are, each attempting to appropriate the dead 'author' to its own cultural field. This is what successive generations of criticism have done ever since, and never more so than when they have sought to out-play Jonson at his own game, by contrasting Shakespeare with him. It is perverse to ask Jonson to be any 'truer', or even consistent, in his criticism of Shakespeare than we are capable of being ourselves, simply because of the proximity in time of their lives and careers. As I have tried to show, that proximity itself imposed enormous pressures, as the very nature of the written word to which they were both – however differently – so committed was being forged anew on the anvil of the early modern world.

Jonson's criticism of Shakespeare remains intensely valuable precisely because it is so much of its own age and records those pressures so cogently, in that way helping us to understand analogous ones in our own time. The questions Jonson raised and the answers he gave, throughout his critical writings, trace the rise of the literary culture we have inherited, and determined much of its future shape. If we want to understand the tensions and contradictions of our own culture, it will help to examine the tensions and contradictions from which it grew. Paradoxically, too, as we pass out of a world where print has been (for four hundred years) the dominant medium of communication, to one where televisual and electronically-generated systems are usurping that primacy, it will help us to keep our bearings if we attend to the career which – more than that of any other individual author – shaped the orthodoxies we are now having to unlearn.

Appendix

Selected Critical Documents by Jonson, printed in the order and form in which they first saw print, though with spelling, punctuation, etc., modernised (see 'A Note on Texts'). Items not printed in or shortly after Jonson's lifetime are included at the end, to emphasise the difference between public and semi-private perceptions of his criticism

Every Man Out of His Humour

from 'After the Second Sounding'

first printed in quarto, 1600; essentially reprinted in 1616 folio

CORDATUS, ASPER, MITIS

CORDATUS Nay, my dear Asper,
MITIS   Stay your mind . . .
ASPER   Away.
  Who is so patient of this impious world,
  That he can check his spirit, or rein his tongue?
  Or who hath such a dead unfeeling sense,
  That heaven's horrid thunders cannot wake?
  To see the earth, crack'd with the weight of sin,
  Hell gapping under us and o'er our heads
  Black rav'nous ruin, with her sail-stretch'd wings,
  Ready to sink us down, and cover us.
  Who can behold such prodigies as these,
  And have his lips sealed up? not I: my language
  Was never ground into such oily colours,
  To flatter vice and daub iniquity:
  But (with an armed, and resolved hand)

163

I'll strip the ragged follies of the time,
Naked, as at their birth:
CORDATUS   (Be not too bold.
ASPER   You trouble me) and with a whip of steel,
Print wounding lashes in their iron ribs.
I fear no mood stamp'd in a private brow,
When I am pleas'd t'unmask a public vice.
I fear no strumpet's drugs, nor ruffian's stab,
Should I detect their hateful luxuries:
No broker's, usurer's, or lawyer's gripe,
Were I dispos'd to say, they're all corrupt.
I fear no courtier's frown, should I applaud
The easy flexure of his supple hams.
Tut, these are so innate, and popular,
That drunken custom would not shame to laugh
(In scorn) at him, that should but dare to tax 'em.
And yet, not one of these but knows his works,
Knows what damnation is, the devil, and hell,
Yet, hourly they persist, grow rank in sin,
Puffing their souls away in perj'rous air,
To cherish their extortion, pride, or lusts . . .
MITIS   Forbear, good Asper, be not like your name.
ASPER   O, but to such, whose faces are all zeal,
And (with the words of Hercules) invade
Such crimes as these! that will not smell of sin,
But seem as they were made of sanctity:
Religion in their garments, and their hair
Cut shorter than their eyebrows! when the conscience
Is vaster than the ocean, and devours
More wretches than the Counters . . .
MITIS   Gentle Asper,
Contain your spirit in more stricter bounds,
And be not thus transported with the violence
Of your strong thoughts.
CORDATUS   Unless your breath had power
To melt the world, and mould it new again,
It is in vain, to spend it in these moods.
ASPER   I not observ'd this thronged round till now.
Gracious, and kind spectators, you are welcome,
Apollo, and the Muses feast your eyes
With graceful objects, and may our Minerva

Answer your hopes, unto their largest strain.
Yet here, mistake me not, judicious friends.
I do not this, to beg your patience,
Or servilely to fawn on your applause,
Like some dry brain, despairing in his merit:
Let me be censur'd by th'austerest brow,
Where I want art, or judgement, tax me freely:
Let envious censors, with their broadest eyes,
Look through and through me, I pursue no favour;
Only vouchsafe me your attentions,
And I will give you music worth your ears.
O, how I hate the monstrousness of time,
Where every servile imitating spirit,
(Plagu'd with an itching leprosy of wit)
In a mere halting fury, strives to fling
His ulc'rous body in the Thespian spring,
And straight leaps forth a Poet! but as lame
As Vulcan, or the founder of Cripplegate.

MITIS   In faith, this Humour will come ill to some.
You will be thought to be too peremptory.

ASPER   This humour? good; and why this humour, Mitis?
Nay, do not turn, but answer.

MITIS   Answer? what?

ASPER   I will not stir your patience, pardon me,
I urg'd it for some reasons, and the rather
To give these ignorant well-spoken days
Some taste of their abuse of this word humour.

CORDATUS   O, do not let your purpose fall, good Asper,
It cannot but arrive most acceptable.
Chiefly to such, as have the happiness
Daily to see how the poor innocent word
Is rack'd, and tortur'd.

MITIS   Aye, I pray you proceed.

ASPER   Ha? what? what is't?

CORDATUS   For the abuse of humour.

ASPER   O, I crave pardon, I had lost my thoughts.
Why, humour (as 'tis *ens*) we thus define it
To be a quality of air or water,
And in itself holds these two properties,
Moisture, and fluxure: as, for demonstration,
Pour water on this floor, 'twill wet and run:

Likewise the air (forc'd through a horn or trumpet)
Flows instantly away, and leaves behind
A kind of dew; and hence we do conclude,
That whatsoe'er hath fluxure, and humidity,
As wanting power to contain itself,
Is humour. So in every human body
The choler, melancholy, phlegm, and blood,
By reason that they flow continually
In some one part, and are not continent,
Receive the name of humours. Now thus far
It may, by metaphor, apply itself
Unto the general disposition:
As when some one peculiar quality
Doth so possess a man, that it doth draw
All his affects, his spirits, and his powers,
In their confluctions, all to run one way,
This may be truly said to be a humour.
But that a rook, in wearing a pied feather,
The cable hat-band, or the three-piled ruff,
A yard of shoetie, or the Switzer's knot
On his French garters, should affect a humour!
O 'tis more than most ridiculous.
CORDATUS   He speaks pure truth now, if an idiot
Have but an apish, or phantastic strain,
It is his humour.
ASPER   Well I will scourge those apes;
And to these courteous eyes oppose a mirror,
As large as is the stage, whereon we act:
Where they shall see the time's deformity
Anatomiz'd in every nerve, and sinew,
With constant courage, and contempt of fear.
MITIS   Asper, (I urge it as your friend) take heed,
The days are dangerous, full of exception,
And men are grown impatient of reproof.
ASPER   Ha, ha:
You might as well have told me, yond' is heaven,
This earth, these men; and all had mov'd alike.
Do not I know the time's condition?
Yes, Mitis, and their souls, and who they be,
That either will, or can except against me.
None, but a sort of fools, so sick in taste,

That they condemn all physic of the mind,
And, like gall'd camels, kick at every touch.
Good men, and virtuous spirits, that loathe their vices,
Will cherish my free labours, love my lines,
And with the fervour of their shining grace,
Make my brain fruitful to bring forth more objects,
Worthy their serious, and intentive eyes.
But why enforce I this? as fainting? No.
If any, here, chance to behold himself,
Let him not dare to challenge me of wrong,
For, if he shame to have his follies known
First he should shame to act them: my strict hand
Was made to seize on vice, and with a grip
Squeeze out the humour of such spongy natures,
As lick up every idle vanity.
CORDATUS   Why this is right *Furor Poeticus!*
Kind gentlemen, we hope your patience
Will yet conceive the best, or entertain
This supposition, that a madman speaks.
ASPER   What? are you ready there? Mitis sit down:
And my Cordatus. Sound hough, and begin.
I leave you two, as censors, to sit here:
Observe what I present, and liberally
Speak your opinions, upon every scene,
As it shall pass the view of these spectators.
Nay, now, y'are tedious Sirs. For shame begin.
And Mitis, note me, if in all this front,
You can espy a gallant of this mark,
Who (to be thought one of the judicious)
Sits with his arms thus wreath'd, his hat pull'd here,
Cries meow, and nods, then shakes his empty head,
Will show more several motions in his face,
Than the new London, Rome, or Nineveh,
And (now and then) breaks a dry biscuit jest,
Which that it may more easily be chew'd
He steeps in his own laughter.
CORDATUS   Why? will that
Make it be sooner swallow'd
ASPER   O, assure you.
Or if it did not, yet as Horace sings,
'Jeiunus rarò stomachus vulgaria temnit,'

'Mean cates are welcome still to hungry guests.'
CORDATUS 'Tis true, but why should we observe 'em, Asper?
ASPER O I would know 'em, for in such assemblies,
They're more infectious than the pestilence:
And therefore I would give them pills to purge,
And make 'em fit for fair societies.
How monstrous, and detested is't, to see
A fellow, that has neither art, nor brain,
Sit like an Aristarchus, or stark-ass,
Taking men's lines, with a tobacco face,
In snuff, still spitting, using his wry'd looks
(In nature of a vice) to wrest, and turn
The good aspect of those that shall sit near him,
From what they do behold! O, 'tis most vile.
MITIS Nay, Asper.
ASPER   Peace, Mitis, I do know your thought.
You'll say, your guests here will except at this:
Pish, you are too timorous, and full of doubt.
Then, he, a patient, shall reject all physic,
'Cause the physician tells him, you are sick:
Or, if I say, that he is vicious,
You will not hear of virtue. Come, y'are fond.
Shall I be so extravagant to think
That happy judgements and composed spirits
Will challenge me for taxing such as these?
I am asham'd.
CORDATUS   Nay, but good pardon us:
We must not bear this peremptory sail,
But use our best endeavours how to please.
ASPER Why, therein I commend your careful thoughts,
And I will mix with you in industry
To please, but whom? attentive auditors,
Such as will join their profit with their pleasure,
And come to feed their understanding parts:
For these, I'll prodigally spend myself,
And speak away my spirit into air;
For these, I'll melt my brain into invention,
Coin new conceits, and hang my richest words
As polished jewels in their bounteous ears.
But stay, I lose myself, and wrong their patience;
If I dwell here, they'll not begin, I see:

Friends sit you still, and entertain this troupe
With some familiar, and by-conference,
I'll haste them sound. Now gentlemen, I go
To turn an actor, and a humorist,
Where (ere I do resume my present person)
We hope to make the circle of your eyes
Flow with distilled laughter: if we fail,
We must impute it to this only chance,
'Art hath an enemy call'd Ignorance.'   [*Exit*]

CORDATUS   How do you like his spirit, Mitis?

MITIS   I should like it much better, if he were less confident.

CORDATUS   Why, do you suspect his merit?

MITIS   No, but I fear this will procure him much envy.

CORDATUS   O, that sets the stronger seal on his desert; if he had
no enemies, I should esteem his fortunes most wretched at this
instant.

MITIS   You have seen his play, Cordatus? pray you, how is't?

CORDATUS   Faith sir, I must refrain to judge, only this I can say
of it, 'tis strange, and of a particular kind by itself, somewhat
like *Vetus Comoedia*: a work that hath bounteously pleased me,
how it will answer the general expectation, I know not.

MITIS   Does he observe all the laws of comedy in it?

CORDATUS   What laws mean you?

MITIS   Why, the equal division of it into acts, and scenes, according to the Terentian manner, his true number of actors; the furnishing of the scene with grex, or chorus, and that the whole
argument fall within compass of a day's business.

CORDATUS   O no, these are too nice observations.

MITIS   They are such as must be received, by your favour, or it
cannot be authentic.

CORDATUS   Troth, I can discern no such necessity.

MITIS   No?

CORDATUS   No, I assure you, Signior. If those laws you speak of,
had been delivered us, *ab initio*, and in their present virtue and
perfection, there had been some reason of obeying their powers:
but 'tis extant, that that which we call *comoedia*, was at first
nothing but a simple and continued song, sung by one only
person, till Susario invented a second, after him Epicharmus a
third, Phormus and Chionides devised to have four actors, with
a prologue and chorus; to which Cratinus (long after) added a
fifth and sixth, Eupolis more; Aristophanes more than they: every

man in the dignity of his spirit and judgement, supplied something. And (though that in him this kind of poem appeared
absolute, and fully perfected) yet how is the face of it changed
since, in Menander, Philemon, Cecilius, Plautus, and the rest;
who have utterly excluded the chorus, altered the property of
the persons, their names, and natures, and augmented it with
all liberty, according to the elegance and disposition of those
times, wherein they wrote? I see not then, but we should enjoy
the same licence, or free power, to illustrate and heighten our
invention as they did; and not be tied to those strict and regular forms, which the niceness of a few (who are nothing but
form) would thrust upon us.

MITIS   Well, we will not dispute of this now: but what's his scene?

CORDATUS   Marry, *Insula Fortunata*, Sir.

MITIS   O, the Fortunate Island? Mass, he has bound himself to a
strict law there.

CORDATUS   Why so?

MITIS   He cannot lightly alter the scene, without crossing the seas.

CORDATUS   He needs not, having a whole island to run through,
I think.

MITIS   No? how comes it then, that in some one play we see so
many seas, countries, and kingdoms, pass'd over with such
admirable dexterity?

CORDATUS   O, that but shows how well the authors can travail
in their vocation, and outrun the apprehension of their audi-
tory. But leaving this, I would they would begin once: this pro-
traction is able to sour the best-settled patience in the theatre.
[*The third sounding.*]

MITIS   They have answered your wish, sir: they sound.

Every Man in his Humour

from Act V, Scene iii (lines 312–43 in H&S)

published in the quarto, 1601; omitted from the 1616 folio

LORENZO JUNIOR

If it may stand with your most wish'd content,
I can refell opinion, and approve
The state of poesy, such as it is,
Blessed, eternal, and most true divine.
Indeed, if you will look on poesy
As she appears in many, poor and lame,
Patch'd up in remnants and old worn rags,
Half-starv'd for want of her peculiar food,
Sacred invention, then I must confirm
Both your conceit and censure of her merit;
But view her in her glorious ornaments,
Attired in the majesty of art,
Set high in spirit with the precious taste
Of sweet philosophy, and, which is most,
Crown'd with the rich traditions of a soul
That hates to have her dignity profan'd
With any relish of an earthly thought:
Oh, then how proud a presence doth she bear!
Then is she like herself, fit to be seen
Of none but grave and consecrated eyes.
Nor is it any blemish to her fame
That such lean, ignorant, and blasted wits,
Such brainless gulls, should utter their stol'n wares
With such applauses in our vulgar ears;
Or that their slubber'd lines have current pass
From the fat judgments of the multitude;
But that this barren and infected age
Should set no difference 'twixt these empty spirits,
And a true poet; than which reverend name
Nothing can more adorn humanity.

From B. Jon: His Part of King James His Royal and Magnificent Entertainment through his Honourable City of London (specifically the Arch at Fenchurch)

first printed in the quarto of 1604; reprinted in the 1616 folio as Part of The King's Entertainment in Passing to His Coronation

The nature and property of these devices being, to present always some one entire body, or figure, consisting of distinct members, and each of those expressing itself, in the own active sphere, yet all, with the general harmony so connexed and disposed, as no one little part can be missing to the illustration of the whole: where also is to be noted, that the symbols used, are not, neither ought to be, simply hieroglyphics, emblems, or impresas, but a mixed character partaking somewhat of all, and peculiarly apted to these more magnificent inventions: wherein, the garments and ensigns deliver the nature of the person, and the word after the present office. Neither was it becoming, or could it stand with the dignity of these shows (after the most miserable and desperate shift of the puppets) to require a truchman, or (with the ignorant painter) one to write, *This is a Dog*; or, *This is a Hare*; but so to be presented, as upon the view, they might, without cloud, or obscurity, declare themselves to the sharp and learned: and for the multitude, no doubt but their grounded judgements did gaze, said it was fine, and were satisfied.

To the Readers, prefacing *Sejanus*

first printed in the 1605 quarto

The following and voluntary labours of my friends, prefixed to my book, have relieved me in much, whereat (without them) I should necessarily have touched: now, I will only use three or four short, and needful notes, and so rest.

First, if it be objected that what I publish is no true poem, in the strict laws of time, I confess it: as also in the want of a proper chorus, whose habit and moods are such, and so difficult, as not any whom I have seen since the Ancients (no, not they who have most presently affected laws) have yet come in the way of. Nor is it needful, or almost possible, in these our times, and to such auditors as commonly things are presented, to observe the old state and splendour of dramatic poems, with preservation of any popular delight. But of this I shall take more seasonable cause to speak, in my observations upon Horace his *Art of Poetry*, which (with the text translated) I intend shortly to publish. In the meantime, if in truth of argument, dignity of persons, gravity and height of elocution, fullness and frequency of sentence, I have discharged the other offices of a tragic writer, let not the absence of these forms be imputed to me, wherein I shall give you occasion hereafter (and without my boast) to think I could better prescribe, than omit the due use, for want of a convenient knowledge.

The next is, lest in some nice nostril, the quotations might savour affected, I do let you know that I abhor nothing more; and have only done it to show my integrity in the story, and save myself in those common torturers, that bring all wit to the rack: whose noses are ever like swine spoiling and rooting up the Muses' gardens, and their whole bodies, like moles, as blindly working under earth to cast any, the least, hills upon virtue.

Whereas they are in Latin and the work in English, it was presupposed, none but the learned would take the pains to confer them, the authors themselves being all in the learned tongues, save one, with whose English side I have had little to do: to which it may be required, since I have quoted the page, to name what editions I followed. *Tacit. Lips.* in 4°. *Antwerp. edit. 600. Dio. Folio Hen. Step. 92.* For the rest, as *Sueton, Seneca*, etc. the chapter doth sufficiently direct, or the edition is not varied.

Lastly I would inform you that this book, in all numbers, is not the same with that which was acted on the public stage, wherein a second pen had good share: in place of which I have rather chosen to put weaker (and no doubt less pleasing) of mine own, than to defraud so happy a genius of his right, by my loathed usurpation.

Fare you well, And if you read farther of me, and like, I shall not be afraid of it though you praise me out.

Neque enim mihi cornea fibra est.
['I am the last man, I say, to fear praise. My entrails are not made of horn!]

But that I should plant my felicity, in your general saying *Good*, or *Well*, etc. were a weakness which the better sort of you might worthily condemn, if not absolutely hate me for.
BEN. JONSON and no such,
Quem Palma negata macrum, donata reducit opimum.
[Whom denial of the palm sends home lean, its bestowal plump.]

From preface to *Hymenaei*

first printed in 1606 quarto; text essentially reprinted in 1616

It is a noble and just advantage that the things subjected to understanding have of those which are objected to sense that the one sort are but momentary and merely taking, the other impressing and lasting. Else the glory of all these solemnities had perished like a blaze and gone out in the beholders' eyes. So short lived are the bodies of all things in comparison of their souls. And, though bodies ofttimes have the ill luck to be sensually preferred, they find afterwards the good fortune, when souls live, to be utterly forgotten. This it is hath made the most royal princes and greatest persons, who are commonly the personators of these actions, not only studious of riches and magnificence in the outward celebration or show, which rightly becomes them, but curious after the most high and hearty inventions to furnish the inward parts, and those grounded upon antiquity and solid learnings; which, though their voice be taught to sound to present occasions, their sense or doth or should always lay hold on more removed mysteries. And howsoever some may squeamishly cry out that all endeavour of learning and sharpness in these transitory devices, especially where it steps beyond their little or (let me not wrong 'em) no brain at all, is superfluous, I am contented these fastidious stomachs should leave my full tables and enjoy at home their clean empty trenchers, fittest for such airy tastes, where perhaps a few Italian herbs picked up and made into a salad may find sweeter acceptance than all the most nourishing and sound meats of the world. For these men's palates let me not answer, O muses, It is not my fault if I fill them out nectar and they run to metheglin.

Vaticana bibant, si delectentur.
[Let them drink rotgut if it pleases them.]

All the courtesy I can do them is to cry again,

Praetereant, si quid non facit ad stomachum.
[Let them pass by anything which doesn't suit their stomach.]

As I will, from the thought of them to my better subject.

Volpone: EPISTLE AND PROLOGUE

first printed in the 1607 quarto; reprinted in the 1616 folio with amendments to the Epistle

EPISTLE
TO THE
MOST NOBLE AND MOST EQUAL SISTERS,
THE TWO FAMOUS UNIVERSITIES,
FOR THEIR
LOVE AND ACCEPTANCE SHOWN TO HIS POEM
IN THE PRESENTATION;
BEN. JONSON,
THE GRATEFUL ACKNOWLEDGER,
DEDICATES BOTH IT AND HIMSELF.

There follows an Epistle, if you dare venture on the length.

Never, most equal sisters, had any man a wit so presently excellent as that it could raise itself; but there must come both matter, occasion, commenders, and favourers to it. If this be true, and that the fortune of all writers doth daily prove it, it behoves the careful to provide well toward these accidents, and, having acquired them, to preserve that part of reputation most tenderly wherein the benefit of a friend is also defended. Hence is it that I now render myself grateful and am studious to justify the bounty of your act, to which, though your mere authority were satisfying, yet, it being an age wherein poetry and the professors of it hear so ill on all sides, there will a reason be looked for in the subject. It is certain, nor can it with any forehead be opposed, that the too much licence of poetasters in this time hath much deformed their mistress, that, every day, their manifold and manifest ignorance doth stick unnatural reproaches upon her; but for their petulancy it were an act of the greatest injustice either to let the learned suffer, or so divine a skill (which indeed should not be attempted with unclean hands) to fall under the least contempt. For if men will impartially, and not asquint, look toward the offices and function of a poet, they will easily conclude to themselves the impossibility of any man's being the good poet without first being a good man. He that is said to be able to inform young men to all good disciplines, inflame grown men to all great virtues, keep old men in their best and supreme state, or, as they decline to childhood, recover them to their first strength; that comes forth the interpreter and arbiter of nature, a teacher of things divine no less than human, a master in manners, and can alone, or with a few, effect the business of mankind: this, I take him, is no subject for pride and ignorance to exercise their railing rhetoric upon. But it will here be hastily answered that the writers of these days are other things: that not only their manners, but their natures, are inverted, and nothing remaining with them of the dignity of poet but the abused name, which every scribe usurps; that now, especially in dramatic, or, as they term it, stage poetry, nothing but ribaldry, profanation, blasphemy, all licence of offence to God and man is practised. I dare not deny a great part of this, and am sorry I dare not, because in some men's abortive features (and would they had never boasted the light) it is over-true; but that all are embarked in this bold adventure for hell is a most uncharitable thought, and, uttered, a more malicious slander. For my particular, I can, and from a most clear conscience, affirm that I have ever trembled to think toward the least profaneness, have loathed the use of such foul and unwashed bawdry as is now made the food of the scene. And, howsoever I cannot escape, from some, the imputation of sharpness, but that they will say I have taken a pride, or lust, to be bitter, and not my youngest infant but hath come into the world with all his teeth; I would ask of these supercilious politics, what nation, society, or general order, or state I have provoked? what public person? whether I have not (in all these) preserved their dignity, as mine own person, safe? My works are read, allowed (I speak of those that are entirely mine); look into them. What broad reproofs have I used? Where have I been particular? Where personal? except to a mimic, cheater, bawd, or buffoon, creatures (for their insolencies) worthy to be taxed? Yet, to which of these so pointingly, as he might not, either ingenuously have confessed, or wisely dissembled his disease? But it is not rumour can make men guilty, much less entitle me to other men's crimes. I know that nothing can be so innocently writ or carried, but may be made obnoxious to construction; marry, whilst I bear mine innocence about me, I fear it not. Application is now grown a trade with many, and there are that profess to have a key for the deciphering of everything; but let wise and noble persons take heed how they be too credulous, or give leave to these invading interpreters to be over-familiar with their fames, who cunningly, and often, utter their own virulent malice under other men's simplest meanings. As for those that will (by faults which charity hath raked up, or common honesty concealed) make themselves a name with the multitude, or (to draw their rude and beastly claps) care not whose living faces they entrench with their petulant styles, may they do it without a rival, for me. I choose rather to lie graved in obscurity than share with them in so preposterous a fame. Nor can I blame the wishes of those severe and wiser patriots, who, providing the hurts these licentious spirits may do in a state, desire rather to see fools and devils, and those antique relics of barbarism retrieved, with all other ridiculous and exploded follies, than behold the wounds of private men, of princes, and nations. For, as Horace makes Trebatius speak, among these:

– *Sibi quisque timet, quamquam est intactus, et odit.*

And men may justly impute such rages, if continued, to the writer, as his sports. The increase of which lust in liberty, together with the present trade of the stage, in all their misc'line interludes, what learned or liberal soul doth not already abhor? where nothing but the filth of the time is uttered, and that with such impropriety of phrase, such plenty of solecisms, such dearth of sense, so bold prolepses, so racked metaphors, with brothelry able to violate the ear of a pagan, and blasphemy to turn the blood of a Christian to water. I cannot but be serious in a cause of this nature, wherein my fame and the reputations of divers honest and learned are the question; when a name so full of authority, antiquity, and all great mark, is, through their insolence, become the lowest scorn of the age; and those men subject to the petulancy of every vernaculous orator that were wont to be the care of kings and happiest monarchs. This it is that hath not only rapt me to present indignation, but made me studious heretofore, and by all my actions to stand off from them; which may most appear in this my latest work – which you, most learned Arbitresses, have seen, judged, and, to my crown, approved – wherein I have laboured, for their instruction and amendment, to reduce not only the ancient forms, but manners of the scene: the easiness, the propriety, the inno-cence, and last the doctrine, which is the principal end of poesy, to inform men in the best reason of living. And though my catas-trophe may in the strict rigour of comic law meet with censure, as turning back to my promise, I desire the learned and chari-table critic to have so much faith in me to think it was done of industry: for with what ease I could have varied it nearer his scale (but that I fear to boast my own faculty) I could here insert. But my special aim being to put the snaffle in their mouths that cry out: We never punish vice in our interludes, &c., I took the more liberty; though not without some lines of example drawn even in the ancients themselves, the goings-out of whose comedies are not always joyful, but oft-times the bawds, the servants, the rivals, yea, and the masters are mulcted, and fitly, it being the office of a comic poet to imitate justice, and instruct to life, as well as purity of language, or stir up gentle affections. To which, upon my next opportunity toward the examining and digesting of my notes, I shall speak more wealthily, and pay the world a debt. For the present, most reverenced Sisters, as I have cared to be thankful for your affections past, and here made the under-standing acquainted with some ground of your favours, let me not despair their continuance, to the maturing of some worthier fruits; wherein, if my muses be true to me, I shall raise the de-spised head of poetry again, and, stripping her out of those rotten and base rags wherewith the times have adulterated her form, restore her to her primitive habit, feature, and majesty, and render her worthy to be embraced and kissed of all the great and master-spirits of our world. As for the vile and slothful, who never affected an act worthy of celebration or are so inwards with their own vicious natures, as they worthily fear her and think it a high point of policy to keep her in contempt with their declamatory and windy invectives: she shall out of just rage incite her servants (who are *genus irritabile*) to spout ink in their faces, that shall eat, farther then their marrow, into their fames; and not Cinnamus the barber, with his art, shall be able to take out the brands, but they shall live, and be read, till the wretches die, as things worst deserving of themselves in chief, and then of all mankind.

From my house in the Blackfriars this 11 of February 1607.

PROLOGUE

Now, luck yet send us, and a little wit
    Will serve to make our play hit;
According to the palates of the season,
    Here is rhyme not empty of reason.
This we were bid to credit from our poet,
    Whose true scope, if you would know it,
In all his poems still hath been this measure:
    To mix profit with your pleasure;
And not as some, whose throats their envy failing,
    Cry hoarsely, 'All he write is railing,'
And when his plays come forth, think they can flout them,
    With saying, 'He was a year about them.'
To these there needs no lie but this his creature,
    Which was two months since no feature;
And though he dares give them five lives to mend it,
    'Tis known, five weeks fully penned it,
From his own hand, without a coadjutor,
    Novice, journeyman, or tutor.
Yet thus much I can give you as a token
    Of his play's worth: no eggs are broken;
Nor quaking custards with fierce teeth affrighted,
    Wherewith your rout are so delighted;

Nor hales he in a gull, old ends reciting,
To stop gaps in his loose writing;
With such a deal of monstrous and forced action
As might make Bedlam a faction;
Nor made he his play for jests stol'n from each table,
But makes jests to fit his fable.
And so presents quick comedy refined,
As best critics have designed;
The laws of time, place, persons he observeth,
From no needful rule he swerveth.
All gall and copperas from his ink he draineth,
Only a little salt remaineth,
Wherewith he'll rub your cheeks, till red with laughter,
They shall look fresh a week after.

From preface to *The Masques* of *Blackness* and of *Beauty*

first printed in 1608 quarto; essentially reprinted in 1616 folio

The honour and splendour of these spectacles was such in the performance as, could those hours have lasted, this of mine now had been a most unprofitable work. But, when it is the fate even of the greatest and most absolute births to need and borrow a life of posterity, little had been done to the study of magnificence in these if presently with the rage of the people, who, as a part of greatness, are privileged by custom to deface their carcases, the spirits had also perished. In duty, therefore, to that Majesty who gave them their authority and grace, and, no less than the most royal of predecessors, deserves eminent celebration for these solemnities, I add this later hand to redeem them as well from ignorance as envy, two common evils, the one of censure, the other of oblivion.

From the preface to *The Masque of Queens*

first printed in the 1609 quarto; essentially reprinted in the 1616 folio

It increasing now to the third time of my being used in these services to her Majesty's personal presentations, with the ladies whom she pleaseth to honour, it was my first and special regard to see that the nobility of the invention should be answerable to the dignity of their persons. For which reason I chose the argument to be a celebration of honourable and true fame bred out of virtue, observing that rule of the best artist, to suffer no object of delight to pass without his mixture of profit and example. And because her Majesty (best knowing that a principal part of life in these spectacles lay in their variety) had commanded me to think on some dance or show that might precede hers and have the place of a foil or false masque, I was careful to decline not only from others', but mine own steps in that kind, since the last year I had an anti-masque of boys; and therefore now devised that twelve women in the habit of hags or witches, sustaining the persons of Ignorance, Suspicion, Credulity, etc., the opposites to good Fame, should fill that part, not as a masque but a spectacle of strangeness, producing multiplicity of gesture, and not unaptly sorting with the current and whole fall of the device.

To the Reader, prefacing *The Alchemist*

first printed in the 1612 quarto; omitted from the 1616 folio

If thou beest more, thou art an understander, and then I trust thee. If thou art one that tak'st up, and but a pretender, beware at what hands thou receiv'st thy commodity; for thou wert never more fair in the way to be cozened than in this age in poetry, especially in plays: wherein now the concupiscence of dances and antics so reigneth, as to run away from nature and be afraid of her is the only point of art that tickles the spectators. But how out of purpose and place do I name art, when the professors are grown so obstinate condemners of it, and presumers on their own naturals, as they are deriders of all diligence that way, and by simple mocking at the terms, when they understand not the things, think to get off wittily with their ignorance. Nay, they are esteemed the more learned and sufficient for this by the many, through their excellent vice of judgement. For they commend writers as they do fencers or wrestlers, who, if they come in robustiously, and put for it with a great deal of violence, are received for the braver fellows; when many times their own rudeness is the cause of their disgrace, and a little touch of their adversary gives all that boisterous force the foil. I deny not but that these men, who always seek to do more than enough, may sometime happen on something that is good and great, but very seldom; and when it comes it doth not recompense the rest of their ill. It sticks out perhaps and is more eminent because all is sordid and vile about it, as lights are more discerned in a thick darkness than a faint shadow. I speak not this out of a hope to do good on any man against his will; for I know, if it were put to the question of theirs and mine, the worse would find more suffrages, because the most favour common errors. But I give thee this warning, that there is a great difference between those that, to gain the opinion of copy, utter all they can, however unfitly, and those that use election and a mean. For it is only the disease of the unskilful to think rude things greater than polished, or scattered more numerous than composed.

Dedication and prefaces to *Catiline His Conspiracy*

first printed in the 1611 quarto; 'To the Reader in Ordinary' and 'Extraordinary' both omitted from the 1616 folio

TO THE GREAT EXAMPLE OF HONOUR AND VIRTUE,
THE MOST NOBLE
WILLIAM, EARL OF PEMBROKE,

My Lord, – In so thick and dark an ignorance, as now almost covers the age, I crave leave to stand near your light, and by that to be read. Posterity may pay your benefit the honour and thanks, when it shall know that you dare, in these jig-given times, to countenance a legitimate poem. I must call it so, against all noise of opinion; from whose crude and airy reports I appeal to that great and singular faculty of judgment in your lordship, able to vindicate truth from error. It is the first, of this race, that ever I dedicated to any person; and had I not thought it the best, it should have been taught a less ambition. Now it approacheth your censure cheerfully, and with the same assurance that innocency would appear before a magistrate. Your lordship's most faithful honourer,

BEN JONSON

TO THE READER IN ORDINARY

The muses forbid that I should restrain your meddling, whom I see already busy with the title, and tricking over the leaves: it is your own. I departed with my right, when I let it first abroad; and now, so secure an interpreter I am of my chance, that neither praise nor dispraise from you can affect me. Though you commend the two first acts with the people, because they are the worst; and dislike the oration of Cicero, in regard you read some pieces of it at school, and understand them not yet: I shall find the way to forgive you. Be any thing you will be, at your own charge. Would I had deserved but half so well of it in translation, as that ought to deserve of you in judgment, if you have any. I know you will pretend, whosoever you are, to have that, and more: but all pretenses are not just claims. The commendation of good things may fall within a many, their approbation but in a few; for the most commend out of affection, self-tickling, an easiness, or imitation: but men judge only out of knowledge. That is the trying faculty: and to those works that will bear a judge, nothing is more dangerous than a foolish praise. You will say, I shall not have yours therefore: but rather the contrary, all vexation of censure. If I were not above such molestations now, I had great cause to think unworthily of my studies, or they had so of me. But I leave you to your exercise. Begin.

TO THE READER EXTRAORDINARY

You I would understand to be the better man, though places in court go otherwise: to you I submit myself and work. Farewell.

BEN JONSON

Prologue to *Every Man in his Humour*

first printed in the 1616 folio

Though need make many poets, and some such
As art, and nature have not bettered much;
Yet ours, for want, hath not so lov'd the stage,
As he dare serve th'ill customs of the age:
Or purchase your delight at such a rate,
As, for it, he himself must justly hate.
To make a child, now swaddled, to proceed
Man, and then shoot up, in one beard, and weed,
Past three score years: or, with three rusty swords,
And help of some few foot-and-half-foot words,
Fight over York, and Lancaster's long jars:
And in the tiring-house bring wounds, to scars.
He rather prays, you will be pleas'd to see

One such, today, as other plays should be.
Where neither Chorus wafts you o'er the seas;
Nor creaking throne comes down, the boys to please;
Nor nimble squib is seen to make afear'd
The gentlewomen; nor roll'd bullet heard
To say, it thunders; nor tempestuous drum
Rumbles, to tell you when the storm doth come;
But deeds, and language, such as men do use:
And persons, such as comedy would choose,
When she would show an image of the times,
And sport with human follies, not with crimes.
Except, we make them such by loving still
Our popular errors, when we know they're ill.
I mean such errors, as you'll all confess
By laughing at them, they deserve no less:
Which when you heartily do, there's hope left, then,
You, that have so grac'd monsters, may like men.

Poetaster: The Apologetical Dialogue

*written 1601/2; first published in the 1616 folio,
after the play*

TO THE READER

If, by looking on what is past, thou hast deserved that name, I
am willing thou should'st yet know more, by that which follows;
an *Apologetical Dialogue*: which was only once spoken upon the
stage, and all the answer I ever gave, to sundry impotent libels
then cast out (and some yet remaining) against me, and this play.
Wherein I take no pleasure to revive the times, but that posterity
may make a difference, between their manners that provok'd me
then, and mine that neglected them ever. For, in these strifes,
and on such persons, were as wretched to affect a victory, as it is
unhappy to be committed with them. [It is not the grey hairs but
the manners of age which must be praised.]

The Persons

NASUTUS, POLYPOSUS, AUTHOR

I pray you let's go see him, how he looks
After these libels.
POLYPOSUS   O, vex'd vex'd, I warrant you.
NASUTUS Do you think so? I should be sorry for him,
If I found that.
POLYPOSUS   O, they are such bitter things,
He cannot choose.
NASUTUS   But, is he guilty of 'em?
POLYPOSUS Fuh! that's no matter.
NASUTUS   No?
POLYPOSUS   No.
                                        Here's his lodging;
We'll steal upon him: or, let's listen, stay.
He has a humour oft to talk t'himself,
NASUTUS They are your manners lead me, not mine own.
AUTHOR   The Fates have not spun him the coarsest thread
That (free from knots of perturbation)
Doth yet so live, although but to himself,
As he can safely scorn the tongues of slaves;
And neglect Fortune, more than she can him.
It is the happiest thing, this not to be
Within the reach of malice; it provides
A man so well, to laugh off injuries:
And never sends him farther for his vengeance
Than the vex'd bosom of his enemy.
Aye, now, but think, how poor their spite sets off.
Who, after all their waste of sulphurous terms,
And burst-out thunder of their charged mouths,
Have nothing left, but the unsav'ry smoke
Of their black vomit, to upbraid themselves:
Whilst I, at whom they shot, sit here shot-free
And as unhurt of envy, as unhit.
POLYPOSUS Aye, but the multitude, they think not so, sir,
They think you hit, and hurt: and dare give out
Your silence argues it, in not rejoining
To this, or that late libel?
AUTHOR   'Las, good rout!

I can afford them leave, to err so still:
And, like the barking students of Bears' College,
To swallow up the garbage of the time
With greedy gullets, whilst my self sit by,
Pleas'd, and yet tortur'd, with their beastly feeding.
'Tis a sweet madness runs along with them,
To think, all that are aim'd at, still are struck:
Then, where the shaft still lights, make that the mark,
And so, each fear, or fever-shaken fool
May challenge Teucer's hand in archery.
Good troth, if I knew any man so vile,
To act the crimes these whippers reprehend,
Or what their servile apes gesticulate,
I should not then much muse, their shreds were lik'd;
Since ill men have a lust t'hear others' sins,
And good men have a zeal to hear sin sham'd.
But when it is all excrement they vent,
Base filth, and offal: or thefts, notable
As Ocean piracies, or highway stands:
And not a crime there tax'd, but is their own,
Or what their own foul thoughts suggested to them,
And that in all their heat of taxing others
Not one of them, but lives himself (if known)
[Worse than a sodomite writing satires].
What should I say, more? then turn stone with wonder!
NASUTUS I never saw this play bred all this tumult.
What was there in it could so deeply offend?
And stir so many hornets?
AUTHOR   Shall I tell you?
NASUTUS Yes, and ingenuously.
AUTHOR   Then, by the hope,
Which I prefer unto all other objects,
I can profess, I never writ that piece
More innocent, or empty of offence.
Some salt it had, but neither tooth, nor gall,
Nor was there in it any circumstance,
Which, in the setting down, I could suspect
Might be perverted by an enemy's tongue.
Only, it had the fault to be call'd mine.
That was the crime.
POLYPOSUS   No? Why, they say you tax'd

The law, and lawyers; captains; and the players
By their particular names.
AUTHOR   It is not so.
I used no name. My books have still been taught
To spare the persons, and to speak the vices.
These are mere slanders, and enforc'd by such
As have no safer ways to men's disgraces,
But their own lies, and loss of honesty.
Fellows of practis'd and most laxative tongues,
Whose empty and eager bellies, i' the year,
Compel their brains to many desp'rate shifts,
(I spare to name 'em: for, their wretchedness,
Fury itself would pardon.) These, or such,
Whether of malice, or of ignorance,
Or itch, t'have me their adversary (I know not)
Or all these mix'd; but sure I am, three years
They did provoke me with their petulant styles
On every stage: And I at last, unwilling,
But weary, I confess, of so much trouble,
Thought I would try, if shame could win upon 'em.
And therefore chose Augustus Caesar's times,
When wit and arts were at their height in Rome,
To show that Virgil, Horace, and the rest
Of those great master-spirits did not want
Detractors, then, or practicers against them:
And by this line (although no parallel)
I hop'd at last they would sit down, and blush.
But nothing could I find more contrary.
And though the impudence of flies be great,
Yet this hath so provok'd the angry wasps,
Or as you said, of the next nest, the hornets;
That they fly buzzing, mad, about my nostrils:
And like so many screaming grasshoppers,
Held by the wings, fill every ear with noise.
And what? those former calumnies you mention'd.
First, of the law. Indeed, I brought in Ovid,
Chid by his angry father, for neglecting
The study of the laws, for poetry:
And I am warranted by his own words.
[Often, Father said, 'Why do you pursue a useless study?
    Maeonides himself left no wealth.']

And in far harsher terms elsewhere, as these:
[I do not learn the ill-written laws, nor have I
  Prostituted my voice before the carping bar.]
But how this should relate unto our laws,
Or their just ministers, with least abuse,
I reverence both too much, to understand!
  Then, for the captain; I will only speak
An *Epigram* I here have made: It is
Unto true Soldiers. That's the *lemma.* Mark it.
  Strength of my Country, whilst I bring to view
    Such as are miscall'd Captains, and wrong you,
  And your high names; I do desire, that thence,
    Be nor put on you, nor you take offence:
  I swear by your true friend, my Muse, I love
    Your great profession, which I once did prove;
  And did not shame it with my actions, then,
    No more than I dare, now, do with my pen.
  He that not trusts me, having vow'd thus much,
    But's angry for the Captains, still: is such.
Now, for the players, it is true, I tax'd 'em,
And yet, but some; and those so sparingly,
As all the rest might have sat still, unquestion'd,
Had they but had the wit, or conscience,
To think well of themselves. But impotent they
Thought each man's vice belong'd to their whole tribe:
And much good do't 'em. What they're done 'gainst me,
I am now mov'd with. If it gave 'em meat,
Or got 'em clothes, 'tis well: that was their end.
Only amongst them, I am sorry for
Some better natures, by the rest so drawn,
To run in that vile line.
POLYPOSUS   And is this all?
Will you not answer then the libels?
AUTHOR   No.
POLYPOSUS   Nor the untrussers?
AUTHOR   Neither.
POLYPOSUS   Y'are undone them.
AUTHOR   With whom?
POLYPOSUS   The world.
AUTHOR   The bawd!
POLYPOSUS   It will be taken

To be stupidity, or tameness in you.
AUTHOR   But, they that have incens'd me, can in soul
   Acquit me of that guilt. They know I dare
   To spurn, or baffle 'em; or squirt their eyes
   With ink, or urine: or I could do worse,
   Arm'd with Archilochus' fury, write iambics,
   Should make the desperate lashers hang themselves,
   Rhyme 'em to death, as they do Irish rats
   In drumming tunes. Or, living, I could stamp
   Their foreheads with those deep and public brands,
   That the whole company of Barber-Surgeons
   Should not take off, with all their art and plasters.
   And these my prints should last, still to be read
   In their pale fronts: when what they write 'gainst me
   Shall like a figure, drawn in water, fleet,
   And the poor wretched papers be employ'd
   To cloth tobacco, or some cheaper drug.
   This I could do, and make them infamous.
   But, to what end? when their own deeds have mark'd 'em,
   And, that I know, within his guilty breast
   Each slanderer bears a whip, that shall torment him,
   Worse than a million of these temporal plagues:
   Which to pursue were but a feminine humour,
   And far beneath the dignity of a man.
NASUTUS   'Tis true: for to revenge their injuries,
   Were to confess you felt 'em. Let 'em go,
   And use the treasure of the fool, their tongues,
   Who makes his gain, by speaking worst of best.
POLYPOSUS   O, but they lay particular imputations –
AUTHOR   As what?
POLYPOSUS   That all your writing is mere railing.
AUTHOR   Ha! If all the salt in the old comedy
   Should be so censur'd, or the sharper wit
   Of the bold satire, termed scolding rage,
   What age could then compare with those, for buffoons?
   What should be said of Aristophanes?
   Persius? or Juvenal? whose names we now
   So glorify in schools, at least pretend it.
   Ha' they no other?
POLYPOSUS   Yes: they say you are slow,
   And scarce bring forth a play a year.

AUTHOR   'Tis true,
I would they could not say that I did that,
There's all the joy that I take i' their trade,
Unless such scribes as they might be proscrib'd
Th'abused theatres. They would think it strange, now,
A man should take but coltsfoot for one day
And, between whiles, spit out a better poem
Than e'er the master of art, or giver of wit,
Their belly made. Yet, this is possible
If a free mind had but the patience,
To think so much, together, and so vile.
But, that these base, and beggarly conceits
Should carry it, by the multitude of voices,
Against the most abstracted work, oppos'd
To the stuff'd nostrils of the drunken rout!
O, this would make a learn'd and liberal soul
To rive his stained quill, up to the back,
And damn his long-watch'd labours to the fire;
Things that were born, when none but the still night
And his dumb candle saw his pinching throes:
Were not his own free merit a more crown
Unto his travails, than their reeling claps.
This 'tis, that strikes me silent, seals my lips,
And apts me rather to sleep out my times,
Than I would waste it in condemned strifes,
With these vile Ibides, these unclean birds,
That make their mouths their clysters, and still purge
From their hot entrails. But I leave the monsters
To their own fate. And, since the comic muse
Hath proved so ominous to me, I will try
If tragedy have a more kind aspect.
Her favours in my next I will pursue,
Where if I prove the pleasure but of one,
So he judicious be; he shall b'alone
A theatre unto me: Once, I'll say,
To strike the ear of time, in those fresh strains,
As shall, beside the cunning of their ground,
Give cause to some of wonder, some despair,
And unto more, despair, to imitate their sound.
I, that spend half my nights, and all my days,
Here in a cell, to get a dark, pale face.

To come forth worth the ivy, or the bays,
And in this age can hope no other grace –
Leave me. There's something come into my thought,
That must and shall be sung, high and aloof,
Safe from the wolf's black jaw, and the dull ass's hoof.
NASUTUS   I reverence these raptures, and obey 'em.

Dedication to *Sejanus*

first printed in the 1616 folio

TO THE NO LESS NOBLE, BY VIRTUE, THAN BLOOD:

ESMÉ, L. AUBIGNY

MY LORD,
If ever any ruin were so great, as to survive, I think this be one
I send you: the *Fall of Sejanus*. It is a poem that (if I well remember) in your Lordship's sight, suffered no less violence from our
people here, than the subject of it did from the rage of the people
of Rome; but, with a different fate, as (I hope) merit: for this
hath out-lived their malice, and begot itself a greater favour than
he lost, the love of good men. Amongst whom, if I make your
Lordship the first it thanks, it is not without a just confession of
the bond your benefits have, and ever shall hold upon me.
                    Your Lordship's most faithful honourer,
                                        Ben. Jonson.

Dedication to *Epigrams*

first printed in the 1616 folio

TO THE GREAT EXAMPLE OF HONOUR AND VIRTUE, THE MOST
NOBLE WILLIAM, EARL OF PEMBROKE, L[ORD] CHAMBERLAIN, etc.

My Lord: While you cannot change your merit, I dare not change
your title; it was that made it, and not I. Under which name, I
here offer to your Lo[rdship] the ripest of my studies, my *Epigrams*, which, though they carry danger in the sound, do not therefore seek your shelter; for when I made them I had nothing in
my conscience to expressing of which I did need a cipher. But if
I be fallen into those times wherein, for the likeness of vice and
facts, everyone thinks another's ill deeds objected to him, and
that in their ignorant and guilty mouths the common voice is, for
their security, 'Beware the poet' – confessing therein so much love
to their diseases as they would rather make a party for them
than be either rid or told of them – I must expect at your
Lo[rdship's] hand the protection of truth and liberty while you
are constant to your own goodness. In thanks whereof I return
you the honour of leading forth so many good and great names
as my verses mention on the better part, to their remembrance
with posterity; amongst whom if I have praised, unfortunately,
anyone that doth not deserve, or if all answer not in all numbers
the pictures I have made of them, I hope it will be forgiven me,
that they are no ill pieces, though they be not like the persons.
But I foresee a nearer fate to my book than this: that the vices
therein will be owned before the virtues (though there I have
avoided all particulars, as I have done names) and that some will
be so ready to discredit me as they will have the impudence to
belie themselves; for if I meant them not, it is so. Nor can I hope
otherwise; for why should they remit anything of their riot, their
pride, their self-love, and other inherent graces, to consider truth
or virtue? but with the trade of the world lend their long ears
against men they love not, and hold their dear mountebank or
jester in far better condition than all the study or studiers of humanity. For such, I would rather know them by their vizards still,

than they should publish their faces at their peril in my theatre,
where Cato, if he lived, might enter without scandal.

Your Lo[rdship's] most faithful honourer,

Ben Jonson

From *Mr William Shakespeare's Comedies, Histories, and Tragedies*, 1623

To the Memory of My Beloved, The Author, Mr William Shakespeare, And What He Hath Left Us

To draw no envy, Shakespeare, on thy name,
    Am I thus ample to thy book and fame;
While I confess thy writings to be such
    As neither man nor muse can praise too much:
'Tis true, and all men's suffrage. But these ways
    Were not the paths I meant unto thy praise:
For silliest ignorance on these may light,
    Which, when it sounds at best, but echoes right;
Or blind affection, which doth ne'er advance
    The truth, but gropes, and urgeth all by chance;
Or crafty malice might pretend this praise,
    And think to ruin where it seemed to raise.
These are as some infamous bawd or whore
    Should praise a matron: what could hurt her more?
But thou art proof against them, and indeed
    Above the ill fortune of them, or the need.
I therefore will begin. Soul of the age!
    The applause, delight, the wonder of our stage!
My Shakespeare, rise: I will not lodge thee by
    Chaucer or Spenser, or bid Beaumont lie
A little further, to make thee a room;
    Thou art a monument without a tomb,
And art alive still while thy book doth live,
    And we have wits to read, and praise to give.
That I not mix thee so, my brain excuses:

I mean with great, but disproportioned, muses;
For if I thought my judgement were of years
   I should commit thee surely with thy peers:
And tell how far thou didst our Lyly outshine,
   Or sporting Kyd, or Marlowe's mighty line.
And though thou hadst small Latin, and less Greek,
   From thence to honour thee I would not seek
For names, but call forth thundering Aeschylus,
   Euripides, and Sophocles to us,
Pacuvius, Accius, him of Cordova dead,
   To life again, to hear thy buskin tread
And shake a stage; or, when thy socks were on,
   Leave thee alone for the comparison
Of all that insolent Greece or haughty Rome
   Sent forth, or since did from their ashes come.
Triumph, my Britain, thou hast one to show
   To whom all scenes of Europe homage owe.
He was not of an age, but for all time!
   And all the muses still were in their prime
When like Apollo he came forth to warm
   Our ears, or like a Mercury to charm!
Nature herself was proud of his designs,
   And joyed to wear the dressing of his lines,
Which were so richly spun and woven so fit
   As, since, she will vouchsafe no other wit.
The merry Greek, tart Aristophanes,
   Neat Terence, witty Plautus, now not please,
But antiquated and deserted lie
   As they were not of nature's family.
Yet must I not give nature all: thy art,
   My gentle Shakespeare, must enjoy a part.
For though the poet's matter nature be,
   His art doth give the fashion. And that he
Who casts to write a living line must sweat
   (Such as thine are) and strike the second heat
Upon the muses' anvil: turn the same
   (And himself with it) that he thinks to frame;
Or for the laurel he may gain a scorn:
   For a good poet's made, as well as born;
And such wert thou. Look how the father's face
   Lives in his issue: even so, the race

Of Shakespeare's mind and manners brightly shines
    In his well-turnèd and true-filèd lines:
In each of which he seems to shake a lance,
    As brandished at the eyes of ignorance.
Sweet swan of Avon! What a sight it were
    To see thee in our waters yet appear,
And make those flights upon the banks of Thames
    That so did take Eliza, and our James!
But stay, I see thee in the hemisphere
    Advanced, and made a constellation there!
Shine forth, thou star of poets, and with rage
    Or influence chide or cheer the drooping stage;
Which, since thy flight from hence, hath mourned like night,
    And despairs day, but for thy volume's light.

From *BARTHOLOMEW FAIR: Induction, Prologue and Epilogue*

written 1614; first printed in the abortive folio of 1631; reprinted in the 1640 Second Folio

THE INDUCTION ON THE STAGE

[*Enter* STAGE-KEEPER.]

STAGE-KEEPER Gentleman, have a little patience, they are e'en upon coming, instantly. He that should begin the play, Master Littlewit, the Proctor, has a stitch new fall'n in his black silk stocking; 'twill be drawn up ere you can tell twenty. He plays one o' the Arches, that dwells about the Hospital, and he has a very pretty part. But for the whole play, will you ha' the truth on't (I am looking, lest the poet hear me, or his man, Master Brome, behind the arras) it is like to be a very conceited scurvy one, in plain English. When't comes to the Fair once, you were e'en as good go to Virginia, for anything there is of Smithfield. He has not hit the humours, he does not know 'em; he has ne'er a sword-and-buckler man in his Fair, nor a little Davy to take toll o' the bawds there, as in my time, nor a Kindheart, if anybody's teeth should chance to ache in his play. Nor a juggler with a well-educated ape to come over the chain for the King of England and back again for the Prince, and sit still on his arse for the Pope and the King of Spain! None o' these fine sights! Nor has he the canvas-cut i' the night for a hobby-horse man to creep in to his she-neighbour and take his leap there! Nothing! No, and some writer (that I know) had had but the penning o' this matter, he would ha' made you such a jib-a-job i' the booths, you should ha' thought an earthquake had been i' the Fair! But these masters-poets, they will ha' their own absurd courses; they will be informed of nothing! He has, sir reverence, kicked me three of four times about the tiring-house, I thank him, for but offering to put in, with my experience. I'll be judged by you, gentlemen, now, but for one conceit of mine! Would not a fine pump upon the stage ha' done well for a property now! And a punk set under upon her head, with her stern upward, and ha' been soused by my witty young masters o' the Inns o' Court? What think you o' this for a show, now? He will not hear o' this! I am an ass, I? And yet I kept the stage in Master Tarlton's time, I thank my stars. Ho! an' that man had lived to have played in *Barthol'mew Fair*, you should ha' seen him ha' come in, and ha' been cozened i' the cloth-quarter, so finely. And Adams, the rogue, ha' leaped and capered upon him, and ha' dealt his vermin about as though they had cost him nothing. And then a substantial watch to ha' stol'n in upon 'em, and taken 'em away with mistaking words, as the fashion is in the stage-practice.

[*Enter* BOOK-HOLDER *and* SCRIVENER *to him.*]

BOOK-HOLDER   How now? What rare discourse you are fall'n upon, ha! Ha' you found any familiars here, that you are so free? What's the business?

STAGE-KEEPER   Nothing, but the understanding gentlemen o' the ground here asked my judgement.

BOOK-HOLDER   Your judgement, rascal? For what? Sweeping the stage? Or gathering up the broken apples for the bears within? Away rogue, it's come to a fine degree in these spectacles when such a youth as you pretend to a judgement.

[*Exit* STAGE-KEEPER.]

And yet he may, i' the most o' this matter i' faith; for the author hath writ it just to his meridian, and the scale of the grounded judgements here, his play-fellows in wit. – Gentlemen, not for want of a prologue, but by way of a new one, I am sent out to you here with a scrivener, and certain articles drawn out in haste between our author and you; which if you please to hear, and as they appear reasonable, to approve of, the play will follow presently. Read, scribe, gi' me the counterpane.

SCRIVENER [*reading*] 'Articles of Agreement indented between the spectators or hearers at the Hope on the Bankside, in the county of Surrey, on the one party, and the author of *Barthol'-mew Fair* in the said place and county, on the other party, the one and thirtieth day of October 1614, and in the twelfth year of the reign of our Sovereign Lord, James, by the grace of God King of England, France and Ireland, Defender of the Faith; and of Scotland the seven and fortieth.

INPRIMIS, It is covenanted and agreed, by and between the parties above-said, and the said spectators and hearers, as well the curious and envious as the favouring and judicious, as also the grounded judgements and understandings do for themselves severally covenant and agree, to remain in the place their money or friends have put them in, with patience, for the space of two hours, and an half and somewhat more. In which time the author promiseth to present them, by us, with a new sufficient play called *Barthol'mew Fair*, merry, and as full of noise as sport, made to delight all, and to offend none; provided they have either the wit or the honesty to think well of themselves.

'It is further agreed that every person here have his or their free-will of censure, to like or dislike at their own charge, the author having now departed with his right: it shall be lawful for any man to judge his six pen'orth, his twelve pen'orth, so to his eighteen pence, two shillings, half a crown, to the value of his place; provided always his place get not above his wit. And if he pay for half a dozen, he may censure for all them too, so that he will undertake that they shall be silent. He shall put in for censures here as they do for lots at the lottery; marry, if he drop but sixpence at the door, and will censure a crown's worth, it is thought there is no conscience or justice in that.

'It is also agreed that every man here exercise his own judgement, and not censure by contagion, or upon trust, from another's voice or face that sits by him, be he never so first in the commission of wit; as also, that he be fixed and settled in his censure, that what he approves or not approves today, he will do the same tomorrow, and if tomorrow, the next day, and so the next week (if need be), and not to be brought about by any that sits on the bench with him, though they indict and arraign plays daily. He that will swear *Jeronimo* or *Andronicus* are the best plays yet, shall pass unexcepted at here, as a man whose judgement shows it is constant, and hath stood still these five and twenty, or thirty years. Though it be an ignorance, it is a virtuous and staid ignorance; and next to truth, a confirmed error does well; such a one, the author knows where to find him.

'It is further covenanted, concluded, and agreed that how great soever the expectation be, no person here is to expect more than he knows, or better ware than a Fair will afford; neither to look back to the sword-and-buckler age of Smithfield, but content himself with the present. Instead of a little Davy to take toll o' the bawds, the author doth promise a strutting horse-courser with a leer drunkard, two or three to attend him in as good equipage as you would wish. And then for Kindheart, the tooth-drawer, a fine oily pig-woman with her tapster to bid you welcome, and a consort of roarers for music. A wise Justice of Peace meditant, instead of a juggler with an ape. A civil cut-purse searchant. A sweet singer of new ballads allurant; and as fresh an hypocrite as ever was broached rampant. If there be never a servant-monster i' the Fair, who can help it? he says; nor a vest of actics? He is loth to make nature afraid in his plays, like those that beget *Tales*, *Tempests*, and such like drolleries, to mix his head with other men's heels, let the concupiscence of jigs and dances reign as strong as it will amongst you; yet if the puppets will please anybody, they shall be entreated to come in.

'In consideration of which, it is finally agreed by the foresaid hearers and spectators that they neither in themselves conceal, nor suffer by them to be concealed, any state-decipherer, or politic picklock of the scene, so solemnly ridiculous as to search out who was meant by the gingerbread-woman, who by the hobby-horse-man, who by the costermonger, nay, who by their wares. Or that will pretend to affirm, on his own inspired ignorance, what Mirror of Magistrates is meant by the Justice, what great lady by the pig-woman, what concealed statesman by the seller of mousetraps, and so of the rest. But that such person or persons, so found, be left discovered to the mercy of the author, as a forfeiture to the stage and your laughter afore-said. As also, such as shall so desperately or ambitiously play the fool by his place aforesaid, to challenge the author of scurrility because the language somewhere savours of Smithfield, the booth, and the pig-broth; or of profaneness because a madman cries, 'God quit you', or 'bless you'. In witness whereof, as you have preposterously put to your seals already (which is your money), you will now add the other part of suffrage, your hands. The play shall presently begin. And though the Fair be not kept in the same region that some here, perhaps, would have it, yet think that therein the author hath observed a special decorum, the place being as dirty as Smithfield, and as stinking every whit.

'Howsoever, he prays you to believe his ware is still the same; else you will make him justly suspect that he that is so loath to look on a baby or an hobby-horse here, would be glad to take up a commodity of them, at any laughter, or loss, in another place.'

[*Exeunt.*]

THE PROLOGUE TO THE KING'S MAJESTY

Your Majesty is welcome to a Fair;
Such place, such men, such language and such ware,
You must expect: with these, the zealous noise
Of your land's faction, scandalized at toys,
As babies, hobby-horses, puppet-plays,
And suchlike rage, whereof the petulant ways
Yourself have know, and have been vexed with long.
These for your sport, without particular wrong,
Or just complaint of any private man,
(Who of himself, or shall think well or can)
The maker doth present: and hopes tonight
To give you for a fairing, true delight.

THE EPILOGUE

Your Majesty hath seen the play, and you
   can best allow it from your ear, and view.
You know the scope of writers, and what store
   of leave is given them, if they take not more,

And turn it into licence: you can tell
  if we have used that leave you gave us well:
Or whether we to rage, or licence break,
  or be profane, or make profane men speak?
This is your power to judge (great Sir) and not
  the envy of a few. Which if we have got,
We value less what their dislike can bring,
  if it so happy be, to have pleased the King.

From *Neptune's Triumph for the Return of Albion*

first published in quarto in 1624, despite the fact that the masque was not actually given

His majesty being set, and the loud music ceasing. All that is discovered of a scene are two erected pillars dedicated to Neptune, with this inscription upon the one, NEP. RED.; on the other, SEC. IOV. The POET entering on the stage to disperse the argument is called to by the MASTER-COOK.

COOK   Do you hear, you creature of diligence and business! What is the affair that you pluck for so under your cloak?

POET   Nothing but what I colour for, I assure you, and may encounter with, I hope, if Luck favour me, the gamester's goddess.

COOK   You are a votary of hers, it seems by your language. What went you upon? May a man ask you?

POET   Certainties, indeed, sir, and very good ones; the presentation of a masque. You'll see't anon.

COOK   Sir, this is my room and region too, the Banqueting House! And in matter of feast and solemnity nothing is to be presented here but with my acquaintance and allowance to it.

POET   You are not his majesty's confectioner, are you?

COOK   No, but one that has as good title to the room, his master-cook. What are you, sir?

POET   The most unprofitable of his servants, I, sir, the poet. A kind of a Christmas engine, one that is used at least once a year for a trifling instrument of wit, or so.

COOK   Were you ever a cook?

POET   A cook? No, surely.

COOK   Then you can be no good poet, for a good poet differs nothing at all from a master-cook. Either's art is the wisdom of the mind.

POET   As how, sir?

COOK   Expect. I am by my place to know how to please the palates of the guests; so, you are to know the palate of the times, study the several tastes, what every nation, the Spaniard, the Dutch, the French, the Walloon, the Neapolitan, the Briton, the Sicilian can expect from you.

POET   That were a heavy and hard task, to satisfy Expectation, who is so severe an exactress of duties, ever a tyrannous mistress, and most times a pressing enemy.

COOK   She is a powerful great lady, sir, at all times, and must be satisfied. So must her sister, Madam Curiosity, who hath as dainty a palate as she, and these will expect.

POET   But what if they expect more than they understand?

COOK   That's all one, Master Poet, you are bound to satisfy them. For there is a palate of the understanding as well as of the senses. The taste is taken with good relishes, the sight with fair objects, the hearing with delicate sounds, the smelling with pure scents, the feeling with soft and plump bodies, but the understanding with all these, for all which you must begin at the kitchen. There the art of poetry was learned and found out, or nowhere, and the same day with the art of cookery.

POET   I should have given it rather to the cellar, if my suffrage had been asked.

COOK   O, you are for the oracle of the bottle, I see; Hogshead Trismegistus, he is your Pegasus. Thence flows the spring of your muses, from that hoof.

Seducèd poet, I do say to thee,
A boiler, range and dresser were the fountains
Of all the knowledge in the universe,
And that's the kitchen, where a master-cook –
Thou dost not know the man, nor canst thou know him
Till thou hast served some years in that deep school
That's both the nurse and mother of the arts,

And hear'st him read, interpret and demonstrate!
A master-cook! why he is the man of men
For a professor! He designs, he draws,
He paints, he carves, he builds, he fortifies,
Makes citadels of curious fowl and fish;
Some he dry-ditches, some moats round with broths,
Mounts marrowbones, cuts fifty-angled custards,
Rears bulwark pies, and for his outer works,
He raiseth ramparts of immortal crust,
And teacheth all the tactics at one dinner,
What ranks, what files to put his dishes in:
The whole art military! Then he knows
The influence of the stars upon his meats,
And all their seasons, tempers, qualities,
And so, to fit his relishes and sauces!
He'as nature in a pot! 'bove all the chemists,
Or bare-breeched brethren of the Rosy Cross!
He is an architect, an engineer,
A soldier, a physician, a philosopher,
A general mathematician!
POET   It is granted.
COOK   And, that you may not doubt him for a poet –
POET   This fury shows, if there were nothing else.
      And 'tis divine!
COOK   Then, brother poet –
POET   Brother!

COOK   But where's your antimasque now, all this while?
   I hearken after them.
POET   Faith, we have none.
COOK   None?
POET   None, I assure you, neither do I think them
   A worthy part of presentation,
   Being things so heterogene to all device,
   Mere by-works, and at best outlandish nothings.
COOK   O, you are all the heaven awry, sir!
   For blood of poetry running in your veins,
   Make not yourself so ignorantly simple.
   Because, sir, you shall see I am a poet

No less than cook, and that I find you want
A special service here, an antimasque,
I'll fit you with a dish out of the kitchen
Such as I think will take the present palates,
A metaphorical dish! And do but mark
How a good wit may jump with you. Are you ready, child?
(Had there been masque or no masque, I had made it.)
Child of the boiling-house!   [*Enter child.*]
CHILD   Here, father.
COOK   Bring forth the pot. It is an *olla podrida*,
But I have persons to present the meats.
POET   Persons!
COOK   Such as do relish nothing but *di stato*,
But in another fashion than you dream of,
Know all things the wrong way, talk of the affairs,
The clouds, the curtains and the mysteries
That are afoot, and from what hands they have 'em –
The Master of the Elephant or the Camels –
What correspondences are held, the posts
That go and come, and know almost their minutes,
All but their business: therein they are fishes,
But ha' their garlic, as the proverb says.
They are our quest of enquiry after news.
POET   Together with their learnèd authors?
CHILD   Yes, sir,
And of the epicoene gender, hes and shes:
Amphibion Archy is the chief.
COOK   Good boy!
The child is learnèd too: note but the kitchen!
Have you put him into the pot for garlic?
CHILD   One in his coat shall stink as strong as he, sir,
And his friend Giblets with him.
COOK   They are two
That give a part of the seasoning.
POET   I conceive
The way of your gallimaufry.
COOK   You will like it
When they come pouring out of the pot together.
CHILD   O, if the pot had been big enough!
COOK   What then, child?

CHILD   I had put in the elephant, and one camel
  At least, for beef.
COOK   But whom ha' you for partridge?
CHILD   A brace of dwarfs, and delicate plump birds!
COOK   And whom for mutton and kid?
CHILD   A fine laced mutton
  Or two, and either has her frisking husband
  That reads her the coranto every week.
  Grave Master Ambler, newsmaster of Paul's,
  Supplies your capon, and grown Captain Buz,
  His emissary, underwrites for turkey;
  A Gentleman of the Forest presents pheasant,
  And a plump poult'rer's wife in Grace's Street
  Plays hen with eggs i' the belly, or a cony,
  Choose which you will.
COOK   But where's the bacon, Tom?
CHILD   Hogrel the butcher and the sow his wife
  Are both there.
COOK   It is well; go dish 'em out.
  Are they well boiled?
CHILD   *Podrida*!
POET   What's that, rotten?
COOK   O, that they must be. There's one main ingredient
  We have forgot, the artichoke.
CHILD   No, sir.
  I have a fruiterer with a cold red nose
  Like a blue fig performs it.
COOK   The fruit looks so.
  Good child, go pour 'em out, show their concoction.
  They must be rotten boiled – the broth's the best on't –
  And that's the dance: the stage here is the charger.
  And brother poet, though the serious part
  Be yours, yet envy not the cook his art.

*The antimasque is danced by the persons described, coming out of
the pot.*

On *The New Inn*: Ode. To Himself

first printed in the 1631 octavo text of **The New Inn**

Come, leave the loathèd stage,
And the more loathsome age,
Where pride and impudence, in faction knit,
    Usurp the chair of wit:
Indicting and arraigning every day
    Something they call a play.
    Let their fastidious, vain
    Commission of the brain
Run on and rage, sweat, censure, and condemn:
They were not made for thee, less thou for them.

Say that thou pour'st them wheat,
And they will acorns eat:
'Twere simple fury still thyself to waste
    On such as have no taste:
To offer them a surfeit of pure bread
    Whose appetites are dead.
    No, give them grains their fill,
    Husks, draff to drink, and swill;
If they love lees, and leave the lusty wine,
Envy them not, their palate's with the swine.

No doubt some mouldy tale
Like *Pericles*, and stale
As the shrieve's crusts, and nasty as his fish –
    Scraps out [of] every dish,
Thrown forth, and raked into the common tub,
    May keep up the play club:
    There sweepings do as well
    As the best-ordered meal.
For who the relish of these guests will fit
Needs set them but the alms-basket of wit.

And much good do't you then:
Brave plush and velvet men

Can feed on orts; and safe in your stage-clothes
 Dare quit, upon your oaths,
The stagers and the stage-wrights too (your peers)
 Or larding your large ears
 With their foul comic socks,
 Wrought upon twenty blocks:
Which, if they're torn and turned and patched enough,
The gamesters share your guilt, and you their stuff.

 Leave things so prostitute,
 And take the Alcaic lute,
Or thine own Horace, or Anacreon's lyre;
 Warm thee by Pindar's fire:
And though thy nerves be shrunk and blood be cold
 Ere years have made thee old,
 Strike that disdainful heat
 Throughout, to their defeat:
As curious fools, and envious of thy strain,
May, blushing, swear no palsy's in thy brain.

 But when they hear thee sing
 The glories of thy king,
His zeal to God, and his just awe o'er men:
 They may, blood-shaken, then
Feel such a flesh-quake to possess their powers,
 As they shall cry: Like ours
 In sound of peace or wars
 No harp e'er hit the stars,
In tuning forth the acts of his sweet reign:
And raising Charles' chariot 'bove his wain.

From *The Magnetic Lady*

first printed in the 1640 Second Folio

Chorus, after Act 1

[*Enter* BOY, PROBEE, DAMPLAY.]

BOY   Now, gentlemen, what censure you of our *protasis*, or first act?

PROBEE   Well, boy, it is a fair presentment of your actors. And a handsome promise of somewhat to come hereafter.

DAMPLAY   But, there is nothing done in it, or concluded: therefore I say, no act.

BOY   A fine piece of logic! Do you look Master Damplay, for conclusions in a *protasis*? I thought the law of comedy had reserved 'em to the *catastrophe*: and that the *epitasis*, as we are taught, and the *catastasis*, had been intervening parts to have been expected. But you would have all come together, it seems: the clock should strike five, at once, with the acts.

DAMPLAY   Why, if it could do so, it were well, boy.

BOY   Yes, if the nature of a clock were to speak, not strike. So, if a child could be born, in a play, and grow up to a man i' the first scene, before he went off the stage: and then after to come forth a squire, and be made a knight: and that knight to travel between the acts, and do wonders i' the Holy Land, or elsewhere; kill paynims, wild boars, dun cows, and other monsters; beget him a reputation, and marry an emperor's daughter for his mistress; convert her father's country; and at last come home, lame, and all-to-be-laden with miracles.

DAMPLAY   These miracles would please, I assure you: and take the people! For there be of the people that will expect miracles, and more than miracles from this pen.

BOY   Do they think this pen can juggle? I would we had Hocus Pocus for 'em then, your people; or Travitanto Tudesko.

DAMPLAY   Who's that, boy?

BOY   Another juggler, with a long name. Or that your expectors would be gone hence, now, at the first act; or expect no more hereafter than they understand.

DAMPLAY   Why so, my peremptory jack?

BOY   My name is John, indeed – Because, who expect what is impossible or beyond nature defraud themselves.

PROBEE   Nay, there the boy said well: they do defraud themselves indeed.

BOY   And therefore, Master Damplay, unless, like a solemn justice of wit, you will damn our play unheard or unexamined; I shall entreat your Mistress Madam Expectation, if she be among these ladies, to have patience but a pissing while: give our springs leave to open a little, by degrees! A source of ridiculous matter may break forth anon that shall steep their temples and bathe their brains in laughter, to the fomenting of stupidity itself, and the awaking any velvet lethargy in the house.

PROBEE   Why do you maintain your poet's quarrel so with velvet and good clothes, boy? We have seen him in indifferent good clothes, ere now.

BOY   And may do in better, if it please the King, his master, to say Amen to it, and allow it, to whom he acknowledgeth all. But his clothes shall never be the best thing about him, though; he will have somewhat beside, either of humane letters or severe honesty, shall speak him a man though he went naked.

PROBEE   He is beholden to you, if you can make this good, boy.

BOY   Himself hath done that, already, against envy.

DAMPLAY   What's your name, sir? Or your country?

BOY   John Trygust my name: a Cornish youth, and the poet's servant.

DAMPLAY   West-country bred, I thought, you were so bold.

BOY   Or rather saucy: to find out your palate, Master Damplay. Faith we do call a spade a spade, in Cornwall. If you dare damn our play, i' the wrong place, we shall take heart to tell you so.

PROBEE   Good, boy.   [*Exeunt.*]

Chorus, after Act 2

[*Enter* DAMPLAY, BOY, PROBEE.]

DAMPLAY   But whom doth your poet mean now by this – Master Bias? What lord's secretary doth he purpose to personate or perstringe?

BOY   You might as well ask me what alderman or alderman's mate he meant by Sir Moth Interest? Or what eminent lawyer by the ridiculous Master Practice? Who hath rather his name invented for laughter than any offence or injury it can stick on the reverend professors of the law: and so the wise ones will think.

PROBEE   It is an insidious question, Brother Damplay! Iniquity itself would not have urged it. It is picking the lock of the scene; not opening it the fair way with a key. A play, though it apparel and present vices in general, flies from all particularities in persons. Would you ask of Plautus and Terence, if they both lived now, who were Davus or Pseudolus in the scene? Who Pyrgopolinices or Thraso? Who Euclio or Menedemus?

BOY   Yes, he would: and inquire of Martial, or any other epigramatist, whom he meant by Titius or Seius (the common John à Noke, or John à Style), under whom they note all vices and errors taxable to the times. As if there could not be a name for a folly fitted to the stage but there must be a person in nature found out to own it.

DAMPLAY   Why, I can fantasy a person to myself, boy: who shall hinder me?

BOY   And, in not publishing him, you do no man an injury. But if you will utter your own ill meaning on that person, under the author's words, you make a libel of his comedy.

DAMPLAY   Oh, he told us that in a prologue long since.

BOY   If you do the same reprehensible ill things, still the same reprehension will serve you, though you heard it afore. They are his own words. I can invent no better, nor he.

PROBEE   It is the solemn vice of interpretation, that deforms the figure of many a fair scene, by drawing it awry; and indeed is the civil murder of most good plays. If I see a thing vively presented on the stage, that the glass of custom, which is comedy, is so held up to me, by the poet, as I can therein view the daily examples of men's lives, and images of truth, in their manners, so drawn for my delight or profit as I may, either way, use them: and will I, rather than make that true use, hunt out the persons to defame, by my malice of misapplying? And imperil the innocence and candour of the author, by his calumny? It is an unjust way of hearing and beholding plays, this, and most unbecoming a gentleman to appear malignantly witty in another's work.

BOY They are no other but narrow and shrunk natures, shrivelled up, poor things, that cannot think well of themselves, who dare to detract others. That signature is upon them, and it will last. A half-witted barbarism, which no barber's art, or his balls, will ever expunge or take out!

DAMPLAY Why, boy? This were a strange empire, or rather a tyranny, you would entitle your poet to, over gentlemen, that they should come to hear and see plays, and say nothing for their money.

BOY Oh, yes; say what you will: so it be to purpose and in place.

DAMPLAY Can anything be out of purpose at a play? I see no reason, if I come here and give my eighteen pence or two shillings for my seat, but I should take it out in censure on the stage.

BOY Your two shilling worth is allowed you: but you will take your ten shilling worth, your twenty shilling worth, and more: and teach others about you to do the like, that follow your leading face; as if you were to cry up or down every scene by confederacy, be it right or wrong.

DAMPLAY Who should teach us the right or wrong at a play?

BOY If your own science cannot do it, or the love of modesty and truth; all other entreaties or attempts – are vain. You are fitter spectators for the bears than us, or the puppets. This is a popular ignorance indeed, somewhat better apparelled in you than the people: but a hard-handed and stiff ignorance, worthy a trowel or a hammer-man; and not only fit to be scorned but to be triumphed o'er.

DAMPLAY By whom, boy?

BOY No particular, but the general neglect and silence. Good Master Damplay, be yourself still, without a second. Few here are of your opinion today, I hope; tomorrow, I am sure there will be none, when they have ruminated this.

PROBEE Let us mind what you come for, the play, which will draw on to the epitasis now.

[*Exeunt.*]

Chorus, after Act 4

[*Enter* DAMPLAY, BOY, PROBEE.]

DAMPLAY   Troth, I am one of those that labour with the same longing, for it is almost puckered, and pulled into that knot, by your poet, which I cannot easily, with all the strength of my imagination, untie.

BOY   Like enough, nor is it in your office to be troubled or perplexed with it, but to sit still, and expect. The more your imagination busies itself, the more it is entangled, especially if (as I told, in the beginning) you happen on the wrong end.

PROBEE   He hath said sufficient, Brother Damplay; our parts that are the spectators, or should hear a comedy, are to await the process and events of things, as the poet presents them, not as we would corruptly fashion them. We come here to behold plays, and censure them, as they are made and fitted for us; not to beslaver our own thoughts, with censorious spittle tempering the poet's clay, as we were to mould every scene anew: that were a mere plastic, or potter's ambition, most unbecoming the name of a gentleman. No, let us mark, and not lose the business on foot by talking. Follow the right thread, or find it.

DAMPLAY   Why, here his play might have ended, if he would ha' let it; and have spared us the vexation of a fifth act yet to come, which everyone here knows the issue of already, or may in part conjecture.

BOY   That conjecture is a kind of figure-flinging, or throwing the dice, for a meaning was never in the poet's purpose perhaps. Stay, and see his last act, his *catastrophe*, how he will perplex that, or spring some fresh cheat to entertain the spectators with a convenient delight, till some unexpected and new encounter break out and rectify all, and make good the conclusion.

PROBEE   Which, ending here, would have shown dull, flat, and unpointed; without any shape, or sharpness, Brother Damplay.

DAMPLAY   Well, let us expect then: and wit be with us, o' the poet's part.

Letter to the Earl of Salisbury, over the *Eastward Ho* affair

written between May and October 1605; not published in Jonson's lifetime

TO THE MOST NOBLY-VIRTUOUS AND THRICE-HONOUR'D
EARL OF SALISBURY

Most truly honourable,

It hath still been the tyranny of my fortune so to oppress my endeavours that before I can show myself grateful (in the least) for former benefits, I am enforced to provoke your bounties for more. May it not seem grievous to your Lordship that, now, my innocence calls upon you (next the Deity) to her defence; God himself is not averted at just men's cries; and you, that approach that divine goodness, and supply it here on earth in your place and honours, cannot employ your aids more worthily, than to the common succour of honesty and virtue, how humbly soever it be plac'd. I am here (my most honour'd Lord) un-examined, or unheard, committed to a vile prison, and (with me) a gentleman (whose name may perhaps have come to your Lordship), one Mr George Chapman, a learned and honest man; the cause (would I could name some worthier, though I wish we had known none worthy our imprisonment) is, a (the work irks me, that our fortune hath necessitated us to so despis'd a course) a play, my Lord; whereof, we hope, there is no man can justly complain that hath the virtue to think but favourably of himself, if our judge bring an equal ear; marry, if with prejudice we be made guilty, afore our time, we must embrace the asinine virtue, patience. My noble Lord, they deal not charitably who are too witty in another man's works, and utter sometimes their own malicious meanings, under our words. I protest to your Honour, and call God to testimony (since my first error, which (yet) is punish'd in me more with my shame than it was then with my bondage) I have so attempered my style, that I have given no cause to any good man of grief; and, if to any ill, by touching at any general vice, it hath always been with a regard, and sparing of particular persons: I may be otherwise reported, but if all that be accused should be presently guilty, there are few men would stand in the state of innocence.

I beseech your most honourable Lordship, suffer not other men's errors, or faults past, to be made my crimes; but let me be examin'd, both by all my works past, and this present, and not trust to rumour but my books (for she is an unjust deliverer both of great and small actions) whether I have ever (in any thing I have written, private or public) given offence to a nation, to any public order or state, or any person of honour or authority, but have equally labour'd to keep their dignity, as mine own person, safe; if others have transgress'd, let not me be entitled to their follies. But lest in being too diligent for my excuse I may incur the suspicion of being guilty: I become a most humble suitor to your Lordship, that with the honourable Lord Chamberlain (to whom I have in like manner petition'd) you will be pleas'd to be the grateful means of our coming to answer; or if in your wisdoms it shall be thought unnecessary, that your Lordships will be the most honour'd cause of our liberty, where freeing us from one prison you shall remove us to another, which is eternally to bind us and our Muses to the thankful honouring of you and yours to posterity; as your own virtues have by many descents of ancestors ennobled you to time.

Your Lordship's most devoted in heart as words.

Ben. Jonson

An Expostulation w[i]th Inigo Jones

written in or after July 1631; not published in Jonson's lifetime, or in the 1640 Second Folio

M[aste]r Survey[o]r, you that first began
From thirty pound in pipkins, to the man
You are: from them leaped forth an architect
Able to talk of Euclid, and correct
Both him and Archimede; damn Archytas,
The noblest engineer that ever was;
Control Ctesibius, overbearing us
With mistook names out of Vitruvius;

Drawn Aristotle on us: and thence shown
How much architectonike is your own!
(Whether the building of the stage or scene,
Or making of the properties it mean,
Vizors or antics, or it comprehend
Something your sirship doth not yet intend!)
By all your titles and whole style at once
Of tire-man, mountebank, and Justice Jones
I do salute you! Are you fitted yet?
Will any of these express your place or wit?
Or are you so ambitious 'bove your peers,
You would be an asinigo, by your ears?
Why, much good do't you! Be what beast you will,
You'll be, as Langley said, an Inigo still.
    What makes your wretchedness to bray so loud
In town and court; are you grown rich and proud?
Your trappings will not change you: change your mind.
No velvet sheath you wear will alter kind;
A wooden dagger is a dagger of wood,
Though gold or ivory hafts would make it good.
What is the cause you pomp it so? (I ask)
And all men echo, You have made a masque.
I chime that too; and I have met with those
That do cry up the machine, and the shows,
The majesty of Juno in the clouds,
And peering-forth of Iris in the shrouds!
The ascent of Lady Fame, which none could spy,
Not they that sided her, Dame Poetry,
Dame History, Dame Architecture, too,
And Goody Sculpture, brought with much ado
To hold her up. O shows! Shows! Mighty shows!
The eloquence of masques! What need of prose,
Or verse, or sense, to express immortal you?
You are the spectacles of state! 'Tis true
Court hieroglyphics, and all arts afford
In the mere perspective of an inch-board.
You ask no more than certain politic eyes,
Eyes that can pierce into the mysteries
Of many colours, read them, and reveal
Mythology there painted on slit deal.
Oh, to make boards to speak! There is a task!

Painting and carpentry are the soul of masque.
Pack with your peddling poetry to the stage:
This is the money-get, mechanic age!
To plant the music where no ear can reach,
Attire the persons as no thought can teach
Sense what they are: which, by a specious, fine
Term of the architects, is called *design*!
But in the practised truth destruction is
Of any art beside what he calls his.
Whither, O whither will this tire-man grow?
His name is Σχενοποιοζ we all know,
The maker of the properties, in sum,
The scene, the engine! But he now is come
To be the music-master, fabler, too;
He is, or would be, the main Dominus Do –
All in the work! And so shall still, for Ben:
Be Inigo the whistle, and his men.
He's warm on his feet now, he says, and can
Swim without cork: why, thank the good Queen Anne.
I am too fat to envy him; he too lean
To be worth envy. Henceforth I do mean
To pity him, as smiling at his feat
Of lantern-lurry: with fuliginous heat
Whirling his whimsies, by a subtlety
Sucked from the veins of shop-philosophy.
What would he do now, giving his mind that way,
In presentation of some puppet-play
Should but the king his justice-hood employ
In setting-forth of such a solemn toy?
How would he firk, like Adam Overdo,
Up and about, dive into cellars, too,
Disguised, and thence drag forth enormity:
Discover vice, commit absurdity
Under the moral? Show he had a pate
Moulded, or stroked up, to survey a state?
O wise surveyor! Wiser architect!
But wisest Inigo! Who can reflect
On the new priming of thy old sign-posts,
Reviving with fresh colours the pale ghosts
Of thy dead standards; or (with miracle) see
Thy twice-conceived, thrice-paid-for imagery

And not fall down before it, and confess
Almighty architecture: who no less
A goddess is, than painted cloth, deal-boards,
Vermilion, lake, or cinnabar affords
Expression for; with that unbounded line
Aimed at in thy omnipotent design.
What poesy e'er was painted on a wall,
That might compare with thee? What story shall,
Of all the Worthies, hope to outlast thy one,
So the materials be of Purbeck stone?
Live long the Feasting Room! And ere thou burn
Again, thy architect to ashes turn!
Whom not ten fires nor a parliament can,
Will all remonstrance, make an honest man.

Notes

Notes to the Preface

1. See A. L. Beier and R. Findlay (eds), *London, 1500–1700: The Making of the Metropolis* (London, 1986); also Kevin Sharpe (ed.), *Faction and Parliament: Essays on Early Stuart History* (Oxford, 1978); Linda Levy Peck, *Court Patronage and Corruption in Early Stuart England* (London, 1991).
2. On new historicism, cultural materialism and their differences, see R. Wilson and R. Dutton (eds), *The New Historicism and Renaissance Drama* (London, 1992).
3. Richard Levin has some typically trenchant things to say about 'new historicist' claims about the status of 'literature' in the Renaissance in 'Unthinkable Thoughts in the New Historicizing of English Renaissance Drama', *New Literary History*, 21 (1990), 433–47.

Notes to the Chronology of Jonson's Life and Work

1. On the date of Jonson's birth – there has been some doubt whether it was 1572 or 1573 – see Rosalind Miles, *Ben Jonson: His Life and Work* (London, 1986), Appendix, pp. 280–2. See below, 1604 and note 2, on the spelling of Jonson's name.
2. Herford and Simpson took the date of Jonson's imprisonment for debt to be January 1599 New Style, and this is still widely repeated. But Mark Eccles has established that it was 1599 Old Style: i.e. 1600 New Style. See Mark Eccles, 'Ben Jonson, "Citizen and Bricklayer"', *Notes and Queries*, 233 (1988), 445–6.
3. We now know that *Mercury Vindicated from the Alchemists at Court* was performed in 1615 and *The Golden Age Restored* in 1616, though Herford and Simpson assumed that these datings were reversed – an assumption commonly reiterated. See John Orrell, 'The London Stage in the Florentine Correspondence 1604–1618', *Theatre Research International*, 3 (1977–8), 173–4; also Martin Butler, 'Jonson's Folio and the Politics of Patronage', *Criticism*, 35 (1993), 377–90, pp. 381–2.
4. Herford and Simpson originally suggested that Jonson suffered two strokes, one in 1626 and another in 1628. They later retracted this, but note has not widely been taken of the retraction. See W. David Kay, *Ben Jonson: A Literary Life* (Basingstoke and New York, 1995), pp. 169–70, and note 28, p. 224.
5. See Richard Dutton, *Mastering the Revels: the Regulation and Censorship of English Renaissance Drama* (London and Basingstoke, 1991), p. 203; and Martin Butler, 'Ecclesiastical Censorship of Early Stuart Drama: the Case of Jonson's *The Magnetic Lady*', *Modern Philology*, 89 (1992), 469–81.

Notes to Chapter 1: The Lone Wolf

1. David Riggs, *Ben Jonson: A Life* (Cambridge, Mass., and London, 1989), p. 3.
2. Alvin Kernan, *Printing Technology, Letters and Samuel Johnson* (Princeton, N.J., 1987), p. 4.
3. Patrick Parrinder, *Authors and Authority: A Study of English Literary Criticism and Its Relation to Culture, 1750–1900* (London, Henley and Boston, 1977), p. 5; see Terry Eagleton, *The Function of Criticism: From 'The Spectator' to Post-Structuralism* (London, 1984).
4. See, for example, Arthur Marotti, *John Donne, Coterie Poet* (Madison, Wisconsin, 1986).
5. See Richard Dutton, *Mastering the Revels: The Regulation and Censorship of English Renaissance Drama* (London and Basingstoke, 1991).
6. See Timothy Murray, 'From Foul Sheets to Legitimate Model: Antitheater, Text, Ben Jonson', *New Literary History*, 14 (1983), 641–64; Richard C. Newton, 'Jonson and the (Re-)Invention of the Book', in *Classic and Cavalier: Essays on Jonson and the Sons of Ben*, eds Claude J. Summers and Ted-Larry Pebworth (Pittsburgh, 1982), pp. 31–58; Andrew Gurr, *Playgoing in Shakespeare's London* (Cambridge, 1987).
7. Michel Foucault, 'What is an Author?', in *The Foucault Reader*, ed. Paul Rabinow (New York, 1984), p. 101.
8. George Watson, *The Literary Critics: A Study of English Descriptive Criticism* (Harmondsworth, reprinted with revisions 1964), pp. 14–15.
9. For a wider discussion of the limitations of 'descriptive criticism', see Jerome J. McGann, *A Critique of Modern Textual Criticism* (Chicago and London, 1983).
10. Eliot used the phrase in 'The Function of Criticism', first published in 1923; see T. S. Eliot, *Selected Essays*, 3rd edn (London, 1951), p. 25. F. R. Leavis adopted *The Common Pursuit* as the title for a collection of his own essays, first published in 1952. See also Raman Selden, *Criticism and Objectivity* (London, 1984).
11. T. S. Eliot, 'Imperfect Critics', in T. S. Eliot, *The Sacred Wood*, 7th edn (London, 1950), pp. 17–46, first published 1920.
12. David Klein, *Literary Criticism from the Elizabethan Dramatists: Repertory and Synthesis* (New York, 1910), p. 152. Chapter 3 of Klein's book is a useful, if unsearching survey of Jonson's criticism.
13. See Watson, *The Literary Critics*, referred to in note 8, above.
14. Paul Sellin, *Daniel Heinsius and Stuart England* (Leiden, 1968), p. 148; see also J. E. Spingarn, 'The Sources of Jonson's "Discoveries"', *Modern Philology*, 1 (1905), pp. 450–60.
15. Ian Donaldson (ed.), *Ben Jonson*, Oxford Authors series (Oxford, 1985), p. xiv.
16. Timothy Murray, *Theatrical Legitimation: Allegories of Genius in Seventeenth-Century England and France* (Oxford, 1987), p. 48.
17. On the rhyme controversy, see pp. 58, 127–8; on the discussion of Shakespeare in *Discoveries*, see pp. 152–62; on Jonson and Bacon, see pp. 10, 33. On Heinsius, see Sellin, *Daniel Heinsius and Stuart England*,

pp. 149–53; on the incidents and the book, see Donaldson (ed.), *Ben Jonson*, Oxford Authors series, p. 735.

18. Sellin, *Daniel Heinsius and Stuart England*, p. 162.

19. John Dryden, *An Essay of Dramatick Poesie*, ed. James T. Boulton (Oxford, 1964), p. 90.

20. Donaldson (ed.), *Ben Jonson*, Oxford Authors series, p. 694.

21. Freda L. Townshend, *Apologie for Bartholomew Fayre* (New York, 1947).

22. Michael McCanles, *Jonsonian Discriminations: The Humanist Poet and the Praise of True Nobility* (Toronto, 1992), p. 89.

23. McCanles, *Jonsonian Discriminations*, pp. 89–90, 93.

24. See Bernard Weinberg, *A History of Literary Criticism in the Italian Renaissance*, 2 vols (Chicago, 1961), vol. I, pp. 71–2. Dryden rather patronised Jonson's translation as 'a metaphrase, or turning an author word by word, and line by line, from one language into another. Thus, or near this manner, was Horace his *Art of Poetry* translated by Ben Jonson' (Preface to his *Translation of Ovid's Epistles*, 1680). See also W. K. Wimsatt Jr and Cleanth Brooks, *Literary Criticism: A Short History* (New York, 1965), p. 94, for a lukewarm modern view of the translation, which has never in fact aroused much interest.

25. Dryden, *Essay of Dramatick Poesie*, p. 90.

26. See Annabel Patterson, *Censorship and Interpretation: The Conditions of Writing and Reading in Early Modern England* (Madison, Wisconsin, 1984), esp. Introduction and chapter 1. Also Richard Burt, *Licensed by Authority: Ben Jonson and the Discourses of Censorship* (Ithaca and London, 1993).

27. George Puttenham, *Arte of Englishe Poesie* (1589), eds. G. D. Willcock and A. Walker (Cambridge, 1936), p. 38; my modernisation. See H&S, I, p. 264, on Jonson's own copy of Puttenham.

28. *The Defence of Poesy*, in *Sir Philip Sidney: Selected Writings*, ed. Richard Dutton (Manchester, 1987), p. 102.

29. See Elizabeth Eisenstein, *The Printing Press as an Agent of Change* (Cambridge, 1979); Newton, 'Jonson and the (Re-)Invention of the Book'; but also see Martin Butler, 'Jonson's Folio and the Politics of Patronage', *Criticism*, 35 (1993), 377–90, where he argues that 'Even though the Folio seems a testimony to the power of print, the emergent market place and bourgeoisification of the author, it was still very much bound up in the old economies and politics of patronage' (p. 388).

30. Riggs, *Ben Jonson: A Life*, p. 266.

31. Klein, *Literary Criticism from the Elizabethan Dramatists*, p. 152.

32. *Calendar of Venetian State Papers*, XI, p. 86. Cited in *H&S*, X, p. 457.

33. John Florio, *Queen Anna's New World of Words, or Dictionary of the Italian and English Tongues* (1611).

34. For a wider consideration of the extent to which masques in which Queen Anne participated might have been perceived as 'her' works, see Barbara Lewalski, 'Anne of Denmark and Masquing', *Criticism*, 35 (1993), 341–55; Marion Wynne-Davies, 'The Queen's Masque: Renaissance Women and the Seventeenth-Century Court Masque', in S. P. Cerasano and M. Wynne-Davies (eds), *Gloriana's Face: Women,*

Public and Private, in the English Renaissance (Detroit, 1992), pp. 79–104; and Leeds Barroll, 'The Court of the First Stuart Queen', in Linda Levy Peck (ed.), *The Mental World of the Jacobean Court* (Cambridge, 1991), pp. 191–208.

35. *Calendar of Venetian State Papers*, xi, pp. 74, 76.

36. Florio, *Queen Anna's New World of Words*, 1611 edition, English dedication, p. 2 verso.

37. Evelyn B. Tribble, *Margins and Marginality: The Printed Page in Early Modern England* (Charlottesville and London, 1993), p. 145.

38. On Jonson's insistence on establishing a distinct identity for himself as writer *of plays*, see George E. Rowe, *Distinguishing Jonson: Imitation, Rivalry, and the Direction of a Dramatic Career* (Lincoln, Nebraska, and London, 1988).

39. See *UV* XXXIV, 'An Expostulation with Inigo Jones' (Appendix, pp. 214–17), and D. J. Gordon, 'Poet and Architect: The Intellectual Setting of the Quarrel between Ben Jonson and Inigo Jones', *Journal of the Warburg and Courtauld Institutes*, 12 (1949), 152–78, reprinted in *The Renaissance Imagination*, ed. Stephen Orgel (Berkeley and Los Angeles, 1975).

40. The City of London authorities originally employed Dekker to compose the pageants which King James was to confront on his ceremonial progress to his coronation, and to publish an account of it. But the plague intervened; the coronation went ahead with a minimum of ceremony, and the royal progress through the city was deferred for almost a year, in which time Jonson was commissioned to prepare two pageants for it (plus a third outside the city itself, on the way to Westminster), in addition to Dekker's work. Jonson published an account of his own part in the proceedings, heavily annotated with classical and other sources and references. Dekker then published his own account of *The Magnificent Entertainment*, with only a sketchy account of Jonson's part and none of his text; indeed, Jonson is never mentioned by name, but his annotations are taken to task: 'To make a false flourish here with the borrowed weapons of all the old masters of the noble science of poesy, and to keep a tyrannical coil, in anatomizing Genius, from head to foot, (only to show how nimbly we can carve up the whole mess of the poets) were to play the executioner, and to lay our City's household god on the rack, to make him confess, how many pair of Latin sheets we have shaken and cut into shreds to make him a garment'. Dekker then used the authority of his original commission to have Jonson's volume 'called in'. See Richard Dutton (ed.), *Jacobean Civic Pageants* (Keele University Press, forthcoming), Introduction to *The Magnificent Entertainment*.

41. 'To the Right Honourable, the Lady Lucy, Countess of Bedford', prefacing *The Vision of the Twelve Goddesses* in *The Complete Works in Verse and Prose of Samuel Daniel*, edited by A. B. Grosart, 5 vols (London, 1885; reissued New York, 1963), vol. III, pp. 187–96, p. 187. All subsequent references to the works of Daniel are to this edition. Richard Helgerson, *Self-Crowned Laureates: Spenser, Jonson,*

Milton and the Literary System (Berkeley, CA, 1983), p. 28. On the complexities of the social status of print, see J. W. Saunders, 'The Stigma of Print: A Note on the Social Bases of Tudor Poetry', *Essays in Criticism*, 1 (1951), pp. 139–54, and 'The Social Situation of Seventeenth-Century Poetry', in *Metaphysical Poetry*, edited by M. Bradbury and D. J. Palmer (London, 1970), pp. 237–59; also Phoebe Sheavyn, *The Literary Profession in Elizabethan England*, revised by J. W. Saunders (Manchester, 1967). Steven W. May is over-categorical in declaring the stigma of print to be 'mythical' but demonstrates how unstable the codes were in these matters ('Tudor Aristocrats and the Mythical "Stigma of Print"', *Renaissance Papers 1980* (1981), pp. 11–18).

42. Letter dedicating the *Arcadia* to the Countess of Pembroke, printed in the 1590 quarto and subsequent folio editions. Cited from *Arcadia* by Sir Philip Sidney, edited by Maurice Evans (Harmondsworth, 1977), p. 57.

43. See pp. 135, 152–3.

44. See Martin Elsky, *Authorising Words: Speech, Writing, and Print in the English Renaissance* (Ithaca and London, 1989), pp. 184–208.

45. Whether Daniel's *The Tragedy of Cleopatra* was ever performed, or even meant for performance, is a moot point. But it seems certain that it was never performed commercially: see the Apology to his *Philotas*.

46. See R. C. Bald, *John Donne: A Life* (Oxford, 1970), pp. 168 note, 241–2, 296.

47. On the non-dramatic verse, see Richard S. Peterson, *Imitation and Praise in the Poems of Ben Jonson* (New Haven and London, 1981).

48. See Stephen Orgel, *The Jonsonian Masque* (Cambridge, Mass., 1965).

49. McCanles, *Jonsonian Discriminations*, especially chapters 1 and 2; see also McCanles' index, under 'contrastivity'.

50. On Jonson's marginality, see Elsky, *Authorising Words*, pp. 95–8, 101–9; on his self-effacement, see Stanley Fish, 'Authors–Readers: Jonson's Community of the Same', *Representations*, 7 (1984), 26–58.

51. Jonas Barish, *Ben Jonson and the Language of Prose Comedy* (Cambridge, Mass., 1960), p. 87.

52. 'Pembroke and his lady discoursing, the Earl said the women were men's shadows, and she maintained them. Both appealing to Jonson, he affirmed it true; for which my lady gave a penance to prove it in verse: hence his epigram' (*Drummond*, 308–11). See Michael G. Brennan, *Literary Patronage in the English Renaissance: The Pembroke Family* (London, 1988); Robert C. Evans, *Ben Jonson and the Poetics of Patronage* (Lewisburg, 1989); and Martin Butler, 'Jonson's Folio and the Politics of Patronage', *Criticism*, 35 (1993), 377–90.

53. See Riggs, *Ben Jonson*, pp. 215–21.

54. On the Stationers' Company cartel and the licensing process, see Richard Dutton, 'Buggeswords: The Licensing, Suppression and Afterlife of Dr John Hayward's *Life and Reign of Henry IV*', *Criticism*, 35 (1993), 305–39.

55. See below, pp. 98, 198.

56. Burt, *Licensed by Authority*, p. 64.
57. On theories of the source/derivation of honour, see Richard C. McCoy, *The Rites of Knighthood: The Literature and Politics of Elizabethan Chivalry* (Berkeley, Los Angeles and London, 1989), pp. 12–24, 89.
58. See McCanles, *Jonsonian Discriminations, passim*. Jonson goes out of his way to link virtue and ancestry in the letter he wrote to the East of Salisbury at the time of his imprisonment over *Eastward Ho*: 'as your own virtues have by many descents of ancestors enabled you to time' (Appendix, p. 214). In fact, the Cecils had no very distinguished ancestry, and this enforced obsequiousness probably rankled with Jonson later (see below, p. 62).
59. On the honour culture, and its decline in Jonson's time, see Mervyn James, *Society, Politics and Culture: Studies in Early Modern England* (Cambridge, 1986). Ian Donaldson's suggestion that the 'hundred letters' relate to the recusancy hearings was made in an unpublished paper at the Ben Jonson conference at the University of Leeds, July 1995.
60. *The Advancement of Learning*, I.vii.21, cited from *Francis Bacon*, ed. Arthur Johnston (London, 1965), pp. 55–6.
61. Don E. Wayne, *Penshurst: The Semiotics of Place and the Poetics of History* (London, 1984), p. 30, see also pp. 147–50; Elsky, *Authorising Words*, p. 108.
62. See R. S. Crane, 'English Neoclassical Criticism: An Outline Sketch', in *Critics and Criticism Ancient and Modern*, ed. R. S. Crane (Chicago, 1952), pp. 372–88; Michel Foucault, *The Order of Things: An Archaeology of the Human Sciences*, English edition (London, 1970), especially pp. 46–67; Peter Womack, *Ben Jonson* (Oxford, 1986), p. 109.
63. Elsky, *Authorising Words*, p. 108. His reference is to Timothy Murray, 'From Foul Sheets to Legitimate Model: Antitheater, Text, Ben Jonson', *New Literary History*, 14 (1983), 641–64, p. 650.
64. See Burt, *Licensed by Authority*, p. 53.
65. 'What is Criticism', in Roland Barthes, *Critical Essays*, translated from the French by Richard Howard (Evanston, Ill., 1972), pp. 255–60, pp. 258–9. I am indebted to my colleague Scott Wilson, for pointing out the relevance of Barthes here.
66. See, for example, Isabel Rivers, *The Poetry of Conservatism, 1600–1745: A Study of Poets and Public Affairs from Jonson to Pope* (Cambridge, 1973).
67. Don E. Wayne, 'Drama and Society in the Age of Jonson: A Different View', *Renaissance Drama*, 13 (1982), 103–29, p. 129.
68. See A. R. Dutton, 'The Sources, Text, and Readers of *Sejanus*: Jonson's "integrity in the Story"', *Studies in Philology*, 75 (1978), 181–98.
69. Dryden, *An Essay of Dramatick Poesie*, p. 64.
70. Newton, 'Jonson and the (Re-)Invention of the Book', p. 46.
71. See J. F. Bradley and J. O. Adams, *The Jonson Allusion Book* (New Haven, 1922) for a collection of Dryden's references to Jonson, Index, pp. 456–7. He could be very positive, as in 'I prefer the *Silent Woman* before all other plays, I think justly, as I do its author, in judgment, above all other poets' (p. 346); but he is best remembered for putting

him in Shakespeare's critical shade: 'I must acknowledge him the more correct poet, but Shakespeare the greater wit. . . . I admire him, but I love Shakespeare'(p. 344); and his dismissal of Jonson's verses to the memory of Shakespeare as 'an insolent, sparing, and invidious panegyric' (p. 442) and of his last plays as 'but his dotages' (p. 343) had a serious long-term effect on his reputation.

72. Preface to the Translation of *Horace His Art of Poetry*, printed in John Oldham, *Works* (1703), p. 401. Edward Howard's 'Second Prologue' to *The Women's Conquest* is quoted from *H&S*, XI, p. 532.

73. Thomas Rymer, Preface to Rapin's *Reflections on Aristotle's Treatise of Poesie*, quoted in *Ben Jonson: The Critical Heritage*, ed. D. H. Craig (London and New York, 1990), p. 331. Jeremy Collier's *A Short View of the Immorality and Profaneness of the English Stage* is quoted from *H&S*, XI, p. 551.

74. *The Jonson Allusion Book*, p. 412.

75. See below, Chapter 5.

Notes to Chapter 2: Poet and Critic

1. On the 1616 folio as a conscious *version* of Jonson's career, see W. David Kay, 'The Shaping of Ben Jonson's Career: A Re-examination of Facts and Problems', *Modern Philology*, 67 (1970), 224–37.

2. See David Riggs, *Ben Jonson: A Life* (Cambridge, Mass., and London, 1989), pp. 28–32, on the dating and early comments.

3. *The Case is Altered* cannot originally have been for the Children of the Chapel, as Rosalind Miles, for one, suggests (*Ben Jonson: His Life and Work*, London, 1986, pp. 33–4), since the troupe was not revived until late 1599 at the earliest, by which time the play was well known. The fact that the Children of the Queen's Revels had lost that title by 1606 (they were the Children of the Whitefriars by 1609) suggests that they had acted the revised play some time before it was published.

4. See Glynne Wickham, 'The Privy Council Order of 1597 for the Destruction of all London's Theatres', in *The Elizabethan Theatre, I* ed. David Galloway (London, 1969), pp. 21–44.

5. See Richard Dutton, 'The Birth of the Author', forthcoming in *Look About You: Elizabethan Theatre – Essays in Honor of Sam Schoenbaum*. ed. R. B. Parker and Sheldon Zitner (Newark, Delaware, 1996).

6. See W. David Kay, 'The Shaping of Ben Jonson's Career', *Modern Philology*, 67 (1969), 224–37.

7. See G. E. Bentley, *The Profession of Dramatist in Shakespeare's Time, 1590–1642* (Princeton, 1971), chapter X, pp. 264–92, esp. pp. 288–91; Joseph Loewenstein, 'The Script in the Market-place', *Representations*, 12 (1985), 101–15; Timothy Murray, 'From Foul Sheets to Legitimate Model: Anti-theater, Text, Ben Jonson', *New Literary History*, 14 (1983), 641–64.

8. No documentary evidence of this status survives, but the known

facts of his career after 1594 square with the kind of contractual arrangements entered into in the 1630s, for which evidence survives. See Bentley, *The Profession of Dramatist in Shakespeare's Time*, chapter VI, pp. 111–44.

9. For other possible explanations about the pace of Shakespeare's playwriting, see Leeds Barroll, *Politics, Plague, and Shakespeare's Theater: The Stuart Years* (Ithaca and London, 1991).

10. Now in Edinburgh University Library. See John F. Andrews's entry on Shakespeare in the *Dictionary of Literary Biography*, volume 62, *Elizabethan Dramatists*, ed. Fredson Bowers (Detroit, 1987), 267–353, p. 304.

11. For some of Jonson's views of Fletcher, see *UV* VIII, and *Drummond*, 41, 134, 184–5.

12. *Poetaster*, III.iv.201; V.iii.123–5. I have discussed these matters further in 'Ben Jonson and the Master of the Revels', in *Theatre and Politics under the Early Stuarts*, eds J. R. Mulryne and M. Shewring (Cambridge, 1993), pp. 57–86.

13. See Jonas A. Barish, 'Jonson and the Loathed Stage', in *A Celebration of Ben Jonson*, eds William Blissett, Julian Patrick and R. W. Van Fossen (Toronto, 1973); John Gordon Sweeney, III, *Jonson and the Psychology of Public Theatre* (Princeton, 1985).

14. Heywood makes this claim in an address to the reader in *The English Traveller* (1633).

15. See below, p. 152.

16. 'Ode Upon Ben Jonson', *Hesperides* (1648).

17. *H&S*, V, pp. 291, 431. See David Wiles, *Shakespeare's Clown* (Cambridge, 1987), pp. 43–60.

18. On the vexed question of the audiences of Elizabethan/Jacobean playhouses, see Ann Jennalie Cook, *The Privileged Playgoers of Shakespeare's London, 1576–1642* (Princeton, 1981); but also Martin Butler's riposte in *Theatre and Crisis, 1632–42* (Cambridge, 1984), pp. 293–306; and Andrew Gurr's very different approach and conclusions in *Playgoing in Shakespeare's London* (Cambridge, 1987).

19. See below, Chapter 3, pp. 80, 82, and note 10.

20. Wiles, *Shakespeare's Clown*, p. 110. Wiles here acknowledges C. L. Barber's *Shakespeare's Festive Comedy* (Princeton, 1959); Northrop Frye's *Anatomy of Criticism* (Princeton, 1957), 'The argument of comedy', in *Shakespeare: Modern Essays in Criticism*, ed. L. F. Dean (New York, 1967), and 'Old and New Comedy', *Shakespeare Survey* 22 (1971); and Neil Rhodes's *Elizabethan Grotesque* (London, 1980), as instrumental in elevating such a view 'to the status of critical orthodoxy'. Subsequently (pp. 172–7) he reviews the contributions of the cultural historians Peter Burke (*Popular Culture in Early Modern Europe*, London, 1978) and Mikhail Bakhtin (*Rabelais and His World*, translated by H. Iswolsky, Cambridge, Mass., 1968), and of the anthropologists, Victor Turner (*The Ritual of Process*, Chicago, 1969) and Clifford Geertz (*The Interpretation of Cultures*, New York, 1973), to later ramifications of this approach.

21. See Burke, *Popular Culture in Early Modern Europe*, p. 182; Clifford

Geertz, 'Deep Play: Notes on the Balinese Cockfight', in *The Interpretation of Cultures*, pp. 412–53, p. 449.

22. On dancing after a performance of *Julius Caesar* at the Globe, see the account by Thomas Platter of Basle, in S. Schoenbaum, *William Shakespeare: A Compact Documentary Life*, revised edition (Oxford, 1987), p. 209.

23. See the Chronology.

24. See Phoebe Sheavyn, *The Literary Profession in Elizabethan England* (1909), revised by J. W. Saunders (Manchester, 1967).

25. Chapman's bitterness, at any rate, is apparent in the 'Invective of Mr George Chapman against Mr Ben Johnson', c.1624, though he never published it. By then Chapman's whole career was 'an agony of hope deferred' (Rosalind Miles, *Ben Jonson: His Life and Work*, p. 226). Christopher Marlowe was something of a precursor for Jonson and Chapman as a writer for the theatre who also pursued aristocratic patronage, but he was dead before Jonson's career began to take shape.

26. See Michael G. Brennan, *Literary Patronage in the English Renaissance: The Pembroke Family* (London, 1988), esp. pp. 103–27, 145–7.

27. See Riggs, *Ben Jonson: A Life*, p. 232.

28. On the pervasive influence of the patronage system on the mindset of the day, see Robert C. Evans, *Ben Jonson and the Poetics of Patronage* (Lewisburg, 1989).

29. See Riggs, *Ben Jonson: A Life*, pp. 191–2.

30. See Chapter 3, below.

31. See E. B. Partridge, 'Jonson's *Epigrammes*: The Named and the Nameless', *Studies in the Imagination*, 6 (1973), 153–98; Richard Dutton, *Ben Jonson: To the First Folio* (Cambridge, 1983), pp. 86–92.

32. More broadly on the *Works* and its place in Jonson's career, see *Ben Jonson's 1616 Folio*, eds Jennifer Brady and W. H. Herendeen (Newark, Delaware, 1991).

33. All of these comments are printed in H&S, X, p. 13.

34. For a suggestive exploration of the relationship between Sidney's politics and his creative writing, see Alan Sinfield, 'Power and Ideology: An Outline Theory and Sidney's *Arcadia*', *English Literary History*, 52 (1985), 259–79. This relates specifically to the *Arcadia*, but might profitably be expanded to other works, including the *Defense*.

35. Meres's comment is in his *Palladis Tamia* (1598).

36. See Riggs, *Ben Jonson: A Life*, pp. 109–12, on the differences between Jonson's contribution to these festivities and Dekker's.

37. He rushed so much that his text ignores the fact that bad weather delayed the show by three days; see Richard Dutton, '*King Lear, The Triumphs of Reunited Britannia* and "The Matter of Britain"', *Literature and History*, 12 (1986), 139–51, note 9, p. 150.

38. See Riggs, *Ben Jonson: A Life*, pp. 113–14.

39. On the Renaissance conventions for printing plays, see T. H. Howard-Hill, 'The Evolution of the Form of Plays in English during the Renaissance', *Renaissance Quarterly*, 43 (1990), 112–45. On the classic status of Chaucer etc., see pp. 67, 194.

40. See *Drummond*, 137–41, and James A. Riddell and Stanley Stewart, 'Jonson Reads "The Ruines of Time"', *Studies in Philology*, 87 (1990), 427–55.
41. Margaret P. Hannay, *Philip's Phoenix: Mary Sidney, Countess of Pembroke* (Oxford, 1990), pp. 69ff.
42. In this, Jonson associates Sidney with Lucan and Guarini, whom he considered guilty of the same fault: *Drummond*, 47–8, 537–8.
43. King James's dismissal of Sidney is coupled with praise for 'the sculler', Taylor the Water Poet, whom Jonson could scarcely take seriously: see *Discoveries*, 612–21, and *Drummond*, 533.
44. *Aubrey's Brief Lives*, ed. Oliver Lawson Dick (Harmondsworth, 1972), p. 338. Strictly speaking, Aubrey actually only notes '*Every Man . . .*' as 'his first good one', but it is fairly clear that he had swallowed Jonson's propaganda. Certainly Nicholas Rowe had swallowed it shortly later in *Some Account of the Life of Mr William Shakespear*, which prefaces his 1709 edition of Shakespeare's plays: see below, p. 143.

   On the revision of the play, see my 'The Significance of Jonson's Revision of *Every Man In His Humour*', *Modern Language Review*, 69 (1974), 241–9. I am more convinced now than I was then that Percy Simpson was right in dating the revision in 1612/13 with an eye to its place in the folio; see p. 242, and notes 3 and 4.
45. Herford and Simpson assumed that *The Golden Age Restored* could not have been performed after the implications of the Overbury case became known, and that Jonson must have reversed its chronological order with that of *Mercury Vindicated from the Alchemists at Court* (see *H&S*, VI, p. 420). But John Orrell established that this was not the case. See *Chronology*, note 3.
46. See Riggs, *Ben Jonson: A Life*, p. 220, and Martin Butler, 'Jonson's Folio and the Politics of Patronage'. It is interesting, in respect of Jonson's position at court, that he was never formally Poet Laureate, though he fulfilled the functions of that office more convincingly than most of its holders have done: see Edmund K. Broadus, *The Laureateship* (Oxford, 1921), pp. 40–4.

Notes to Chapter 3: Poet and State

1. I.iv.4–5. All references to the works of Shakespeare are to *William Shakespeare: the Complete Works*, general editors Stanley Wells and Gary Taylor, Compact Edition (Oxford, 1988).
2. Martin Elsky, *Authorizing Words: Speech, Writing, and Print in the English Renaissance* (Ithaca and London, 1989), pp. 87–8. On Jonson's response to James's authority, see Jonathan Z. Kamholtz, 'Ben Jonson's *Epigrammes* and Poetic Occasions', *Studies in English Literature*, 23 (1983), pp. 77–94, and Jennifer Brady, 'Jonson's "To King James": Plain Speaking in the *Epigrammes* and the Conversations', *Studies in Philology*, 82 (1985), pp. 380–99.

3. See Chapter 1, note 54.
4. See Richard Dutton, *Mastering the Revels: The Regulation and Censorship of English Renaissance Drama* (London, 1991).
5. D. H. Willson, *James VI and I* (London, 1963), p. 198.
6. For an accessible account of Vives's role, and more generally that of humanist thought, in the court of Henry VIII, see Anthony Martienssen, *Queen Katherine Parr* (London, 1975), esp. pp. 31–6, 51–5.
7. I have developed this further in R. Dutton, '"What Ministers Men Must, For Practice, Use": Ben Jonson's Cicero', *English Studies*, 59 (1978), 324–35.
8. *Satiromastix*, in *The Dramatic Works of Thomas Dekker*, ed. Fredson Bowers, 4 volumes (Cambridge, 1953–61), vol. 1, I.ii.376). All references to the works of Dekker are to this edition.
9. The 'missliked' is Dekker's verdict in *Satiromastix*, V.iii.324.
10. There is no evidence that Jonson was actually taken to law over *Poetaster*. In dedicating the play to Richard Martin, he cryptically commends it as a work 'for whose innocence, as for the author's, you were once a noble and timely undertaker, to the greatest justice of this kingdom'. Sir John Popham, the Lord Chief Justice, and Richard Martin were both members of the Middle Temple, Popham by then being its treasurer. If it was specifically Middle Temple lawyers who took offence at the play, it may be that Jonson was asked to account for himself to Popham in that capacity, and that Martin intervened on his behalf. I am grateful to Dr Tom Cain, editor of the forthcoming Revels Plays edition of *Poetaster*, for sharing this insight with me.
11. See Dutton, *Mastering the Revels*, pp. 11–12, 164–5, 171–3.
12. The fact that *Eastward Ho* should have had a licence from the Lord Chamberlain, rather than his functionary, the Master of the Revels who licensed most plays in the London region at this time, must relate to the anomalous status of the Children of the Queen's Revels, who performed it; they were attached to Queen Anne's household and subject to special provisions, at least for a time. See Dutton, *Mastering the Revels*, chapter 7, 'The Question of Authority II: the Boy Companies, 1604–10'.
13. See Rosalind Miles, *Ben Jonson: His Life and Work* (London, 1986), p. 100.
14. Miles, *Ben Jonson: His Life and Work*, p. 102.
15. See Richard Dutton, *Ben Jonson: To the First Folio* (Cambridge, 1983), p. 147, about the dating of *Volpone*. For an unequivocal view of Jonson as a double-agent, see John Archer, *Sovereignty and Intelligence: Spying and Court Culture in English Renaissance Writing* (Stanford, Calif., 1993).
16. The letter to the Earl of Salisbury is reproduced in the Appendix, based on the version in *Eastward Ho*, edited by R. W. Van Fossen (Manchester and Baltimore, 1979), appendix 2, pp. 218–25, pp. 220–1. References to Jonson's other letters (and Chapman's) over the *Eastward Ho* affair are to these versions; I have, as usual, modernised the text.

17. See p. 86 above.
18. I have expanded on this point and its significance in 'Ben Jonson and the Master of the Revels', in *Theatre and Government under the Early Stuarts*, eds J. R. Mulryne and M. Shewring (Cambridge, 1993).
19. See Chapman's second letter to him, *ed.cit.*, p. 219.
20. Strabo, *Geographica*, I.ii.5.
21. See Chapter 4, below.
22. *Ben Jonson's Literary Criticism*, ed. James D. Redwine Jr (Lincoln, Nebraska, 1970), p. xv.
23. See Jonathan Goldberg, *James I and the Politics of Literature* (Baltimore, 1983), esp. pp. 219–30. In Goldberg's contention even Jonson at his most free-minded is subsumed by the authority of the king: 'His fantasy of rebellion is licensed by the king. And throughout his career, that fantasy was very close to the facts. His rebellions were royally countenanced', p. 221.
24. Stanley Fish, *Is There a Text in This Class?* (Cambridge, Mass., and London, 1980), p. 312.
25. See above, p. 62.
26. See pp. 37–9.
27. On the allusions to Shakespeare, in *Much Ado About Nothing* and *Titus Andronicus*, see below, pp. 98, 197.
28. Jonathan Haynes, 'Festivity and the Dramatic Economy of Jonson's *Bartholomew Fair*', ELH, 51 (1984), 645–68, p. 647. On the formal structure of the play, see Richard Levin, 'The Structure of *Bartholomew Fair*', *PMLA*, 80 (1965), 172–9; and Joel Kaplan, 'Dramatic and Moral Energy in Jonson's *Bartholomew Fair*', *Renaissance Drama*, N.S. 3 (1970), 137–56. On the play and festive culture, see Peter Burke, *Popular Culture in Early Modern Europe* (London, 1978), p. 196; also Peter Stallybrass and Allon White, *The Politics and Poetics of Transgression* (London, 1987), 'Smithfield and Authorship', pp. 66–79.
29. The Lord Mayor is usually identified as Sir Thomas Hayes – see, for example, Eugene M. Waith's edition of *Bartholomew Fair* (New Haven, 1963), pp. 190, 192 – but David McPherson has argued that it was Thomas Middleton (no relation to the dramatist). See his 'The Origins of Overdo: a study in Jonsonian Invention', *Modern Language Quarterly*, 37 (1976), 221–33. McPherson is sensible and scholarly about the whole business of 'applications'; for a less circumspect view, see C. G. Thayer, *Ben Jonson: Studies in the Plays* (Norman, Oklahoma, 1963), pp. 144–5.
30. On the theatrical precedents for Overdo's role, see Anne Barton, *Ben Jonson, Dramatist* (Cambridge, 1984), p. 203; Robert N. Watson, *Ben Jonson's Parodic Strategy* (Cambridge, Mass., 1987), pp. 157–8.
31. See Robert C. Evans, *Ben Jonson and the Poetics of Patronage* (Lewisburg, 1989), esp. p. 144, on the range of patrons addressed.
32. See p. 63.
33. For a full exposition of the theory, see W. Todd Furniss, 'Ben Jonson's Masques', in *Three Studies in the Renaissance: Sidney, Jonson, Milton*, ed. B. C. Nangle (New Haven, 1958), pp. 88–179.
34. See 'An Expostulation with Inigo Jones', Appendix, p. 214.

35. *The Masque of Beauty*, Appendix, p. 180; *Hymenaei*, Appendix, p. 174.
36. James wanted the union of crowns compounded by a union of his two Parliaments, a project to which the masque also tactfully alludes; but the Westminster Parliament would have none of it.
37. See David Riggs, *Ben Jonson: A Life* (Cambridge, Mass., and London, 1989), p. 203; also David Lindley, 'Embarrassing Ben: The Masques for Frances Howard', *English Literary Renaissance*, 16 (1986), 343–59; and his defence of the much-maligned Frances Howard in *The Trials of Frances Howard: Fact and Fiction at the Court of King James* (London, 1993).
38. See Dale B. J. Randall, *Jonson's Gypsies Unmasked* (Durham, NC, 1975). Martin Butler has challenged the ironic reading of the masque in '"We Are One Man's All": Jonson's *The Gypsies Metamorphosed*', *Yearbook of English Studies*, 21 (1991), 252–73, primarily because it does not square with the factional politics of the situation to which the masque relates. But in a sense the very fact that Randall can articulate such an ironic reading demonstrates that it was *potentially* available to the Jacobean audience (and, indeed, participants). Which is essentially my point.
39. *The Defence of Poesy*, in R. Dutton (ed.), *Selected Writings of Sir Philip Sidney* (Manchester, 1982), p. 130.

Notes to Chapter 4: The 'Laws' of Poetry

1. The 'affirmation' of order in 'To Penshurst' is certainly not unproblematic, as Don E. Wayne has demonstrated at length in *Penshurst: The Semiotics of Place and the Poetics of History* (Madison, Wisconsin, 1984). My point here is that Jonson starts in the poem from such a notion of order, whether or not he actually succeeds in representing it.
2. See J. T. McCullen, 'Conference with the Queen of Fairies', *Studia Neophilologica*, 23 (1950), 87–95.
3. See O. J. Campbell, *Comicall Satyre and Shakespeare's 'Troilus and Cressida'* (San Marino, California, 1938), pp. 3–8.
4. See J. D. Redwine Jr, *Ben Jonson's Literary Criticism* (Lincoln, Nebraska, 1970), xxii–xxiii, on the equivalence of *summa epitasis* and *catastasis*.
5. See T. W. Baldwin, *Shakespeare's Five-Act Structure* (Urbana, 1947), especially pp. 228–51 and 294–6.
6. See T. H. Howard-Hill, 'The Evolution of the Form of Plays in English during the Renaissance', *Renaissance Quarterly*, 43 (1990), 112–45.
7. See pp. 49–50, 98–9.
8. See J. D. Redwine, 'The Moral Basis of Jonson's Theory of Humour Characterization', *ELH*, 28 (1961), 316–34.
9. See Katharine Eisaman Maus, 'Facts of the Matter: Satiric and Ideal Economies in the Jonsonian Imagination', *English Literary Renaissance*, 19 (1989), 42–64, reprinted in *Ben Jonson's 1616 Folio*, ed. Jennifer Brady and W. H. Herenden (Newark, Delaware, 1991), for a recent

assessment of the 'frustrated murderousness of Jonsonian comedy' (p. 65).

10. A. C. Swinburne, *A Study of Ben Jonson* (London, 1889), p. 39.

11. See the prefatory material to *Catiline*.

12. This is certainly what Jonson has in mind in justifying the anti-masque on the grounds that 'a principal part of life in these spectacles lay in their variety'; see above, p. 22.

13. Dryden's claim about Morose is in *An Essay of Dramatick Poesie*, ed. James T. Boulton (Oxford, 1964), p. 91. On the Induction to *The Magnetic Lady*, see p. 66. Note that Jonson does not entirely disavow humour-characterisation in his tragedies, something which generations of critics who have habitually compared them unfavourably with the supposed psychological realism of Shakespeare's tragedies would doubtless echo. But he never develops this, and in particular never explains how a theory associated with the fictionalised representation of contemporary attitudes might square with the standard Renaissance expectation that tragedy should be both true-to-life and historically verifiable, something alluded to by the foolish Fitzdottrel in *The Devil is an Ass* when he confesses that he gets his history 'from the Play-books / And think they're more authentic' (II.iv.13–14). See J. A. Bryant Jr, 'The Significance of Ben Jonson's First Requirement for Tragedy: Truth of Argument', *Studies in Philology*, 49 (1952), 195–213.

14. See L. C. Knights, *Drama and Society in the Age of Jonson* (London, 1937), especially the chapters 'Social Theory', 'Drama and Society', 'Tradition and Ben Jonson' and 'Jonson and the Anti-Acquisitive Attitude'; also Raymond Williams, *The Country and the City* (London, 1973), pp. 26–45; Don E. Wayne, 'Drama and Society in the Age of Jonson: An Alternative View', *Renaissance Drama*, 13 (1982), 103–29; Walter Cohen, *Drama of a Nation: Public Theater in Renaissance England and Spain* (Ithaca, New York, 1985), pp. 292–301.

15. Anne Barton, *Ben Jonson, Dramatist* (Cambridge, 1984).

16. Susan Wells, 'Jacobean City Comedy and the Ideology of the City', *ELH*, 48 (1981), 37–60, p. 38. Karen Newman has pursued this, in respect of the representation of women as creatures of the city in *Epicoene*, in 'City Talk: Women and Commodification in *Epicoene*', *ELR*, 53 (1989), 503–18, reprinted in her *Fashioning Femininity and English Renaissance Drama* (Chicago, 1991).

17. See Lawrence Danson, 'Jonsonian Comedy and the Discovery of the Social Self', *PMLA*, 99 (1984), 179–93. On the contemporary rationale for what I have called proto-capitalism, see C. B. MacPherson, *The Political Theory of Possessive Individualism* (Oxford, 1962).

18. Wayne, 'Drama and Society in the Age of Jonson: An Alternative View', p. 105.

19. 'Manhood': Jonson professed to respect the reading abilities of at least some women, as when he commends Donne's satires to Lucy, Countess of Bedford, with the observation that 'Rare poems ask rare friends' (*Ep* XCIV). But his public comments always assume male readers, as in the prefaces to *Catiline*. 'To the Reader in Ordinary':

... men judge only out of knowledge. That is the trying faculty'. 'To the Reader Extraordinary': 'You I would understand to be the better man, though places in court go otherwise; to you I commend myself and work.' And see pp. 133–4 on 'women's poets'.

20. See Christopher Ricks, '*Sejanus* and Dismemberment', *Modern Language Notes*, 76 (1961), 301–8.

21. See Richard S. Peterson, *Imitation and Praise in the Poems of Ben Jonson* (New Haven and London, 1981); G. A. E. Parfitt, 'The Nature of Translation in Ben Jonson's Poetry', *SEL*, 13 (1974), 344–59; Robert Shafer, *The English Ode. to 1660* (New York, 1966), pp. 106ff; Paul H. Fry, *The Poet's Calling in the English Ode* (New Haven and London, 1980), chapter 1; Stella P. Revard, 'Pindar and Jonson's Cary-Morison Ode', in *Classic and Cavalier: Essays of Jonson and the Sons of Ben*, ed. C. J. Summers and T-L. Pebworth (Pittsburg, 1982), pp. 17–29.

22. See Richard Dutton, 'The Significance of Jonson's Revision of *Every Man In His Humour*', *Modern Language Review*, 69 (1974), 241–9.

23. Don E. Wayne, *Penshurst: The Semiotics of Place and the Poetics of History* (Madison, Wisconsin, 1984); Stanley Fish, 'Authors–Readers: Jonson's Community of the Same', *Representations*, 7 (Summer 1984), 26–58.

24. See Robert C. Evans, *Ben Jonson and the Poetics of Patronage* (Lewisburg, PA, 1988); William E. Cain, 'The Place of the Poet in Jonson's "To Penshurst" and "To My Muse"', *Criticism*, 21 (1979), 34–48; Don E. Wayne, 'Poetry and Power in Ben Jonson's Epigrammes: The Naming of "Facts" or the Figuring of Social Relations', *Renaissance and Modern Studies*, 23 (1979), 79–103.

25. Downright: c.f. George Downright, 'a plain squire', in the folio *Every Man In His Humour*.

26. On the differences between Spenser and Jonson as would-be laureate-poets, see Richard Helgerson, *Self-Crowned Laureates: Spenser, Jonson, Milton and the Literary System* (Berkeley, CA, 1983).

27. M. McCanles *Jonsonian Discriminations: The Humanist Poet and the Praise of True Nobility* (Toronto, 1992), p. 217. I must not pretend that McCanles's general thesis endorses my own; he goes on to invoke – the theme of his book – 'the centuries-long tradition of the vera nobilitas argument which governed his self-identity and yielded him the means of achieving it'. McCanles finds in 'the vera nobilitas argument' a central validating point of authenticity in his career – a sticking point, in my terms – which eradicates the kinds of tensions which I find in Jonson's work. My own thesis will probably be listed with 'the most recent atacks [sic] on Jonson, those of Rowe, Evans, and Riggs [which] view him in new historicist fashion as driven by the same kinds of self-loathing, *resentment* and obsession with power ascribed to court life in general by [Frank] Wigham' (p. 268).

28. Compare the first half of this with the more considered: 'Words borrowed of antiquity do lend a kind of majesty to style, and are not without their delight sometimes. For they have the authority of years, and out of their intermission do win themselves a kind of

grace like newness. But the eldest of the present and newest of the past language is the best' (1931–6).

29. See above, pp. 52, 56, 101, 123, 131.
30. Davies gets away lightly compared with Sir John Harington, who 'when [he] desired [Jonson] to tell the truth of his epigrams, he answered him that he loved not the truth, for they were narrations, and not epigrams' (37–40). Jonson also said 'Harington's "Ariosto" [*Orlando Furioso*] under all translations was the worst' (35–6).
31. See above, pp. 88, 97.
32. There are analogies to be drawn here with Jonson's reservations about basing a play on Plautus's *Amphitrio*, 'for that he could never find two so like others that he could persuade the spectators they were one' (*Drummond*, 360–2), an impediment that clearly did not weigh so heavily with Shakespeare. See below, p. 157.
33. See Scott Wilson, 'Racked on the Tyrant's Bed: Pleasure and Pain and Elizabethan Sonnet Sequences', *Textual Practice*, 2 (1989), 234–51.
34. Samuel Johnson, 'Abraham Cowley', in *Lives of the Poets*, 2 volumes (London, 1925), vol. I, pp. 1–45, p. 13.
35. Don K. Hedrick, 'Cooking for the Anthropophagi: Jonson and His Audience', *Studies in English Literature*, 17 (1977), 233–45, p. 244.
36. I pursue this further, and the way the two different versions of the poem are subtly adjusted for their different readerships, in R. Dutton, *Ben Jonson: To the First Folio* (Cambridge, 1983), pp. 109–10.

Notes to Chapter 5: Jonson and Shakespeare

1. See S. Schoenbaum, *Shakespeare's Lives* (Oxford and New York, 1970); 'Shakespeare and Jonson: Fact and Myth', *The Elizabethan Theatre*, II, ed. David Galloway (Toronto, 1970), pp. 1–19.
2. S. Schoenbaum, *William Shakespeare: A Compact Documentary Life*, revised edition (Oxford, 1987), pp. 256–7.
3. In the case of Plume's version it would seem that *real* hearsay had taken over, and that he simply got it wrong, not knowing enough about either Jonson or Shakespeare to get the true point of the joke.
4. Thomas Fuller, *The History of the Worthies of England* (1662), p. 126.
5. Schoenbaum, *William Shakespeare: A Compact Documentary Life*, p. 258.
6. 'Some Account of the Life, &c. of Mr. William Shakespear', in Shakespeare, *Works*, ed. Nicholas Rowe (1709), vol. I, p. ix.
7. See above, p. 45.
8. On the 1572 Act for the Punishment of Vagabonds and the 1598 Act for the Punishment of Rogues, Vagabonds and Sturdy Beggars, see E. K. Chambers, *Elizabethan Stage*, IV (Oxford, 1923) pp. 270, 324–5; see also, Richard Dutton, *Mastering the Revels: The Regulation and Censorship of English Renaissance Drama* (London and Basingstoke, 1991), pp. 26, 110.
9. John Cocke, 'A Common Player', quoted in Chambers, *Elizabethan Stage*, IV, pp. 255–7.

10. See Schoenbaum, *William Shakespeare: A Compact Documentary Life*, pp. 227–32.
11. For a fuller account of possible allusions to Shakespeare in *Every Man Out of His Humour* and other early plays, see E. A. J. Honigmann, *Shakespeare's Impact on His Contemporaries* (London, 1982), pp. 100–3.
12. See David Riggs, *Ben Jonson: A Life* (Cambridge, Mass., and London, 1989), p. 20.
13. See pp. 97–9.
14. See David Wiles, *Shakespeare's Clown* (Cambridge, 1987), p. 75, on Kempe as Dogberry, but also more generally on the clowning tradition in the Elizabethan theatre; see particularly his analysis of Jonson's handling of the clown's role in the two versions of *Every Man In His Humour*, pp. 96ff.
15. Hamlet makes much the same point: 'And let those that play your clowns speak no more than is set down for them; for there be of them that will themselves laugh to set on some quantity of barren spectators to laugh too, though in the mean time some necessary question of the play be then to be considered' (III.ii.38–43). There is no telling, however, whether this is specific to that play's obsession with theatrical representation or if Shakespeare was speaking his own mind, Kempe by then having left the company.
16. See Riggs, *Ben Jonson: A Life*, pp. 87–91.
17. Ian Donaldson, *The World Turned Upside-Down* (Oxford, 1970), pp. 47–8.
18. See *The Winter's Tale*, ed. J. H. P. Pafford (London, 1963), p. xxii.
19. On *Bartholomew Fair* as a parody of *The Two Noble Kinsmen*, see Muriel Bradbrook, *The Living Monument: Shakespeare and the Theatre of His Time* (Cambridge, 1976), p. 111; and R. Dutton, *Ben Jonson: To the First Folio* (Cambridge 1983), pp. 168–9.
20. See, for example, J. F. Danby, 'Sidney and the Late-Shakespearian Romance', in *Elizabethan and Jacobean Poets* (London, 1965), 74–107; Northrop Frye, *A Natural Perspective: the Development of Shakespearean Comedy and Romance* (New York, 1965); Howard Felperin, *Shakespearean Romance* (Princeton, 1973); D. L. Peterson, *Time, Tide and Tempest: a Study of Shakespeare's Romances* (San Marino, California, 1973).
21. For a modern attempt to apply 'tragicomedy' to Shakespeare, see Joan L. Hartwig, *Shakespeare's Tragicomic Vision* (Baton Rouge, Louisiana, 1972).
22. W. H. Herendeen, 'A New Way to Pay Old Debts', in *Ben Jonson's 1616 Folio*, eds J. Brady and W. H. Herendeen (Newark, Delaware, 1991), pp. 38–63, p. 60 note 13; see also pp. 44–6.
23. Modern opinion ascribes *The Faithful Shepherdess* solely to Fletcher, but this does not affect the issue. It was in the preface to this (printed *c*.1609), a work which echoes both the theory and the theme of *Il Pastor Fido*, that Fletcher championed 'tragicomedy' in England, against the objections of those, like Philip Sidney, who had objected that 'mongrel tragicomedy', in practice if not necessarily in theory, muddied proper distinctions between tragedy and comedy. (See *The*

Defence of Poesy, ed.cit., p. 141.) And 'tragicomedy' was most commonly used in England in relation to Fletcher's own plays, particularly those he wrote in collaboration with Francis Beaumont. See E. M. Waith, *The Pattern of Tragicomedy in Beaumont and Fletcher* (New Haven, 1952).

24. *William Shakespeare: The Complete Works,* general editors Stanley Wells and Gary Taylor (Oxford, 1988), p. xlv.
25. *Ben Jonson,* The Oxford Authors, ed. Ian Donaldson (Oxford, 1985), p. 742, note to *Discoveries,* line 676, drawing on the discussion in *H&S,* XI, 231–3. It is worth noting, in respect of the general point Jonson was making here, that when Leonard Digges praised *Julius Caesar* and noted 'how the audience / Were ravished', he contrasted this with the effect on them 'Of tedious though well-laboured *Catiline*'. Quoted in *William Shakespeare: The Complete Works,* general editors Stanley Wells and Gary Taylor, p. 599.
26. 'Ode to Himself' (after *The New Inn*), Appendix, p. 206, lines 21–2.
27. See pp. 37, 106.
28. See p. 50.
29. Russ McDonald, *Shakespeare and Jonson / Jonson and Shakespeare* (Lincoln, Nebraska, and London, 1988), pp. 186–7. As McDonald acknowledges, his is not the first challenge to the usual division of the two men into separate camps, though it is one of the most sustained; see his survey of previous work, pp. 190–91, notes 6 and 7.
30. See Alexander Leggatt, *Ben Jonson: His Vision and His Art* (London, 1981), especially pp. xv–xvi and 199–232.
31. In 'A Discourse Concerning the Original and Progress of Satire' (1693). For modern comment on the poem see T. J. B. Spenser 'Ben Jonson on his beloved, the Author Mr. William Shakespeare', in *Elizabethan Theatre, IV,* ed. George Hibbard (London and Basingstoke, 1974), pp. 22–40; Peterson, *Imitation and Praise in the Poems of Ben Jonson,* chapter 4; Lawrence Lipking, *The Life of the Poet* (Chicago, 1981), chapter 3.
32. See Richard Dutton, 'The Birth of the Author', forthcoming in *Look About You: Elizabethan Theatre – Essays in Honor of Sam Schoenbaum* (Newark, Delaware, 1996), ed. R. B. Parker and Sheldon Zitner.

Select Bibliography

This selection makes no attempt to be a comprehensive guide to the very extensive array of work on and by Jonson. It is limited to material specifically relevant to this study.

EDITIONS OF JONSON

Ben Jonson, edited by C. H. Herford, and Percy and Evelyn Simpson, 11 vols (Oxford, 1925–52).

The Complete Plays of Ben Jonson, edited by G. A. Wilkes, 4 vols (Oxford, 1981–2).

Ben Jonson: Five Plays, edited by G. A. Wilkes, The World's Classics (Oxford, 1988).

The Selected Plays of Ben Jonson, vol. 1, edited by Johanna Procter (Cambridge, 1989).

The Selected Plays of Ben Jonson, vol. 2, edited by Martin Butler (Cambridge, 1989).

Ben Jonson, edited by Ian Donaldson, The Oxford Authors (Oxford, 1985), contains *Discoveries* and *Drummond*.

Ben Jonson: Poems, edited by Ian Donaldson, Oxford Standard Authors (Oxford, 1975).

Ben Jonson: The Complete Poems, edited by George Parfitt, The Penguin Poets (Harmondsworth, 1975), contains *Discoveries* and *Drummond*.

Ben Jonson: The Complete Masques, edited by Stephen Orgel (New Haven, 1969).

Ben Jonson's 'Timber, or Discoveries', edited by R. S. Walker (Syracuse, 1953).

Jonson, Ben, *Bartholomew Fair*, edited by Eugene M. Waith (New Haven, 1963).

Jonson, Ben, Chapman, George and Marston, John, *Eastward Ho*, edited by R. W. Van Fossen (Manchester and Baltimore, 1979).

(It is not possible here to list all the single-volume editions of Jonson's plays).

JONSON'S LIFE AND CAREER

Brady, Jennifer, and Herendeen, W. H. (eds), *Ben Jonson's 1616 Folio* (Newark, Delaware, 1991).

Dutton Richard, 'Ben Jonson and the Master of the Revels', in *Theatre and Government under the Early Stuarts*, eds J. R. Mulryne and M. Shewring (Cambridge, 1993).

Kay, W. David, *Ben Jonson: A Literary Life* (Basingstoke and New York, 1995).

——, 'The Shaping of Ben Jonson's Career: A Re-examination of Facts and Problems', *Modern Philology*, 67 (1970), 224–37.

Miles, Rosalind, *Ben Jonson: His Life and Work* (London, 1986).

Orrell, John, 'The London Stage in the Florentine Correspondence, 1604–1618', *Theatre Research International*, 3 (1977–8), 173–4.

Riggs, David, *Ben Jonson: A Life* (Cambridge, Mass., and London, 1989).

JONSON AND LITERARY CRITICISM

Barthes, Roland, 'What is Criticism', in *Critical Essays*, translated from the French by Richard Howard (Evanston, Ill., 1972), pp. 255–60.

Bryant, J. A. Jr, 'The Significance of Ben Jonson's First Requirement for Tragedy: Truth of Argument', *Studies in Philology*, 49 (1952), 195–213.

Clark, Ira, 'Ben Jonson's Imitation', *Criticism*, 21 (1978), 107–27.

Gordon, D. J., 'Poet and Architect: The Intellectual Setting of the Quarrel between Ben Jonson and Inigo Jones', *Journal of the Warburg and Courtauld Institutes*, 12 (1949), 152–78.

Hedrick, Don. K., 'Cooking for the Anthropophagi: Jonson and His Audience', *Studies in English Literature*, 17 (1977), 233–45.

Klein, David, *Literary Criticism from the Elizabethan Dramatists: Repertory and Synthesis* (New York, 1910).

Redwine, J. D. Jr, *Ben Jonson's Literary Criticism* (Lincoln, Nebraska, 1970).

——, 'The Moral Basis of Jonson's Theory of Humour Characterization', *ELH*, 28 (1961), 316–34.

Walker, R. S., 'Literary Criticism in Jonson's Conversations with Drummond', in *Ben Jonson's 'Timber or Discoveries'*, edited by R. S. Walker (Syrause, 1953), pp. 123–35.

Watson, George, *The Literary Critics: A Study of English Descriptive Criticism* (Harmondsworth, 1964).

Weinberg, Bernard, *A History of Literary Criticism in the Italian Renaissance*, 2 vols (Chicago, 1961).

Wimsatt, W. K. Jr, and Brooks, Cleanth, *Literary Criticism: A Short History* (New York, 1965).

JONSON AND THE THEATRE

Barish, Jonas A., 'Jonson and the Loathed Stage', in *A Celebration of Ben Jonson*, edited by William Blissett, Julian Patrick and R. W. Van Fossen (Toronto, 1973).

——, *The Antitheatrical Prejudice* (Berkeley, 1981).

Butler, Martin, *Theatre and Crisis, 1632–42* (Cambridge, 1984).

Carlson, Peter, 'Judging Spectators', *ELH*, 44 (1977), 443–57.

Cook, Ann Jennalie, *The Privileged Playgoers of Shakespeare's London, 1576–1642* (Princeton, 1981).

Gurr, Andrew, *Playgoing in Shakespeare's London* (Cambridge, 1987).

Sweeney, John Gordon, III, *Jonson and the Psychology of Public Theatre* (Princeton, 1985).

Wickham, Glynne, 'The Privy Council Order of 1597 for the Destruction of all London's Theatres', in *The Elizabethan Theatre*, I, edited by David Galloway (London, 1969), pp. 21–44.

Wiles, David, *Shakespeare's Clown* (Cambridge, 1987).

JONSON AND CONDITIONS OF AUTHORSHIP

Archer, John, *Sovereignty and Intelligence: Spying and Court Culture in English Renaissance Writing* (Stanford, Calif., 1993).

Bakhtin, Mikhail, *Rabelais and His World*, translated by H. Iswolsky (Cambridge, Mass., 1968).

Baldwin, T. W., *Shakespeare's Five-Act Structure* (Urbana, 1947).

Bentley, G. E., *The Profession of Dramatist in Shakespeare's Time, 1590–1642* (Princeton, 1971).

Brady, Jennifer, 'Jonson's "To King James": Plain Speaking in the *Epigrammes* and the Conversations', *Studies in Philology*, 82 (1985), 380–99.

Brennan, Michael G., *Literary Patronage in the English Renaissance: The Pembroke Family* (London, 1988).

Burke, Peter, *Popular Culture in Early Modern Europe* (London, 1978).

Burt, Richard, *Licensed by Authority: Ben Jonson and the Discourses of Censorship* (Ithaca and London, 1993).

Butler, Martin, 'Jonson's Folio and the Politics of Patronage', *Criticism*, 35 (1993), 377–90.

——, 'Ecclesiastical Censorship of Early Stuart Drama: the Case of Jonson's *The Magnetic Lady*', *Modern Philology*, 89 (1992), 469–81.

——, '"We Are One Man's All": Jonson's *The Gypsies Metamorphosed*', *Yearbook of English Studies*, 21 (1991), 252–73.

Cerasano, S. P., and Wynne-Davies, M. (eds), *Gloriana's Face: Women, Public and Private, in the English Renaissance* (Detroit, 1992).

Dutton, Richard, *Mastering the Revels: The Regulation and Censorship of English Renaissance Drama* (London, 1991).

Eisenstein, Elizabeth, *The Printing Press as an Agent of Change* (Cambridge, 1979).

Elsky, Martin, *Authorizing Words: Speech, Writing, and Print in the English Renaissance* (Ithaca and London, 1989).

Evans, Robert C., *Ben Jonson and the Poetics of Patronage* (Lewisburg, 1989).

Fish, Stanley E., 'Authors–Readers: Jonson's Community of the Same', *Representations*, 7 (1984), 26–58.

Foucault, Michel, 'What is an Author?', in *The Foucault Reader*, edited by Paul Rabinow (New York, 1984).

Geertz, Clifford, *The Interpretation of Cultures* (New York, 1973).

Howard-Hill, T. H., 'The Evolution of the Form of Plays in English During the Renaissance', *Renaissance Quarterly*, 43 (1990), 112–45.

Helgerson, Richard, *Self-Crowned Laureates: Spenser, Jonson, Milton and the Literary System* (Berkeley, 1983).

Kamholtz, Jonathan Z., 'Ben Jonson's *Epigrammes* and Poetic Occasions', *Studies in English Literature*, 23 (1983), 77–94.

Lewalski, Barbara, 'Anne of Denmark and Masquing', *Criticism*, 35 (1993), 341–55.

Loewenstein, Joseph, 'The Script in the Market-place', *Representations*, 12 (1985), 101–15.

May, Stephen W., 'Tudor Aristocrats and the Mythical "Stigma of Print"', *Renaissance Papers 1980* (1981), 11–18.

McCanles, Michael, *Jonsonian Discriminations: The Humanist Poet and the Praise of True Nobility* (Toronto, 1992).

Murray, Timothy, 'From Foul Sheets to Legitimate Model: Anti-theater, Text, Ben Jonson', *New Literary History*, 14 (1983), 641–64.

Newton, Richard C., 'Jonson and the (Re-)Invention of the Book', in *Classic and Cavalier: Essays on Jonson and the Sons of Ben*, edited by Claude J. Summers and Ted-Larry Pebworth (Pittsburgh, 1982), pp. 31–58.

Patterson, Annabel, *Censorship and Interpretation: The Condition of Writing and Reading in Early Modern England* (Madison, Wiscon., 1984).

Peck, Linda Levy (ed.), *The Mental World of the Jacobean Court* (Cambridge, 1991).

Peterson, Richard S., *Imitation and Praise in the Poems of Ben Jonson* (New Haven, 1981).

Saunders, J. W., 'The Stigma of Print: A Note on the Social Bases of Tudor Poetry', *Essays in Criticism*, 1 (1951), 139–54.

——, 'The Social Situation of Seventeenth Century Poetry', in *Metaphysical Poetry*, edited by M. Bradbury and D. J. Palmer (London, 1970), pp. 237–59.

Sheavyn, Phoebe, *The Literary Profession in Elizabethan England* (1909), revised by J. W. Saunders (Manchester, 1967).

Stallybrass, Peter, and White, Allon, *The Politics and Poetics of Transgression* (London, 1987).

Tribble, Evelyn B., *Margins and Marginality: The Printed Page in Early Modern England* (Charlottesville and London, 1993).

Turner, Victor, *The Ritual of Process* (Chicago, 1969).

RELEVANT CRITICAL STUDIES OF JONSON

Barish, Jonas, *Ben Jonson and the Language of Prose Comedy* (Cambridge, Mass., 1960).

Barton, Anne, *Ben Jonson, Dramatist* (Cambridge, 1984).

Campbell, O. J., *Comicall Satyre and Shakespeare's 'Troilus and Cressida'* (San Marino, California, 1938).

Danson, Lawrence, 'Jonsonian Comedy and the Discovery of the Social Self', *PMLA*, 99 (1984), 179–93.

Donaldson, Ian, *The World Turned Upside-Down* (Oxford, 1970).

Dutton, Richard, *Ben Jonson: To the First Folio* (Cambridge, 1983).

Fry, Paul H., *The Poet's Calling in the English Ode* (New Haven and London, 1980).

Furniss, W. Todd, 'Ben Jonson's Masques', in *Three Studies in the Ren-*

aissance: Sidney, Jonson, Milton, edited by B. C. Nangle (New Haven, 1958), pp. 88–179.

Haynes, Jonathan, *The Social Relations of Jonson's Theater* (Cambridge, 1992).

——, 'Festivity and the Dramatic Economy of Jonson's *Bartholomew Fair*', *ELH*, 51 (1984), 645–68.

Kaplan, Joel, 'Dramatic and Moral Energy in Jonson's *Bartholomew Fair*', *Renaissance Drama*, N.S. 3 (1970), 137–56.

Knights, L. C., *Drama and Society in the Age of Jonson* (London, 1937).

Leggatt, Alexander, *Ben Jonson: His Vision and His Art* (London, 1981).

Levin, Richard, 'The Structure of *Bartholomew Fair*', *PMLA*, 80 (1965), 172–9.

Lindley, David, 'Embarrassing Ben: The Masques for Frances Howard', *English Literary Renaissance*, 16 (1986), 343–59.

Lipking, Lawrence, *The Life of the Poet* (Chicago, 1981).

McDonald, Russ, *Shakespeare and Jonson / Jonson and Shakespeare* (Lincoln, Nebraska, and London, 1988).

McPherson, David, 'The Origins of Overdo: a Study in Jonsonian Invention', *Modern Language Quarterly*, 37 (1976), 221–33.

Parfitt, George, *Ben Jonson: Private Poet and Public Man* (London, 1976).

——, 'The Nature of Translation in Ben Jonson's Poetry', *SEL*, 13 (1974), 344–59.

Partridge, E. B., 'Jonson's *Epigrammes*: The Named and the Nameless', *Studies in the Imagination*, 6 (1973), 153–98.

Revard, Stella P., 'Pindar and Jonson's Cary-Morison Ode', in *Classic and Cavalier: Essays on Jonson and the Sons of Ben*, eds C. J. Summers and T-L. Pebworth (Pittsburg, 1982), pp. 17–29.

Riddell, James. A. and Stewart, Stanley, 'Jonson reads "The Ruines of Time"', *Studies in Philology*, 87 (1990), 427–55.

Rivers, Isabel, *The Poetry of Conservatism, 1600–1745: A Study of Poets and Public Affairs from Jonson to Pope* (Cambridge, 1973).

Rowe, George E., *Distinguishing Jonson: Imitation, Rivalry, and the Direction of a Dramatic Career* (Lincoln, Nebraska, 1988).

Shafer, Robert, *The English Ode, to 1660* (New York, 1966).

Spenser, T. J. B., 'Ben Jonson on his beloved, the Author William Shakespeare', *The Elizabethan Theatre, IV*, edited by George Hibbard (Hamden, Conn., 1974), pp. 22–40.

Thayer, C. G., *Ben Jonson: Studies in the Plays* (Norman, Oklahoma, 1963).

Watson, Robert N., *Ben Jonson's Parodic Strategy* (Cambridge, Mass., 1987).

Wayne, Don, E., *Penshurst: The Semiotics of Place and the Poetics of History* (London, 1984).

——, 'Poetry and Power in Ben Jonson's Epigrammes: The Naming of "Facts" or the Figuring of Social Relations', *Renaissance and Modern Studies*, 23 (1979), 79–103.

——, 'Drama and Society in the Age of Jonson: An Alternative View', *Renaissance Drama*, 13 (1982), 103–29.

Williams, Raymond, *The Country and the City* (London, 1973).

Index

(There is no entry for Jonson himself; his works are entered separately in the alphabetic list. Works by other people are listed under their authors. The names of classical authors are given in their familar modern forms, usually a single word. Royalty are listed by their Christian names. Other aristocrats are entered under their titles, with parenthetic personal names; maiden names of married women are given in brackets.)

133, 222 note 45; *The Vision of the Twelve Goddesses*, 25, 26–7, 221 note 41, *Tethys' Festival*, 25–6, 27; *A Defence of Rhyme*, 127
Danson, Lawrence, 231 note 17
D'Aubigny, Esme Stuart, Seigneur, xv, 14, 52, 55, 58, 100, 101, 123, 131, 192
Davies, Sir John, 131
Day, John, 6
decorum, 134–7
Dekker, Thomas, xiii, xiv, 6, 41, 60, 79–80, 145, 221 note 40; *The Magnificent Entertainment*, 25, 34, 60, 221 note 40, 226 note 36; *Satiromastix*, xiv, 79–80, 145, 228 notes 3 & 9
Descartes, René, 20
Devil is an Ass, The, xvii, xix, 18, 46, 61, 68, 155, 231 note 13
Devonshire, Charles Blount, Earl of (formerly Lord Mountjoy), 10
Digby, Sir Kenelm, xx, 9, 127
Discoveries, xviii, xx, xxii, 5, 10–13, 14, 16, 19, 20, 21, 57–8, 64, 75–6, 77, 78–9, 93, 105–11, 119, 123–4, 125, 126, 129, 130, 133, 134, 135, 140, 141, 147, 152–3, 159, 161
Donaldson, Ian, xxi, 10, 14, 32, 149, 219 note 15, 220 notes 17 & 20, 223 note 59, 234 note 17, 235 note 25
Donatus, 113–14
Donne, John, xiii, xix, 2, 6, 14, 17, 27, 33, 53, 55, 97, 126, 129–38, 152; *Anniversaries*, 27, 130, 132; 'Songs and Sonets', 27; *Pseudo-Martyr*, 27; *Biathanatos*, 27; Sermons, 27; 'Divine Poems', 27; *Satires*, 131
Dorset, Thomas Sackville, Earl of, 89
Drayton, Michael, 6, 128; *Poly-Olbion*, 128
Drummond, William (of Hawthornden), xvii, 3, 5, 6, 7, 44, 68–9, 126, 132, 146, 152, 158; see separate entry for *Conversations with Drummond*
Dryden, John, 4, 16, 34, 37, 38, 96, 117, 119, 142, 159, 235 note 31; *Of Dramatic Poesie*, 3, 5, 13, 37, 142, 220 notes 19 & 25; 223 notes 64 & 71; *Translation of Ovid's Epistles*, 220 note 24

Eagleton, Terry, 2, 219 note 3
Eastward Ho, xv, 62, 67, 83, 84, 85, 86, 87, 88–9, 95, 213–14, 228 notes 12 & 16
Eccles, Mark, 218 Chronology: note 2
Eco, Umberto, 96
Egerton, Sir Thomas, 53
Eisenstein, Elizabeth, 220 note 29
Eliot, T. S., 4, 34, 219 notes 10 & 11
English Grammar, The, xviii, xx, 40
Elizabeth I, xiv, 50, 53, 70–1, 73, 75, 81, 196
Elsky, Martin, 33, 71–3, 94, 222 notes 44 & 50, 223 note 63, 227 note 2
Elyot, Sir Thomas, 20, 72, 73
England's Parnassus, 62
Entertainment at Althorp, xiv, 63
Entertainment at Highgate, The, xiv
Entertainment at the Blackfriars, An, xvii
Entertainment of the King and Queen at Theobalds, An, xvi, 63
Entertainment of the Two Kings at Theobalds, The, xv
Epicoene, or The Silent Woman, xvi, 3, 7, 46, 48, 58, 117–19, 121, 223 note 71
'Epigram on William, Lord Burghley, Lord High Treasurer of England (Presented Upon a Plate of Gold to His Son Robert, Earl of Salisbury, when he was also Treasurer)', 62, 95
Epigrams, xvi, xvii, xxii, 18, 30,

Printed in the United Kingdom by
Lightning Source UK Ltd., Milton Keynes
136551UK00001B/27/A